WINDOWS INTO MY SOUL

Adena Hodges

This book and other titles by Adena Hodges can be found at www.Transformations.Community and on Amazon.com

Other books by Adena Hodges:
Three Easy Steps Toward Revival
The Inheritance

Table of Contents

Acknowledgments

I am alive today only because of the True Lord Jesus Christ my Savior. Words cannot express my gratitude and wonder that He would save one such as I, as Paul says, the chief of sinners. Before my memories came, I was a Christian and believed, but I was good at keeping the rules and really didn't need a Savior, or so I thought! As hard as this journey is, I am glad for it, because it brought me to my desperate need of True Jesus and the incredible grace He offers.

In addition, He has so graciously surrounded me with faithful ones to help me step by step. I am so grateful for Jo Getzinger, my prayer minister, and the profound impact her tender care has had on my life. She regularly reads my journaling and is infinitely patient with me in processing the dark things of my past. Her demonstration of love and forgiveness has forever changed my life. I am amazed at God's goodness in bringing her into my life. Special thanks also to Pamela Tidmore and Debby Samuels who modeled and taught me about True FAMILY and how to connect with Them. Their encouragement and support have helped me through many storms.

Transformations Community would not be a reality if it were not for my dear friends and interns, Nikki Lyn Pugh (also my book and health coach), Muriel Weidemann, and Jennifer Violette. In a major crisis when I was ready to give up ministry entirely, they surrounded me with love and served tirelessly to keep Transformations going while I recovered. They have been my "Aaron and Hur" lifting up my arms in the battle. I am so grateful for their sacrifice of love. Week in and week out, they've been there for me, and I cherish their friendship, love and partnership in ministry. I extend this too to my prayer team, Transformations team and all my clients and groups.

There isn't room to name them all here, but their compassion, care, fervent prayers and love are more than I could ask for. I learn so much from them as they share their hearts and hear mine. They are my safe place where I can be me. I honor each of them.

This book is a window into my soul, but it also is a reflection of so many who have sowed into my life through the years, and I am so very grateful.

Foreword

It is an honor to write this foreword for *Windows Into My Soul.* I have provided counseling and prayer ministry to survivors of Satanic Ritual Abuse (SRA) for over 35 years. I am not aware of another resource to survivors that provides such a wonderful model as this book does for dialoging with the One who truly accomplishes healing. Adena refers to this One as the True Family - the Trinity of Father, Son and Holy Spirit. She selflessly opens such a tender and vulnerable window into intimate conversations between herself, her dissociated parts (i.e. alter personalities), and the True Family.

It is dynamic, inspirational, redemptive, and miraculous to witness the process of healing through the journaling she has shared with us, the readers. Whether you are a survivor, a helper, or a curious reader, you will be enriched to see how the True Family works with Adena and her parts to build her faith and trust. Together They weave understanding and gentle encouragement into her choices (never forced upon her) so that she can courageously face her pain and heal.

In *Windows Into My Soul*, the reader will be blessed to witness how redemption comes from the most horrific circumstances. SRA involves all forms of abuse, including mental, emotional, physical, sexual, and spiritual abuse and torture. It involves mind control of the victim in order to create a slave who will do the bidding of the cult group. This type of abuse often involves generational occult activity from infancy that is prolonged and severe. When a child experiences abuse in this way, his or her mind will fracture into separate parts of "self" in order to hold the trauma until the resources are developed for healing. The brain will dissociate these traumatic experiences into an unconscious region of the brain to house them until the conscious mind can manage the traumatic information, internal conflicts, and distressing emotions that surface with each memory.

I will expound on these internal conflicts a little more here since many of them surface in the dialogues between Adena and the True Family as well as between Adena and her parts. It is necessary to resolve internal conflicts in order for the mind to manage these competing and often opposing views on a conscious level. A common conflict Adena experiences regularly centers around the desire *not* to know the details surrounding painful and traumatic events and her awareness that in order to heal, she must face them. Adena occupies the host position in the "system of parts." The host manages daily life and is generally the most protected by the system from traumatic information. As the reader will see in the journaling, the "system of parts" as well as the host herself (i.e. Adena) fears that, when trauma surfaces, it will overwhelm the host to the point of not being able to function in daily life.

Unresolved internal conflicts, if intense enough, are a big part of why the mind of an SRA survivor will continue to dissociate. True Family frequently reminds Adena that she can choose to put her trust in Them, reassuring her that They can manage the information, timing, and amount of painful memories at a pace that she can handle. As she chooses to trust, she works out her fears and finds relief through the faithful support of the True Family.

Another common conflict SRA survivors face is the internal conflict of wanting to trust in an all-knowing, all-powerful, loving God and also being terrified of being tricked and disappointed.

In dialogues between parts and Adena, she frequently invites parts to accept help from the True Family. They often quip back that it is a trick or that they feel they have some evidence that the True

Family cannot be trusted. This belief comes from many ritual events that manipulate circumstances. In these rituals and other abusive situations, Jesus may appear "random" in His help, not powerful enough to help, or even the source of evil Himself. Cult members often dress up like the Messiah and tell the child that they are Jesus. They enact scenarios of Jesus not showing up in time to help, of Jesus being tethered and powerless to help, or even Jesus directly participating in the evil abuse of the child.

When the reader understands the length that cults will go in order to destroy the trust of a child in a good God, one can begin to appreciate the tremendous courage it takes survivors to begin to trust God again. Even more profoundly, readers can begin to appreciate the courage it takes for Adena and her parts to share this struggle with us. It is my opinion that the enemy of our souls, the devil, knows God is the answer for healing. The devil works hard to deceive survivors into believing God is not the answer. Regardless of how difficult it is, it is worth the effort to go through this journey to develop trust with God. The True Family has not disappointed Adena and, as you will witness yourself as you read, remains trustworthy throughout the journaling.

When extreme abuses have occurred from infancy, it impacts the ability to relate securely with others. God created us to be in relationship with one another because He is relational – He desires relationship with us. When insecure attachments form due to abuse, the individual will also experience fear in relationships with others. This fear will also likely be projected onto God. There is no shortcut to healing attachment wounds. It involves patience, endurance with consistency and love. One way for parts to "test the spirits to see if they are from God" (see 1 John 4:1-4) is to see if the True Family stays true to the Word of God, the Bible. 1 Cor. 13: 4-8 lists the qualities of real love:

> "Love suffers long and is kind, thinks no evil, bears all things, believes all things, hopes all things, endures all things. Love never fails." (NKJV)

These are a few of the qualities of love that are listed in this Scripture. As I followed the dialogue between Adena and True Family, I watched carefully to see how They would respond to her fears as well as to accusations of various parts. Time and time again, the True Family exemplified the love described in 1 Corinthians 13 in Their patience, consistency, kindness, graciousness, and mercy. They take delight in being with her when she is distrusting and fearful just as much as when she is trusting and thankful. True Family's loving patience with Adena in all circumstances endeared me to Them the most and set an example for me to attain. I personally strive to attain that patient consistency in the prayer ministry work I do with survivors. This is not an easy task to maintain. Attachment wounds cause terror in the survivor and often result in a push/pull dynamic within the relationship. This fear dynamic is evident at times in the journaling about me.

I am glad to be a part of sharing with others my involvement in this story in the hope that it might also help other prayer ministers who read Adena's story. This work is not for the faint of heart, but it is worth it. Every now and then a treasure like Adena's journaling appears that challenges us to be like the True Family in love. It renews our hope and faith that the True Family are intimately involved with our lives and desire to lead and guide us into abundant life with Them. Adena's journaling delivers all of this. I am full of gratitude for the loving gift she gives to us through sharing her intimate journey with the True Family.

Jo Getzinger, CARE, Inc.

Introduction

This is a unique book. It is about my journey from Satanic Ritual Abuse and mind control to overcoming and freedom via the lens of personal journal entries. I have found profound healing through writing out my process with what I call the True FAMILY (Father, Holy Spirit and Jesus) as well as with myself and my parts. I don't know if I would have gotten this far in my healing journey without this precious tool and without the relationship with the Living God that it fosters! There is so much programming to forget. Having something "on paper" that I can review periodically has helped me to solidify and remember important key points as well as "hear" again God's voice speaking to me of His love and about who I really am.

There are many ways to process our journey. Some of these ways include art, creativity, dance, just to name a few. Journaling might not benefit all, but I hope that these excerpts from my own journalling will be insightful and help your own process of recovery if you are a survivor. If you are not, then I hope it can help you to better understand someone who is. For counselors, therapists, prayer ministers and church leaders, I hope this book will give you insight into the unique challenges survivors face and how to work compassionately with them for restoration.

Why I Published This Book

Reading an autobiographical account gives you a narrative, but not always the inner struggle, turmoil and victory that journaling does. I am including some narrative to give context and then letting the rest speak for itself. At so many points, survivors feel "crazy" and struggle to believe their own memories. Hearing someone else's wrestling may bring validation and hope. You aren't crazy!

Trigger Warning:

While I've edited out many details, I've chosen to leave in some things that may be triggering. Read as God leads you and feel free to skip anything that is overwhelming. Triggering isn't bad when we walk through it with God's guidance and find the "treasure behind the trigger." When we do it to ourselves, however, - which I've frequently done! - it can be too much and can destabilize our inner realm. I trust you to be led by Holy Spirit in what to read and what to leave for another time.

While a lot of stories from survivors are focused on what was *done to us*, in the cult system, most of us were also forced to do bad things to others. This is a side of the Survivor experience that is not talked about as much. I've chosen to be vulnerable about this part of the Survivor journey for me and the struggle with coming to terms with it. For full healing to occur, I believe we must face this and I hope my testimony will help others to do so. I honor courageous ones like Svali who have shared their stories with us and given us an example to overcome. If you haven't read her blogs or books, I encourage you to go to: https://svalispeaksagain.wordpress.com/

My prayer is that through this book you will better understand yourself, who God is and His tender loving kindness to you. He has a way through anything and nothing is too bad or evil that He can't redeem. We get to fall into His arms of grace over and over again and find the strength for one more day.

How To Read This Book

I've arranged *Windows into My Soul* in sections according to some common themes survivors face. That being said, within the journaling there are often several themes expressed, and it was impossible to totally separate it all out and keep the flow. Feel free to read in the way True FAMILY leads you!

Because my journaling is a "dance" between God, me, and my parts, I've **bolded** what I feel is God speaking, I also put "me" in normal print, and my parts *in italics* for clarity in reading. These are excerpts, so sometimes reading this book may feel like walking up to a conversation that is mid-sentence. I believe you will be able to get the context as you hang around, however. I've also added some clarifying notes where needed. I encourage you to find the nuggets of truth you need.

My Story

For those of you who don't know me personally, I'm including some of my story here so that you can have context for the journaling.

Until age 50, I thought I was pretty normal, albeit in a dysfunctional sort of way. I knew I had struggled in my family of origin. There was also a vague memory and a particular dream that had always been in my consciousness which I labeled as "strange" my whole life. Other than that, however, it seemed to me that I had a fairly good life. My parents were Seventh Day Adventists who were devoted to following God and to keeping the rules. I did not rebel against this but instead thought that if this was what God required, I was happy to comply.

Basically, our family was made up of what I call the "pharisees of the pharisees." We were all about keeping the rules and being good. Admittedly, I cheated occasionally in school if I thought I could get away with it because a 98% was devastating to me. I justified it because I was going to get an "A" anyway, but I couldn't handle being less than perfect. My parents didn't put this on me. Intense perfectionism just came "naturally," or so I thought!

When I was 15, I went to boarding school in another state. After a few months, I collapsed with undiagnosed fibromyalgia and became mostly bedridden for 6+ years. I wanted to die because of the pain, loneliness and isolation. It was a time of wrestling with God.

"Why didn't He heal me?" I thought. "Enough people were praying!"

Throughout this whole lonely time, I also grew in relationship with God. He was the only one I had. Eventually through some medication and diet changes, I got better enough to function mostly normally. I finished college and got married to a pastor in the Seventh-Day Adventist church.

Three kids and two churches later, my husband experienced burnout and depression. We were referred to a prayer counseling ministry through Elijah House. It was my first exposure to anyone Spirit-filled and I was scared. Would we be deceived?

What we found instead through that ministry was such life and freedom! Still, we couldn't understand why they didn't know the "right" doctrines? It seemed like they were hearing from God, but what about "truth?"

In His mercy, God eventually broke through our legalism and brought us into freedom! We left the Seventh-Day Adventist church and enjoyed a number of Spirit-filled churches after that. Raising our kids, spending time as an intercessory missionary in our local House of Prayer and starting a regional ministry teaching on prayer occupied many years for me.

Throughout those years, there were ups and downs as well as times when I'd be back in counseling for what seemed like "normal" dysfunctional things. However, around the time I turned 50, things shifted. In a session with a prayer minister, I was working on integrating a "part" of me. What came up in my spirit is that this part didn't belong to me. The prayer minister asked where or what this part was connected to and I was shocked when out of my mouth came, "It's connected to five planets." I really thought I was talking nonsense and going insane. But the prayer minister simply prayed for me to be disconnected from those planets and amazingly I felt different! This really messed with my theology and began a journey of processing with the Lord as well as listening to other survivor stories.

As memories began to come, they were mostly related to cosmic stuff, being trafficked "off-world," and connections to other beings. I understand now that a lot of this might have been done through virtual reality and other programming set-ups, but I experienced it as real and needed to process it as such. At the time, I thought, "This might be weird but at least it's not as bad as that Satanic Ritual Abuse stuff."

I felt the Lord ask me to start a school for those "trafficked off-world" like me. I had no clue what to do but partnered with some experienced prayer ministers who actually believed me. This was how "Transformations: Becoming Who You Are" was born. I realized trauma is trauma and the things we were sharing would benefit anyone who had experienced it, regardless of what form. That basis gave me the inspiration to open it up to all. We started weekly groups and soon powerful healing experiences began as lives were changed (including mine).

Remember when I said, "at least I didn't have SRA?" Well, that changed too. Six months after starting Transformations and on the eve of our first retreat, memories of being trafficked to high level political figures dropped suddenly and unexpectedly in. I thought I was going crazy! How could this be? Yet, the memories were so distinct, and I felt them clearly in my body, soul and spirit. I couldn't deny that something was going on. The Lord confirmed it as well. I am still on the journey of discovery as memories continue to come in. For me, it has been like puzzle pieces here and there. There's a lot more to go, but I share my journey here in hopes that it can help and bless others.

My family struggled to believe me, and this ultimately led to a divorce. I was programmed to be a functional Christian leader. I didn't struggle with some of the "usual" things survivors encounter: depression, anxiety, panic attacks, flooding of emotions and memories, etc. I looked "normal." I understand why my family and others had a hard time believing my memories. This is often a confusing point for survivors. Many are programmed to be more non-functional and to have the issues I just described. Then, if memories surface, it can be blamed on "mental" issues. Others are programmed to be functional so that if memories surface, no one will believe them. Functional survivors are also used strategically to infiltrate all levels of society as politicians, entertainers, business leaders, church leaders, and so on.

Though difficult, I love my life as I get to see groups and clients being transformed even as I am walking out the journey with them. The power of God's love manifested regularly encourages us all. We are not alone in this journey. I believe that there is coming a "mass exodus" from the cult systems of this world. We get to be a part of that as survivors by releasing forgiveness and restoration to our perpetrators. They were programmed just like us. God loves them and has a plan for them, too. Nothing is impossible with God! If He can bring me out, He can free anyone.

This doesn't mean we don't experience intense and overwhelming feelings, as you will see from my journaling. It is not about "spiritual bypassing," i.e. just focusing on the "good stuff." Instead, it is about bringing it all into the light of God's unconditional love which is the only place we can be set free.

Every journey is unique and similar at the same time. Parts of my journey may resonate with you while others not. I hope you will find the treasure that inspires you to know that you are not alone and that the Lord has a way through for you, too, no matter how you feel. There is hope and healing, truth and justice, peace and rest as we trust in True FAMILY.

Hearing From God

Journaling did not come easy for me. Neither did hearing God's voice. I don't want anyone to be discouraged reading this and think "this is impossible for me." It *is* possible for you! God's promise is that His sheep hear His voice. (John 10:27) Don't use this verse to assume then that if you don't hear, you aren't His sheep! My point is that God speaks to *all* of His children, even those who can't yet hear Him.

All that being said, there are usually concrete reasons for the blocks. It is not an unwillingness on God's part, but often pain, trauma and programming we might not even be aware of which blocks His voice and His presence from coming through to our conscious awareness. There are also ways to make it easier. Most of us are trained primarily from the left side of our brain, where our abilities of logic and reasoning reside. However, hearing God's voice happens primarily through the relational center in the right side of our brain. This side is also where intuition and creativity flow and where memories are stored. For survivors and others who have experienced extreme trauma, these memories can directly interfere with hearing from God.

I have found that letting go of trying to "make something happen" or trying to "figure it out" and instead simply resting in His love and flow has really helped. When I am worried about getting it wrong (which you will see I do a lot of!) it can cut off that flow. The result is we can't hear accurately. Two books that have really helped me in this process are *Joyful Journey: Listening to Immanuel* by Dr. James Wilder and *4 Keys to Hearing God's Voice* by Mark Virkler. I was first exposed to two-way journaling through Mark, and I so resisted it! It took years of starts and stops-- here a little, there a little-- until it began to take root for me as a regular practice. As my own journey opened up, I discovered I also had parts of me that had a voice longing to be heard, and it became a three-way conversation. I'm glad I persisted in pursuing this format for journaling.

We all hear God through our own filters. I am not claiming this is a "new" testament. This is simply God's personal revelation to me in a language I understand. God knows each of us uniquely. He speaks in a way that we "get" because He loves us so much. When you start journaling, you might feel that some of it sounds like mine and be tempted to think you are "copying" me. This is part of the enemy's attempts to stop or distract us. Yours will be both unique and similar because He is the same God, speaking to you in language that is meaningful to you.

Trauma and programming interfere significantly with us hearing God's voice clearly. Don't be discouraged if it takes some time and healing to get there. Also, some people are more visual, or "sensing" (just feeling or knowing), than actually hearing, so celebrate how you do "hear" from Him in your unique way. You can also go to our website: www.Transformations.Community and find resources for hearing God's voice.

About Mind Control

If all of this is new to you, here's a few basic terms and information for you to know. People who haven't experienced this cannot fully comprehend the complexity of issues and the depth in which mind control programming can go. God is fully able to heal and set free, but it is usually a lengthy process because of His tender mercy to gently deal with each layer of our pain. At the same time, He draws us near with incredible kindness and love which makes it all well worth the journey! I've come to know the love of God in a way that I never knew before my memories surfaced and I had to face indescribable horror.

It can be easy for those who don't understand these dynamics to say things like:

"Just pray more."

"Just get over it."

"Just give it to Jesus." or

"Focus on the positive."

However, these surface actions and attitudes won't get to the deep core pain and lies that we've been trained in, some of us from the womb. Breaking these lies and helping us step into His Truth is what True Jesus is after!

Why?: For "normal" people, probably the first question is "Why?" I mean, why would anyone want to do horrendous things to other people?

There is a range for each group depending on ideology, but it boils down to money, power, control and "ascension," i.e. the striving to becoming "gods," ascended masters, or immortals. Child trafficking is extremely lucrative. As opposed to drugs or guns which are a one-time sale, children can be used over and over and when they are "done" their organs can be harvested, adrenochrome can be acquired, and ultimately their bodies cremated to create diamonds. Mind controlled slaves are incredibly useful as assassins, spies, mules, sex slaves and more. Because of the ability to dissociate (see below), memories and key information can be stored in compartments in the mind and brought out with the right codes or suppressed. Depending on a group's ideology, the goal could also be for the "betterment of humanity," which usually means for the elites and the special privileges that come from "ascension."

Disassociation and Parts: Disassociation is the foundation of how mind control is perpetuated. God has given us the ability to dissociate because when we are infants or children, we do not have the capacity or maturity to handle trauma. We do, however, have the ability to section off that trauma and "hold it in place" until we are old enough to process it with God. **Parts** are internal personalities that hold these memories inside until we can integrate them back to wholeness with God as we mature.

Unfortunately, in the cult system "parts" are also programmed for their use. I will refer to parts sometimes as "littles" throughout this book interchangeably. The parts can be different ages, from the womb to older children or teens with various personalities, desires and opinions. They each hold a portion of the person's will. The more cooperation between parts we can get the better. The cult system uses force to program parts, but with Jesus we use gentle invitation. We cannot become like the cult even in our desire to heal. It won't work.

Some prayer ministers try to integrate parts quickly, but I do not recommend this. It will happen naturally when the parts and host are ready. I use the term **"host"** or "presenter" for the one who is consciously functioning in a person's natural life. You could see this as the one who is the driver in a car. You might hear the other parts in the "back seat" and sometimes one of them may take over, but for the most part the "host" or "presenter" drives the car. Managing this with True FAMILY is key. I highly recommend the prayers in *Prayer Warriors* and *Prayer Warrior 2* by CARE, Inc. for help in both understanding parts as well as for healing them with True FAMILY.

You will notice in my journaling that some parts manifest as male and this might surprise you. Parts who have taken on a false identity as a handler or programmer could be male since I was programmed to "do whatever the man says." These parts are a part of me, but they also believe they are male. Protectors can also manifest as male with the belief that men are stronger and more powerful. In working gently with them to recognize their true identity in Jesus, they eventually come to identify fully as me. As a side note, this can be one of the many factors at play for individuals within the transgender community as well. This is also why it is important to love these individuals (and these parts) well. Trauma may be causing them to see themselves and their parts as the opposite gender. Loving care will do more for their overall healing and relationship with God than "righteous" judgment.

In my journaling, sometimes I reference "drifting." This is likely a form of mild dissociation where I am focused on one thing and then find my mind drifting to seeing or hearing other things not in my present reality. This may be parts surfacing a memory or trying to get my attention.

Programming: Programmers in the cult system purposefully shatter the minds of those they are programming over and over through trauma, especially sexual trauma. They then program each part with certain jobs, such as pain or emotion carriers, reporters (report to the cult the activities of the person), punishers, controllers, programmers, and more.

The complexity of programming can be overwhelming. There is often split programming, light and dark sides, or a front Christian host who may be completely unaware of back parts who are still involved in cult activity. This is particularly distressing for Christian survivors to discover and so must be approached with love and care. We would like to think of it as simple, i.e. you are either "in the system" or "out of the system." The reality, however, is that it is much more complicated than that.

Access: If there are still parts who are not healed and have programs running, then there is the potential for access. This access can range from simple harassment to a full-on double life. There is not an "instantly out of the system" moment for most survivors. For most, it is a process of gaining more and more freedom as more parts are healed and set free, and truths replace lies. Many survivors who have believed they are completely free have discovered years later that there was still access and cult activity happening. The only solution is through True Jesus and His protection and trusting Him. This means letting go of our self-protection which we've been operating in all our lives. Self-protection opens the way for cult access. Only Jesus can heal, save, and deliver. Our trust is in Him alone.

False Jesus/Trinity: In the cult's effort to destroy any connection to Jesus, who alone can set us free, they will have many set-ups with someone dressed as Jesus. This "Jesus" then may rape the child repeatedly or appear weak and unable to save the child crying out for help while being tortured. They work hard with anti-

Christian programming to distort Scripture, bring confusion and ultimately break any kind of trust the child could have in Jesus. There may also be those masquerading as Father or Holy Spirit. It takes care and patience to work with parts who feel they cannot trust True Jesus. This is also why throughout I usually use "True Jesus" and "True FAMILY" to distinguish from any counterfeits.

Different Groups: There are multiple groups who perpetuate ritual abuse and mind control, ranging from secret societies like freemasons, to church structures like Mormonism and the Jesuits, to government agencies, medical agencies, international groups, local covens, gangs, and more. There is infiltration at every level and aspect of society including media, entertainment, education, government, and medicine. The good news is that our God has a plan of restoration! This system *will* come down – we are promised this in Revelation 18. We do not need to fear these groups, but to stand with True FAMILY and partner for restoration in the ways They show us.

Early Access: Mind control must begin before the ages of 6-8 while the brain is still forming. For some groups it starts in the womb. Some of us were genetically created by groups and experienced incredible traumas even before we were born. Because of this, we believe we don't have any choice but to do what the cult tells us, and it is not easy to undo the lies. It requires patience and unconditional love. It isn't a simple fix, of just "thinking the right thoughts." Only Jesus, who is the Way, the Truth, and the Life, can heal and transform us.

Because early access is key, many groups are multi-generational. This is the easiest way to perpetuate cult philosophy and ideology to the next generation. Because of the way programming works, most families look like respectable citizens, including Christian families who may be leaders of churches and other philanthropic organizations. Those involved in SRA are not typically crazy, sleazy, people that you could tell were "off." Most appear as normal as you or I. They may be your next-door neighbor. I'm not saying this to make you paranoid, but instead to help you be aware and trust more in Jesus as our *only* Protector.

Mass Mind Controlled: All of us have experienced some level of broad mass mind control through media, entertainment, sports, music, and more. Subtle and not so subtle programming can be seen in every industry, shifting cultural norms and affecting families. Many events such as concerts and the Super Bowl are actual rituals being played out in public. More and more they are doing things in plain sight.

Again, this is not to instill fear, but to become aware of the enemy's tactics and to trust in True Jesus. Fear opens more doors to the enemy. Faith in True FAMILY closes them!

Forced Perpetration and "Double Binds:" Because the goal of the cult is willing victims who don't resist, double binds are used to control and manipulate. Examples of double binds are: "Kill this rabbit or we will kill your brother" or "kill this child or we will kill your friend." This is done progressively until the child feels they have no choice but to do the "lesser" of two evils. With young children, at first adults assist and hold the hands of the child around the knife (for example), but eventually the child graduates to doing evil things on their own. This occurs after many double binds that leverage attachment bonds and devastate the child emotionally and mentally. Eventually specific parts may be trained to be "killers" or assassins on command, all for the "greater good."

Don't Remember, Don't Tell: The key to keeping everything hidden in the cult system is for survivors to keep silent. Most do this very effectively. When loved ones are threatened if we remember and tell anyone, we suppress and "forget" in numerous ways. The only way we survived was to bury the memories, pain, and emotions very deep behind amnesic walls. Thankfully, True Jesus has a way through, and He so lovingly and gently brings memories to the surface as we are ready to handle them with Him. He can provide protection for us and also for our loved ones as we put our trust fully in Him. Again, this is a process. Have patience with yourself and others. Each journey is unique and only God knows the timetable.

Inner Healing and Deliverance: Most churches are familiar with some form of inner healing and deliverance. The focus is often on "fixing" a problem or making someone better. I see this very differently as a journey of growing in trust and intimacy with God. This way of looking at the healing process makes it ongoing and beautiful. When I start to focus on "fixing" me, I get impatient and miss what God is doing. In my impatience, sometimes I even end up slowing down the process.

Another issue is that with mind control, often parts are programmed to believe they are demons. This is why traditional deliverance is often unsuccessful. It may be a part manifesting, not a demon. Deliverance is important, but it is not necessary to shout, yell, etc., which actually damages parts. We have authority in Jesus' name to separate out any demonic from parts and to speak gently with parts. Sometimes in my journaling, I refer to the demonic as "yuckies" since this is a gentler term that doesn't scare parts, i.e. our "little ones" inside. Often, they are willing to bring their "yuckies" to Jesus and there is no need for a long, drawn-out struggle. I find that wounded parts can act as a magnet for the demonic, but once the parts receive what they need from Jesus, that access is closed, and deliverance is simple.

You will notice that when I use the word magick in the journaling it is spelled with a "k." Aleister Crawley, an English occultist who founded the religion of Thelema, coined this term to distinguish the difference between magic tricks and occult magick that is used extensively in SRA and mind control.

God's Plan: I believe God has an incredible plan of recovery and restoration for both victims and perpetrators within the cult system. We are all survivors, and this system is coming down. We can be a part of it!

This is what fuels my own journey. When I am tempted to "quit," forget or plateau, True FAMILY reminds me of the bigger picture and what we get to have a part in. Because we know the depths of pain and trauma, we understand the glories of God's love, forgiveness and restoration in a way that "normal" people do not. There is a great reward promised. Paul said, "For our momentary, light affliction is producing for us an eternal weight of glory far beyond all comparison, while we look not at the things which are seen, but at the things which are not seen; for the things which are seen are temporal, but the things which are not seen are eternal." (2Co 4:17-18 NASB20)

Take heart and do not be afraid. We are called to overcome.

Preface

This book is particularly hard to release publicly because of the intensely personal nature of it. It is the raw and real struggle with God and my parts. In addition, shortly before publishing this a few new things came to light which caused me to question some details of the journaling.

Did I get it right? Is it accurate?

I've chosen to share this portion of my journal here as a Preface so you can understand God's view on it and hopefully find encouragement for your own journey.

About "Windows Into My Soul"

You are troubled with some things that you aren't expressing. You can talk with Us about it.

It is just about some possible inconsistencies with what I've written in my journaling and possibly some things that might disprove it. It shakes my confidence in hearing You clearly. I am also troubled about making mistakes. Then I question the book and all of that as well. Run. Hide. Go away. You know it all.

We do [know it all] and We understand the struggle. There are filters and veils that all people have. This is not to be distressed over. Remember Paul's words in 1Co 13:12, "For now we see in a mirror, dimly, but then face to face. Now I know in

part, but then I shall know just as I also am known." You hear and see well. There are also times when your own filters can cause distortion or inaccuracy, or parts or programming can interfere. We are not discouraged by this, and We can work it all for good. This is Our promise. You bring everything to Us and We can walk it out with you step by step. You want to get it perfectly. The training in the system is that anything less than that is punished. We do not work that way. We are holding you gently through all of this and Our love is steadfast, immovable, constant, faithful. You cannot miss this.

Okay. But I don't want to publish the book if parts of it are wrong.

Does the book express Our love?

Yes, it does… but…

You are afraid of being put to shame with details that might not be 100% accurate or that you find out later has additional information…

Yes, I am.

Think about a 2-year-old. She views things from a 2-year-old perspective. Many things she believes are inaccurate until she is old enough to understand more. You would not punish her for this. It is developmental. We know where you are and what you are capable of understanding at this time. This is not shameful. You have put down faithfully to the best of your ability what you have heard and seen. This is beautiful and We honor this. You don't see everything clearly and there is no blame. You are still on your journey. There are many puzzle pieces that are not clear yet. Can you receive this?

Yes, but…

Have grace for yourself and know that We are pleased with the book. You can publish it as is. You also can choose to

remove some portions or things that you aren't ready to share. You get to choose. This is the main point.

I want it to be just right, to impact others in the way You intend…

Can you believe that We can do that regardless of what you put in or take out?

Oh. Yes, I see that. I don't have to get it perfect. You do the work.

Yes. We can cover what needs to be covered and reveal what needs to be revealed for each person. We can work it all for good. This takes the pressure off of you.

But I do want to be as accurate as possible.

Yes. We understand this. And We are helping you on this journey. To accept your less-than-perfect self, who is perfect in Us. To just be you and not worry about what others will think or say or do. This is true freedom.

I do want that. So, this is part of that journey to get there?

Remember it is not about "getting there," as you are already "there" in Us. It is the joyful journey with Us, enjoying each step of the way.

I teach this but it is hard to live it.

Yes, We understand. It gets easier. These are mindsets that We are addressing.

I want to live today in the light of Your love, enjoying Your presence and what You bring every step of the way. Keep me there, please.

Yes, We love to do that AND We are not troubled or discouraged when you struggle. We are not disappointed in you. We understand.

Thank you so so so very much!

We delight in this journey with you. Step by step. Held safe in Our hands. That is always true and never changes. We are not bothered if you have some details that are not accurate. Our love is the main thing.

I am grateful for You exposing more wrong beliefs in my heart and programming. I give this to You. Thank you for Your love that never leaves me!

My hope for this book is that you experience the powerful love of True FAMILY that never changes, holds you steady and never fails!

Windows Into My Soul

Journal Entries

Section I

Being Loved

One prominent thing that survivors struggle with is receiving love. We can feel so degraded and dirty. After all, we've done such horrendous things, how could God *ever* love us? Or we may feel that no one is safe. No one can be trusted, and we must flee from any kind of care. Below are some glimpses into my own struggle to believe God could love me and that He was safe.

Bold = True FAMILY (Father, Holy Spirit and Jesus)

Normal print = me

Italics = my parts

Afraid of Love

It is not wrong to want to be cared for and loved for who you are.

But it isn't possible. I can't go there. It hurts too bad. Please hold this for me until I can handle it.

Yes, we wanted you to see this today. I am a man (True JESUS) who tenderly cares for you and deeply understands you. You are completely loved and known. You can learn to receive this.

Not from a man. Or a woman. Everyone is dangerous.

This is what you've experienced, but it is not truth. If you want truth, then you will need to let Our love in.

How can I? I want the truth in every part of me, but we've been so abused. It's too hard. No one is safe.

We understand and We are gently wooing you to receive Our love. You know in your head that you are completely loved by Us, but it is the many parts who resist this. Wholeness comes when you can agree. This means facing the pain, the terror, the things done to you and the things you've done in the light of Our love that will not let you go, not from force or control, but in the deepest love that doesn't condemn.

I do want this. I don't know how.

You don't have to figure it out. We know. We know the inner workings of your heart and mind, and We love you. We are not here to overwhelm you, but to hold you gently as you receive Our truth and love. Can you receive this?

I want to. Please help me.

What if We are Too Bad to Be Loved?

Now is your time for deep healing and joy. Yes, joy in what We are doing in you. The path is difficult, but We are with you step by step and We will give you joy unspeakable and full of glory. Taste and see Our goodness.

I am overwhelmed by Your goodness, my True and living Lord. I am so very grateful.

Trust the process and trust Us. We are at work in you and through you. You get to be you.

What is the priority for today? I feel stuck.

How about just receiving Our love and delight in you. Setting your gaze on Us first is priority. You can linger here.

Thank you. I want to do that. I want to seek You and Your kingdom first. Please show me what that looks like.

It is more glorious than you know. We delight to show you the boundless depths of Our love for you. It never fails. It goes on and on and on.

Why do You love someone like me who has done so many bad things? I have really hurt others.

We see the end from the beginning. You chose a very difficult assignment, and you are fulfilling it. It is not a surprise to Us. We have such beautiful plans for you each step of the way.

Is the journey for You spontaneous? Are you able to enjoy the moments with us while knowing all about it?

Yes, We do. It seems impossible to you but it is a fresh journey for Us while also being known. This is Our delight. It is a beautiful paradox.

I don't understand but I choose to believe. How can I experience Your love today?

Find Our grace in your every moment. Know that We are with you always. Grace is poured out abundantly.

Thank you. I choose You. How come I struggle to connect even for a short time?

You have a lot going on and distractions inside and out. We know this and do not condemn you. The invitation is always open all day and all night.

Am I doing bad things in the night?

Have you asked Us to be night managers?

Yes, although some nights I forget.

Do We know that is the intent of your heart?

Yes.

Then that is the truth. We only allow what is needed for healing and for Our glory.

It can't be for Your glory for me to do bad things.

Yes, but there is more to it than you know. We work all things for good. We work with your will and your parts and Our sovereign plan. It is such a glorious arrangement!

I want to see it that way. I want to see from Your perspective. I can see it for others, but it is harder to see it for myself.

We know and understand. There is a place of resting in Us and of walking by faith. We love this journey with you! We will show you the way. Trust and rest. We delight to open Our hearts to you in this way.

Loved Because of Who We Are

We have a way through.

But I can't see it right now!

It is okay. Take it step by step. You do hear Us, and it is about taking it step by step, listening and following what We share with you.

But what if You are a false jesus?

Do you trust Us?

I want to. I try to.

Thank you for being honest. We are at work in you. This is not something for you to work up. It is Our faith, love and grace that will see you through. You are distressed in any way that you would further the cause of the cult. We understand this. Can you trust Us?

If it is really You. I don't want to hurt anyone.

You can't avoid pain for you or others. It is not about avoiding pain but facing the pain and overcoming through Our help, grace and love. You know this.

Yes. But it is hard.

It is but it becomes "light" when you give this to Us and trust and rest.

Okay. I say yes, again. Thank you for not getting tired of me.

We love you so much. Feel Our delight in you. Not because of doing things, teaching well or anything else, but just for who you are.

Love and Deep Pain

Please help me today!

It is Our joy to walk you through this day. Stay fervent in prayer and restful in Our love.

Thank you! I put my trust in You. You will see me through…I'm struggling with things. How do I work this out?

It is not about you working it out. It is Our love carrying you through. You can give this to Us. You do not need to struggle through.

What does it look like to give this to You. Will You keep me safe?

Yes, We do. We are holding you and rocking you and nurturing all the parts who need this deep attachment love. It is always available to you. You teach this but have a hard time receiving it yourself.

There's a lot of pain here. I don't know what to do with it.

We are able to take that and help to heal your heart. Don't run from Us or others. It is hard to be vulnerable when you have been through what you have. There's more there than you know. Don't be overwhelmed by this but know that We are surfacing things as you are able to handle it.

I can't do this.

We know. You can't on your own. But We are here to help you through it. We never leave you nor forsake you.

Then why do I feel that way?

That is what they want you to believe. Over and over set-ups for you to believe that We abandoned you and to reinforce so many other things. That is not the truth. You are not alone. We are here for you, and We've provided help for you along the way. Don't turn away from Us or them. It is okay to have feelings. Don't run from vulnerability.

You know the truth about me.

Yes, We do.

I want to ask if you will keep me safe, but on the other hand want you to take me out so I don't hurt anyone. Just take me out. Protect everyone else from me.

Do you remember what We showed you in your restoration? How many lives you would impact?

Yes, but …what if I hurt as many or more? I don't want to! Please, please help me not to hurt anyone.

We love your tender heart! If We took you out now you wouldn't be able to fulfill the destiny We created you for. Many lives would remain untouched. Can you trust Us? This is the question.

I'm terrified. I want to believe that You can work all things for good and what You've showed me will be true. But what if…

You can just give the 'what if's' to Us to handle. There is a lot of grief and pain to process, but you are not alone. Help is here.

I can't receive.

You can and you want to but are afraid.

Can You do it quickly? Like ripping off a band-aid?

We can do a lot of things, but the point is can you trust Us with your unique journey. Your journey is unique. It won't look like others. Be you. Let the fear go so We can hold you.

Okay.

Even Though I Feel Like a Hypocrite...

How do I receive Your love and stay engaged with You? I tell clients this but then I can deflect as much as them. I'm sorry True Jesus.

We understand. We don't see you as a hypocrite. It is parts fleeing from pain and self-triggering. We know this journey is overwhelming and seems impossible, but We have a way through.

It feels like a nightmare.

Yes, and there is a way to see it that is different, through the triumph of Our love.

It feels like a mockery.

Yes, it can feel that way when you see only the bad stuff and not the glory that is coming. See through Our eyes of love and the restoration that is coming.

I just need to feel Your love right now.

We are here. We know it is hard for you to receive.

I want to shut down and blank out and pretend and hide and die. I feel big pain. I don't like it.

We can help with it. It is not yours to carry alone. We are here and We've provided those around you.

But nobody is here right now.

Yes, and you can reach out. They have offered.

I don't want to be a crybaby.

Then you limit yourself. There are others who would gladly be there for you. You do not need to be strong for everyone else.

I don't know any other way.

That isn't true giving and receiving.

I'm sorry for being so needy.

It's okay to be needy. In what is coming, all will be learning how to walk this out. You get a head start.

Can You just help me?

Yes, and you can grow in receiving from the body.

I wish I didn't exist. It hurts too much.

It's okay to be honest, but Our arms are open wide.

I don't know how to receive it. It's the same thing over and over, never making any progress.

That may be how it feels, but you are making progress. It is okay to feel so helpless and needy. We know it is terrifying for you, but it is actually a good place to encounter Our love and supply for you.

I need to know that You will keep me safe. And then there's parts who don't really care and would rather go away.

Facing all the inner conflict is not easy, but it is the open door for freedom. Listen to both sides and work through it with Us. We are committed to you and your eternal safety. There will be challenges, but We are with you through it all. This is

Our promise. To those who just want to disappear, We see your despair, grief and pain. You are not alone, and We will help you through this. Trust and rest. We meet you where you are.

What about the "dead" parts?

That is an illusion. It is not the truth. These parts are told they are lost, dead, gone, junk, but every one of them is precious to Us and a part of you that We love.

It is too much fragmentation…too much shattering…too many parts…too much programming…

You can be overwhelmed, or you can just put your hand in Ours. Feel how that feels. Warm, steady, sure. Let yourself feel that.

Okay. Will You walk me out of all of this?

Yes, step by step. You don't have to figure it out. As you stay in Our timing, We will reveal things as you are ready. You see already how We bring things together for you step by step. If you can focus on Our presence with you, it will not feel so overwhelming.

Okay. I can sort of feel Your hand in the darkness, the swirl, the sludge. Please don't let go!

I won't.

Will You keep me safe through the night?

Yes. We watch over your days and nights tenderly. Angels attend you. You are never alone.

Will You help all of these parts?

Yes, I care for each deeply.

Okay. I give all of this to You.

Rest in Our love today! There is great victory on its way. Stay steady and know that you are deeply loved and surrounded by Our care and protection. When you fear or walk in unbelief, it opens doors of access to the enemy.

Okay. I am asking for Your grace and love to penetrate my whole system as far as is possible. Let them all know of Your care and love. I trust You for today.

The battle is fierce, but you are standing strong, and We are so very proud of you.

It doesn't feel that way, but I take what You are saying. Thank you.

Learning To Trust

Can you trust Us with every part of you?

I can try and I am willing to. I just need to know that You will help me not to hurt others in any way.

Remember that if you focus on this you won't do anything. You will be held back. It is all and always about trust. Do you trust Us? We can take care of the rest. Even if you were, are We powerful enough to transform and restore? And bring glory to Our name?

Yes, even in this…. Please help me. I want to be wholly Yours and wholly committed to what is on Your heart and to the mass exodus and the bringing down of this system. I know it is only You who can do this and I am beyond humbled that You would invite me into the process with You. I can't do this.

See where that is coming from.

I don't want to mess it up. I don't want to hurt anyone. I don't want to be bad. It is too risky. I am not ready. I'm scared. I'm too broken.

Can you give all of that to Us? We have gently led you and given you people to love and support you on this journey.

I know and I can't believe it. You are too good to me. I don't deserve it.

Can you let Us love you? Can you let Us provide for you? Can you partner with Us for great things?

I want to.

Remember it is as easy as putting your hand in Ours and taking the next step? Yes, there is much more work. Trust and rest.

Okay. I'm in. I am taking Your hand. Please lead and guide each step. I surrender my fear of making mistakes and hurting others. I ask that You take down this stronghold and the stronghold of unbelief. Only You can do this. I am so very excited and yet so very scared.

It is okay to feel that. Keep bringing it all to Us. We are here.

Thank you so very much.

Don't think about what others are thinking of you and fearing different scenarios. Keep your eyes on Us and don't look back.

Okay. Help me!

Feeling "Not Good Enough"

I repent for feeling I need to make up for what I did by pouring out to others. It would never be enough anyway. Please cleanse all of this and its effect on others. I only want to do this in purity.

No one can do it purely alone. Everyone has mixed motivations in what they do. There is no condemnation, but We do want you to see this and understand Our grace that has

been poured out through you and in you to bless others. This is Our work.

Yes, I give it all to You. Thank you for washing it thoroughly. You alone are good and perfect. I don't have to make up for what I did. I can't. It would never be enough, and it is like the system thinking.

Yes, it is. And now there is panic inside. Can you see why?

Because we aren't good enough.

Remember who is worthy to open the scroll? There is only One worthy. Only One who is good enough. Only One who is good. Your job is not to be perfect or good or make up for things, but to simply receive what I have done for you and to celebrate My love for you and others. This is true joy, peace and love. You know this.

Yes, how do my parts receive it? I want every part of me to know this.

It is Our great delight to be known by you as We truly are, without the distortions. This takes time. You want to get this right, but it is okay to make mistakes and to be messy and feel out of control because We are tenderly holding you. We have the way through. Your life is a beautiful testimony of Our love. That is how We see it. We don't see it as you do--the horrendous monster.

I am grateful. In awe and wonder. How can it be?

Remember the difference between Mary and Zacharias' response? Choose the heart of Mary.

I repent for my unbelief and doubts. I put my trust in You. Please help me. I can't do this.

Gladly and with great joy. You can go back to bed knowing We've got you safe in Our arms. Held securely. Lovingly.

Remember who you really are. Not a monster, but Our beloved daughter.

Are You mad at me for trying to make up for stuff?

No, precious Adena. We are not. We understand and know why. We did not bring it up to shame you but to show you Our love and a better way. We have covered this so that it does not defile your clients and groups. This is Our grace and mercy.

It is way more than I can imagine or deserve.

Yes, because you can't. It is just receiving it.

Why are You so good to me?

Because We care deeply about you, precious daughter. You know your weak human love for others. Now multiply it by infinity. This is the greatness of Our love. Nothing can compare. There is no possible way of earning any of it. Your only choice is to receive it with a thankful heart.

There is resistance.

We know and We know the reasons why. This doesn't bother Us. Just receive. Feel the sweetness of it. Undeserved, but freely given.

Is this available to all?

Yes, of course. No one or part is excluded.

That is a great big love.

Yes, it is Our delight when you can receive it.

I want to. Show me how.

With great joy. Let Us tuck you in bed tenderly and sleep the rest of the night.

I can only if You help me.

We are here and do this with great joy.

Okay. Thank you!

(Later)

Thank you so much for meeting me through the night. Reviewing this this morning is so precious. I want to receive moment by moment this great love.

You are learning to stay steady in Our love. This doesn't mean to not feel the emotions. There is much to be faced, but it is best done in the light of Our love. This gives you perspective and helps you to overcome. This is why it is key to settle in Our love before doing any work. This is helpful for your clients too.

What about when we can't settle?

This is why it is helpful to bind off any demonic entities and to express to parts that it is okay to rest and to cooperate with True FAMILY. It takes patience and flexibility even with the order of prayers and journaling and other times of engagement. Some parts may need worship and movement first to settle down. Teaching flexibility is important for survivors.

I am realizing that with Strong Girl* and what we've been going through. I like the new flexibility, although it was very hard at first.

Flexibility can only be taught in a place of safety and love. The more you are settled in love the easier it is for the parts to also.

But I can't do any of it.

Yes, that is where instead of your coping strategies you ask for help and receive Our love. We know it is hard. You think you have surrendered a lot, but often it is just settling into another way of coping. This isn't condemnation. This is just speaking truth to you. It is step by step. With patience for yourself and others. Forgiving you.

That is key, isn't it?

Yes. It is.

Why is it so hard?

From conception you experienced great condemnation for anything that wasn't "perfect." These developed habits of performance, etc. You've worked through a lot and there are more levels, parts, etc. to work through. There is no condemnation. We are pleased with you right where you are at. We don't have the expectations that you have of yourself. You can give those to Us. There is more freedom in being able to just be.

You know the parts that are having a really hard time with this.

Yes, and with reasons. There was so much punishment and reinforcement of the deaths that would happen if you weren't perfect. It is very reasonable for them to be resistant and not willing to look at this. Can you have patience for yourself and your parts?

I guess so.

Just take it step by step in Our love. We honor your journey. We are not impatient or expecting you to be more than you are. There is no condemnation, just the gentle invitation to love.

It sounds easy but it isn't.

We know that. We are here and We care. The more you sync with this the easier it will be. Trust and rest. This is the answer. Rest from trying to make up for it all. Rest from trying to be perfect. Rest from trying to be enough. The simplicity is that We supply all that you need. It is Our great love that overcomes. This is the deep longing of all, yet most run from it. You can receive it.

Yes, I want to. I want to understand this and to walk it out. Please help me.

We are delighted to help you on this journey.

* Strong girl appears throughout this volume and is one of my primary identities. See Section IX for more adventures with Strong Girl (and Good Girl)

The Price of Love

Here I am True FAMILY – I so need You. I really need to sleep but so much is swirling. Are You here?

Yes, darling Daughter of Zion, We are here. We've got you safe and secure in Our arms. Nothing can touch you that doesn't go through Us. Can you believe it?

I want to and I am so very grateful. I give everything to you. There's no way for me to do this. You are my sustainer.

It is Our joy to provide for you and to care for you tenderly. This is always Our heart. It is your part to receive.

I'm not very good at that but I want to be. I want to be a joyful receiver.

You know the lies that stand in the way.

Yes. I am asking for You to speak truth to my heart and to all of my parts…

Hey everyone, there's good news! We get to hear the truth from True FAMILY. We've believed so many lies and have been tricked and deceived. I'm learning a new way of life, and I am inviting all of you to participate. We don't have to work hard to try to make up for all the bad things we did. That is something the cult does. We get to receive from True FAMILY Their love and forgiveness. We get to forgive ourselves.

We can't.

Why?

It's just not the way it is done. There's always a price – a payment. It's like the law of gravity.

I know it seems that way, but there is a higher law, the law of grace. True Jesus died and rose again, conquering our sin and death so that we could have life and life more abundantly. Not because we earned it but because of His love.

It can't be possible and even if it was then all the bad things we did were in vain and that is devastating. We can't face that.

I can see how that would feel. However, Their love is so very great. It is Their delight for us to simply receive.

With nothing in return?

When we receive so great a love, we do want to give, but it is not forced, coerced or manipulated. It is our joy and delight to give as a free will offering. No strings attached.

What if we don't give back?

They love us still, and that again evokes such a response to give with joy. This is who we were created to be. They created us with this ability to spontaneously, joyfully give back, not out of obligations but freely.

I don't know. Sounds too good to be true.

I know it feels that way and we have a strong pull to do what the cult says to because of our long bondage. But the truth sets us free. I hear the clamoring. True FAMILY knows your heart and loves to draw us in.

Too scary.

I know it is hard, and you don't even have to make a full commitment. The invitation is to try it out and see how it feels. You can always choose. Anyone want to testify?

We love True FAMILY! We feel safe!

It is really good and worth trying. It is so much easier not to be forced.

I know it is hard to receive, but when you do, it is so good.

Thank you so much for sharing. I hope that encourages you.

We are going through a lot right now. I'm not sure.

It is okay. I understand and I want you to know that the True FAMILY does too. There is no condemnation. You can take your time.

I'm afraid because of the changes we won't be able to pay for counseling. There's no way.

True FAMILY can do miracles. There's a story about a jar of oil that never ran dry during a famine and about ravens bringing food to a hungry man. They can provide in creative and astonishing ways. We are asking that True FAMILY would supply and that the "oil" would not run dry. That there would be enough to pay for sessions and even the intensive.

It's not possible.

I know it seems that way in the natural, but even now, it seems to be happening. Remember how we found that money unexpectedly?

Yes, but that is gone now.

We are trusting Them to supply. Step by step. They are asking us to trust Them. There are many stories in the Bible about people who trusted in God and God came through for them.

That is other people who didn't do all the bad things we have.

Many of them did bad things too. The grace and mercy of the True FAMILY is incredible.

Hmmm… we don't know.

Just know you are welcome to try. It is that simple.

Intrigued. Maybe.

Okay, no pressure, just a gentle invitation.

Thank you.

True FAMILY, anything more? You know I need to get some sleep. Can You help me?

It is always Our delight to do so. We've so enjoyed this conversation you had with the littles. Do not be afraid. It is Our joy to provide.

I believe, help my unbelief.

We will carry you through today. We surround you with songs of deliverance. Rejoice in Us and Our protection of you. Rest in Our care and love.

I am beyond grateful. Keep me steady in Your love. You know the other requests on my heart.

Don't be afraid to ask and ask big. We hear the inside parts and what they are saying. It is Our great joy to demonstrate Our love in this season.

Section II

Questions For God

For every survivor, the question of "Why did God allow this?" will surface. Even if we have an intellectual answer to this question, it is vital to hear from God what He says from His heart. He knows how to respond to our parts and to help us see the bigger picture in the context of His great love. Other questions arise and need to be answered so that our parts can settle and be able to receive from God. Safety is another common question. Will You keep me safe? For a survivor, this is uppermost in the mind. Jesus loves to reassure us and take us on a journey of learning to trust.

Why?

Any parts want to share anything about the goodness of the True FAMILY? Do you feel Their goodness and love for you?

Some of us do and some don't. Lots of bad things happened. How could He allow it? That doesn't seem fair or good. Why did we have to suffer?

True Jesus, I will let You respond.

My dearest ones, you are more deeply loved than you know. I am not surprised by these questions, and I want to honor you for asking. These are at the root of the issues. Love makes a way where there seems to be no way. I experienced it all on the cross and I overcame it as an example for you. You are not

promised the perfect life but help to find the perfect in it. This takes learning love and dependency on Us instead of yourself. We work it all together for good. This is what We love to do! We take the trauma and turn it into triumph. This brings glory to Us and honor to you and such growth and beauty. Do not despise the trials you are going through. Now there are some which are related to the enemy and those you can just say no to.

Thank you, True Jesus. I choose to trust You today. Anyone want to join me? Is there a place they can meet with You and ask more questions or drain out the "yuck?" (note: the "yuck" or the "yuckies" is what my parts and I call the demonic)

Of course, I am always available to each of you in a personal way because you each matter. None of you are insignificant or not needed. We are on this joyful journey of wholeness together. We delight in you.

I open up my heart to receive all You have for me. Thank you so much!

Are You Safe?

Okay. Thank you for helping me. I want to walk out Your love today. How can I receive it and how can I be it?

We love these questions and love to answer! The first part is just to receive.

"Are You safe?" and "Will You hurt me?" comes up immediately.

And We are happy to answer this over and over again as much as you need it, precious Adena and all parts. We are the safest and We do no harm.

But it doesn't look like it in the Bible. I need help to understand.

You've been working through this. Our plan for restoration is key. Also understanding that this physical body, while exceedingly important in fulfilling your mission here, will be replaced with a different body on the other side in the fullness of time. There is full restoration. What happens now is a temporary injustice that will be fully resolved. This is trusting Our way and seeing from Our perspective.

But it feels close to "the ends justify the means" that the cult uses.

All deceptions are close to the Truth. The differences are that We DO know the end, they do not. Also, Our love is unconditional and freely given without force, while there is conditional.

Okay.

So, do you trust Us, looking at it from the big picture of Our love and restoration?

Yes. Please give me the grace to walk through the temporary injustice, including my part in it.

Are you more powerful than Us?

No. But the struggle is my participation in the bad stuff. I don't want that.

Do you believe We have a way through?

Yes. But…

To get through will require trust and rest, because you cannot do this yourself. All of your desire (drive/control) to avoid hurting others will only keep you in. If you fully release this to Us and trust Us to bring you through, We can do this. Your part is the moment by moment surrender to Our love, not getting distracted by fear or unbelief – the what if's, buts, etc.

Okay, I don't know how to do that. I can cognitively agree, but I have all these parts... I don't know what to do with them.

Can you entrust them to Us also?

I want to. I choose to give all that I am to You, every part and trust You to take me step by step. Please help me.

It is Our delight to do so. Rest in Our love and delight in you today.

Okay.

Who Is In Charge?

I believe True FAMILY is ultimately in charge.

But then how come They allow all the bad things to happen?

It is a good question. If you are forced to do something, is it love?

No.

So, They don't force us. They give us a choice.

Then They are powerless against us.

No, They ultimately have a plan that is good. They have a sovereign plan that works in conjunction with free will.

Sounds complicated.

It isn't really and there is more to it, but like we talked about a few days ago, They know the end, They love unconditionally, and They have a way through. We are learning to trust Them.

Okay.

Why Is It So Hard?

Would You please manage today?

It is Our joy to do so. There is more going on than you know, and We have you safe in Our arms. Trust and rest as We gently lead you. Know that We are here whether you feel Us or not.

Some of this (or a lot of this) feels so unreal to me right now. Distant, like it could be someone else's story. I want to be fully present.

Invite all of you that can be to be present.

I invite all of me that is able to be present to be present. Is there anything anyone wants to share? True FAMILY is with us and working through all things with us. We do not need to be afraid. They can heal and restore all things. We can trust them.

We are scared. Lots of things are happening.

Can you tell me what is happening?

They are working hard to do things, so you won't be free.

Thanks for letting me know. I am trusting True FAMILY to help us and keep us safe through this. We can trust Them.

How come They don't just take us out of this?

It is a process. And we can trust Them to lead us gently for the most restoration for the most people. This is what we've asked of Them. I am excited for as many to be restored as possible. This is how we can do the most damage to the enemy's plans.

But we just want it to stop. We want peace.

Only True FAMILY can give that to us.

Then why is it taking so long? We'd rather go back to sleep and know nothing.

It can seem like the best solution, but does that really stop the torture?

No.

Then this is the only way for lasting peace, even though right now it might be hard. We are trusting Them.

It's really hard. They punish us and others.

I am so very sorry. We can ask the True FAMILY for help. They can protect us and help our parts to stop any internal punishment. Who is punishing internally? There is a better way.

No. They will hurt the ones we love. You must get back in line. Don't you see what they are doing?

No, I don't. But I do believe you, AND there is another way.

You keep saying that, but we can't see it. Just bad things and more bad things. If you saw it, you would do the same.

You are probably right, but I am learning to trust True FAMILY. It is the only way to full freedom for all. It doesn't help for you to punish internally. If we learn to cooperate and work together it will go much better and we will be stronger to resist them and to work with True FAMILY for freedom for all, including the ones we love.

Do you know how high the cost is?

I have a little idea, but not fully. However, the cost is higher if we stay in. They will continue to do bad things and spread to the next generation and continue until someone is brave enough to stop it. Alone we are powerless, but working together with True FAMILY, it is possible. We can trust our loved ones, too, with the True FAMILY.

You don't know how bad it is.

You are right, but it will only continue even if we stay in. Do you have the courage to join me? We are stronger together. The greatest victory we can have is for the system to come down and for all those trapped in it to be free.

That is blasphemous. You can't do that.

I can't on my own, but together with True FAMILY and other survivors we can see a completely new way that is life-giving, not life-taking. Wouldn't it be great to not torture people/parts? Wouldn't it be nice to live free, to make our own decisions and not be in such fear?

It is tempting, but we have to hold firm to save the others.

We are not their savior. There is one Savior. That is True Jesus, who was tortured and died and rose again so that we might have life.

That is a fairy tale.

I know you've been told that, but it is true, and we can be free.

We can't believe that. It is blasphemous. Forbidden.

True Jesus lets us choose. He doesn't force us to believe or torture us to believe. He freely gives. We are not locked in and can continue to choose. It is so much better than the torture and torment. Do you enjoy hurting others?

No, of course not, but it must be done.

What if it didn't?

You are torturing us with the thought of freedom. Freedom is bad and dangerous. We must keep everyone in line.

I hear you and I understand why you feel that way and I just want you to consider there is another way that is much better. You can try it and see.

There will be consequences.

We can ask True Jesus to protect us. You've been seeing how He has been doing that, right?

Well, yes, but …

At least consider it. I know you don't like to hurt others. This is a way to help and not hurt.

But you don't know how bad it is.

The only way to stop the cycle of torture is to have the courage to stop and to not comply with them. You can do this.

Maybe.

Thank you for considering. I am happy to talk with you about this anytime and True FAMILY is here also to help. True Jesus, I am trusting You to protect my parts and my loved ones and providing a way through. Please help us.

I am here and I am delighted to work with you and your parts in a new way. Feel My love and My power on your behalf. I do this because I care. I have gifts for anyone who wants them. This is not a bribe, but simply because I love you. Anything that you need is available. Rest, play, food, water, attention, fun and adventure. We love to provide for you all.

Thank you so much.

Just Taking the Next Step?

Should I just give up ministry? Maybe I'm hurting people.

No, that is not what We have for you.... you are helping many, and your journey is unique. Continue until We show you what is next. Your journey will be more public for Our purposes and glory and for more to be set free.

I don't want that! You know that! I want to stay hidden in the cage. Please!

Do you trust Us and are you willing to walk out the destiny We have for you for the most restoration?

I want to, but…

We will give you grace step by step.

Maybe this is all fake… all made up?

You get to choose to believe it or not. You get to trust Us or not. We will not force you. You can stay in the cage. You can go into hiding. We love you no matter what. We always

will. Nothing can change how We feel about you. You've asked for the most restoration possible. You didn't ask for the easiest journey.

I ask for dumb things, I guess…

We love your heart. You are very courageous.

I don't feel like it. I just want to hide forever and ever.

We know you are scared. We do have a way through if you continue to say yes. We have prepared the way. It IS easiest with Us and the greatest rewards are available.

I really do want the system to come down. I want to walk this out in love. I want to be true to You. I do want to see the greatest restoration possible.

Then let's do this together. Just put your hand in Our hand and take the next step.

I'm terrified.

We know. It doesn't have to stop you from putting your hand in Ours. We hold you gently.

Okay.

What If?

Why do I have these tremendously bad images and sensations?

It is because of what was done to you. Do not fear them, but step into Our safe protection.

How do I know You are real and not the ones doing this to me?

We are real and We are here. We are the only Ones who have what it takes to get you completely free. You get to walk this out in faith.

I don't want to hurt anyone. If I am doing anything that is hurting others, please stop me, even if that means you know what.

That is not necessary. We only allow what is needed for healing.

What if something bad happens?

We are with you through it all. Do you want full healing? Let it come. Don't hold back. Be yourself. Trust Us in the process.

I don't want that stuff (memories) to come out right now.

We know that, but if you desire to be set free, it is necessary. You are here for such a time as this. If you want to see the full restoration, you must be willing to surrender it all to Us. The timing and what it looks like. Lay down all pride.

Oh, I see. That is big, isn't it? Okay, I choose to surrender it all to You. I think I have but then You take it to a deeper level. I choose You, True Jesus, and You alone. No other gods. I want to be completely free. I am committed to that. I will trust You.

Will It Hurt?

Here I am True FAMILY – I really need You today! Please help me walk this out.

We are here. We never leave you nor forsake you. It is Our heart to keep you safe and to nurture you in Our love and to help you complete your destiny here.

Am I walking in my purpose?

Yes, you are, and We are so very thrilled. We delight in you in more ways than you can know.

Should I be running this morning? (my exercise routine)

That is not the question.

What is the question?

Why are you afraid to be outside?

Yes, that is the question… Why?

We don't like it outside. More bad things happen outside than inside.

What bad things happened outside?

Hunts, rituals, yuckies… you name it. Rape and torture.

But plenty happened inside too?

Yes, but what you can see is more manageable.

So, are tunnels also part of the "outside" in your way of thinking?

Of course, everyone knows that.

Okay, just checking.

I don't want to talk about those things.

I know they are very painful... oh, and shapeshifting happened outside?

We don't want to talk about that.

I understand. I'm just trying to get a better understanding of what is going on and how we feel about indoors/outdoors.

Indoors is definitely safer. It is more controlled. Outside is crazy bad. We hate outside. We hide inside. But underground is the worst.

What can you tell me about underground?

Why do you want to know?

It will help us to understand each other better.

That is a part you don't want to know. Ever. Scary BAD. Always bad, never good.

Jesus, I need You here. I don't want to make anything up. I want only the true Truth always that is You.

I am here. I can help you every step of the way. Do you trust Me?

I am willing to trust You. Were You in the tunnels with me when I was going through all of that?

Yes, I was. I know every detail of it.

Why?

It is a part of all things that will take place for ultimate glory. There is a bigger story going on. My promises are always yes and amen and they will be fulfilled. Do you believe Me?

I want to.

Keep entering in with Me and you will see this glory and you will understand.

That's baloney! How could You allow such things! That makes You complicit.

I understand how it feels that way, and in a way, it makes sense. However, there is a bigger picture which you cannot see that is true and that will make sense when you can see it all. This is what faith is about.

I don't have any faith.

I understand that trust has been broken over and over and that is why we struggle with faith. There is compassion and grace. It is not about our faith but about the Faith of Jesus. We can rely on His faith when ours is the size of a mustard seed, and it can still accomplish great things. That is the good news.

All I can see is the darkness.

Would you like Jesus to bring the true light?

Will it hurt?

When light comes it can hurt initially, but it is very healing if you are willing to trust.

I want true light.

I'm so glad! Jesus, can You bring true light?

I can. It will not be easy to adjust to the light when there has been so much darkness, but We will supply the grace. You are a brave one. We honor you.

Do it quick before I change my mind.

Jesus, You are the Light of the world, please shine brightly in my dark places. I say yes to You.

It is My delight to do so. Let there be light.

Oh! Oh! Oh! Wow!

Why Won't It Go Away?

I hate this day. Can we erase every 13th of the month?

It is okay. There is a reason your parts blurted this out this morning. Adena, you've not been aware of what this means. Listen to them.

I don't want to. I'm sick of this. I want to bury it all again forever. Can't You make it all go away?

It is okay to express how you feel, and also to be able to come to Us to quiet your heart. We know this is hard. Facing truth is the way for full freedom and healing. You want to be free and to not be accessed. This is the only true way. Burying things never works and only makes this worse.

I know, but it is hard. Please strengthen me to face these things. It hurts.

We know and We are here to comfort you and to help you with the pain. There is a way through. We can help you if you let Us.

I want to. I can't make all of my parts agree to it though.

We know this. It is a process, and We are holding you through the process. Do not be afraid.

That is impossible. How can I not be afraid? This is horrible stuff.

It is not in your own strength, but in Ours. When you can see it from Our perspective, it will help make it easier. You teach this and write on it, but you also must walk it out.

Yes, I know. What if I wanted to stop doing all of that? Never teach again or write anything ever again?

Okay. What would that look like for you?

I would just get a normal job and work like normal people…

And die inside because you wouldn't be doing what you were created for. You know who you are and what We've given you. To bury those gifts would also be a kind of death to you. There may be times when We ask you to take a break, but it is through this crucible of having to live what you teach, and as others see and hear your heart that We've given you, that you overcome… By the blood of the Lamb and the word of your testimony.

I know this is true in my heart, but it is so hard.

It is and We are here to make it much lighter if you will let Us.

I don't want to be a hypocrite.

You aren't [and you won't be] if you continue to walk with Us. We will give you the strength. When you share your personal story and are real in groups and on Sundays, it blesses others. Just like you've been blessed by those We've put you into connection with.

Okay, so please hold me close. I choose to let You hold me. Please quiet me in Your love.

We are here and delight to do so. Listen to the song We are singing over you. Let it fill every part of you with comfort and hope.

Struggling to Connect

Okay, thank you! Littles, I'm here. I'm so sorry when I ignore you. I don't want to do that. I struggle with the stuff too. I'm sorry to leave it with you. The TRUE Family is going to help us.

We hate you. You leave us alone. You are a hypocrite to speak to others about this but don't help us.

I am really sorry. The True FAMILY is here to help us. They will not abandon you or reject you or neglect you. Let's come to Them for help. I know They are eager to help us.

Why should They be? They are bad and mean too. No one is safe. We are staying locked away.

This will not help us to heal. I do understand, though. But I've found the True FAMILY to be safe and good and always there for us. Are You here for us, TRUE FAMILY?

Yes, We are. More than you know. We delight in this day and in your willingness to come.

We didn't say we were willing. You hurt us.

That was not Us but others. If We allow hurt, it is for a purpose and bigger purpose than you know so that all evil will ultimately be defeated.

But didn't You do this on the cross?

Yes, and it is a process of walking this out with you.

Why does it take so long? Can't You speed it up?

We could but you would miss out on some things, and it would be overwhelming. We are being gentle with you so that you can continue to bless others. Step by step. This is the process. We so love you. Do not be afraid or doubt. We are with you.

*Is it a trick? We've experienced this over and over with the "family." **

Yes, but that was not the TRUE FAMILY. The TRUE FAMILY always causes us to triumph. They have helped me so very much and I have been carried by Them through these last few weeks. So very tender and good. I submit to You, TRUE FAMILY. I let go of my pride and all the other things and I choose to trust You. I open my heart to You and all of my parts. Come littles and find rest and peace and trust with the TRUE FAMILY. They will not harm us but will help us.

That's what you think.

True FAMILY, I need help with this one. What is the opposition and hatred? How do I handle this?

Do not be afraid. Release this one to Us and We will help her to know Our love.

I release this hateful one to you, True FAMILY. I know that you are meant to be passionate in love. This is who you really are. Let's give this hatred to Jesus.

He is the one we hate. We hate Him in you. We can't stand Him.

Please tell me why? I'm sorry for what happened to you.

We told you… the upside down cross, the oral sex, the having to be like Jesus. Yuck. No, never. We don't want to be like Him.

That is a distortion of the Real and True Lord Jesus Christ. The Real one would never do that or call you to do that. They are pure and holy.

But They allowed it. They allowed wicked mean men to do this. They could have stopped it.

Jesus, what do You say?

There is a bigger purpose going on.

So, the ends justify the means? That is horrible. How could You?

Remember, I came and experienced it too. I suffered humiliation, betrayal and a horrific death on more levels than you know. I did this for your freedom. You are not still on the

cross. I can take that pain from you. I can take the hatred and the trauma that is tormenting you. I can take it all away. Would you like that?

Yes, but this is a trick.

We don't play tricks. We are true to Our word. Are you willing to trust Us?

Will it make it worse?

No, in the long run it will be so glorious and so much better.

Okay. We accept. There's many of us. This was their favorite game. It is called "dying daily."

Oh, I'm so very sorry. I can see why you would carry so much hatred. Jesus is here to help you and all the others. They will take you to a safe place. They will not trick you. This safe place is good and holy.

But we are not. How can we get there?

Jesus paid for it all and He has a way to bring you rest and to cleanse you from all that stuff. I am also asking for your release from all demonic entities, through the power and by the blood of the True Lord Jesus Christ of Nazareth. No substitutes. No interference.

Okay. We receive it.

Thank you so much, True FAMILY. We love You. Lift this burden of hate and bring Your cleansing in every way. Thank you for delivering me from those entities that tormented so many of my parts.

*Many cult groups call their members "family." This is why I am careful to distinguish by using the term "True FAMILY" for the Trinity.

Section III

Access

The hard reality is that as long as a survivor has unhealed parts and programming, there is the potential for access. This can range from minor harassment to major involvement in rituals. The ONLY safety is in True Jesus and trusting Him. This might sound easy for someone who is not a survivor, but to those of us who were intentionally trained to NOT trust Him, this is not an easy task, and it takes time and process.

Struggling

Here I am True FAMILY – struggled with prayers today, distracted, shifting to other scenes. Why does this happen? Is it just fatigue or was there access last night?

You know the answer, but don't want to face it.

Okay, if it is yes, then what happened, and can You undo it? Is it because I read last night from the book? What is it? How can I protect myself…oops that is the wrong question isn't it? How are You going to protect me?

That is better. We understand, precious Adena, and We know. We are not discouraged by this, but We do have solutions. It is important for you to understand what is going on.

I don't know what to do.

That is okay, because We do. Can you trust Us?

That is always the question isn't it. I do to the best of my ability.

We know this and We are strengthening you, step by step.

Why do I have breakthroughs on some days and on other days, I struggle? I don't know what happens to make one day so different than the next. Sometimes things are so clear, but it doesn't seem to be because of anything I did or did not do. Maybe it is just because of Your sovereign grace? On the other hand, sometimes there is access, and I don't know why. I don't understand this.

It is not about what you do or don't do but your heart in relationship to Us and your ability to receive from Us. When you are trying to do things on your own, you are more accessible.

Then what is my part?

To simply trust and rest. Parts get agitated and you allow it.

Please teach me how to do this…to not "stuff" emotions and to learn how to quiet myself in Your love.

It also has to do with leaning on Jo (my prayer minister) **instead of leaning on Us. She is Our gift to you, and it is important not to idolize the gift or depend on her beyond what We've given to you.**

This is hard. Please help me.

We are and We will. It is not an easy thing because you tend to swing from self-dependence to Jo-dependence instead of resting in Our love. We allow different things to make you aware of what is going on and to help correct you in love.

Thank you. I appreciate it. How do I walk this out today?

We will show you gently.

I can't do this. Just tell me what to do.

We know that is what your parts want. It is easy to swing from one extreme to another – doing it all on your own with "Strong Girl" and "Reckless" * sometimes and at other times swinging the other way in compromise and fear. If We force you to make a decision or just tell you what to do, then you won't grow, and We are no different than the programmers and handlers.

It makes sense but it is hard.

This is why you are writing the book on paradox. ** It is for you too. To learn how not to swing but to hold these beautiful aspects in restful tension and to be aware of the counterfeits. You do need community, and We've placed Jo in your life for a purpose. You are growing in strength to make decisions, but not self-reliance. Rest in Our love.

I'm grateful for You showing me this and I am asking for strength and grace to walk it out. What about Testimony Mountain…Do I go ahead and release this one***?

Do you want to?

Yes, I do.

Is that Reckless or Strong Girl?

Maybe.

It is helpful to explore this. Will this help others?

I believe it will, but can You strip it of any self-promotion and anything in it that promotes the system that is there unknowingly?

Yes, We can cleanse it of anything not of Us and We can help it to be a blessing to those who listen.

Is my life at risk?

Not in the way you are asking. We've got this. You can rest and trust Us, taking it step by step. Go with your intuition.

But is my intuition messed up by the cult too?

The only way you find out is to walk it out. There are elements to be cleansed and restored, but you discover that by the process.

Can't You just tell me?

We can but you will not grow. Trust and rest.

Okay. I choose You.

*More on these parts in Section IX and X

**This is the next book I'm working on, still in progress

***Referring to an interview on a sensitive topic

Held Safe

I am so very grateful, True FAMILY, for all that You are doing for me! I give my days and nights to You. You know what is on my heart before I even say it.

Yes, We do, precious Daughter of Zion. Put your trust in Us and never be put to shame. We've got you safe in Our arms. No weapon formed against you can prosper.

You are my Protector and King. What a beautiful dance of love! Keep me safe in Your arms of love. I am safe with You. Is there more I need to process? It feels lighter but I can't sleep. There's joy bubbling up.

There are times when We give you a rest from what is surfacing. You are working on an important project and transition, and We know what you can handle. Rest and trust in Us.

How do I get back to sleep?

There is much on your mind. Just be for a bit and rest in Us. We give you the strength that you need.

I choose to rest joyfully in You. I give all of this to You. Is there anything I am missing? Was there any access?

Be aware of this, but also trust in Us as your Protector. You have turned a corner, and We are so very proud of you. This doesn't mean smooth sailing from here, but that there is a place of rest. Look to Us for all that you need. We will supply directly or through the body. These are triumphant times as Our love is magnified in you. You are going from glory to glory. Rest in Our love.

There's a lot to do. Do You have a plan for all of that?

Yes, find the rhythms of Our grace. You can "plow through," which is an old pattern for you, or you can do things differently in Our flow and from Our rest. We invite you to a different way of doing things. No condemnation. It will be easy to slip into the old patterns, but joy is found in Our way.

I want to learn this. Show me how.

Glady, with great joy!

Section IV

Doubts, Unbelief, and Internal Conflict

No survivor wants their story to be true. The horrendous trauma and potential things we did to others is not something we want to remember. We'd love to forget it all and pretend. But to find true healing and wholeness, we have to face the pain. Most of us also had specific mind control programming or other techniques done to us as well as threats to keep us from remembering. Denial programming is strong. Amnesia walls can be very thick. A lot of times family and friends may disbelieve us. I don't blame them. I don't want to believe it myself. It usually takes the Lord giving me numerous clues and confirmations before I finally believe my memories. These things aren't just "vain imaginations" to get attention. Here are my struggles to believe my parts and sometimes even what the Lord is revealing.

You Don't Believe Us!

And if that is true, then we get to walk in forgiveness.

See you don't ever believe us. We hate you too.

What does that mean?

You talk a good talk, but you don't love us.

I'm sorry. I want to. I'm learning and working on that. It isn't easy to reconcile everything, and I don't feel like I have all that many memories back. They are just like puzzle pieces, and I don't know where they all go.

If you believed us, it would be easier.

True Jesus, I need help here. I need to return to some joy. I give all of this to You and all of my parts too. I put my trust in You alone. Please meet me here.

We are here, dearest Daughter of Zion. We see and know your heart. Don't feel condemned. Walk in Our love and remember who you are.

It is just hard to one minute feel like me as a leader ministering and then feel like a baby throwing a temper tantrum. Who am I?

We know this is not easy. You are both and We value and treasure both. We honor you and who you are. Take a break from this and worship. Know We are with you and do not be afraid. We will help you to navigate this. It feels really big right now, but We can help you through it.

Is it True?

Help me today, True FAMILY! I want to stay focused on You and in joy. I need some recovery time. But I know I also have these parts that I am struggling to believe. It would help so much to have confirmation. But I give all of this to You.

Dear ones, I want to believe you. I want to hear and honor what you have to say and what you went through. I really do. I am asking the True FAMILY to help me with this. I know we were programmed in ways to be against one another and contradictory. I don't want to have this internal conflict, and I am willing to work through some things so that we can cooperate and collaborate as this is the path to healing.

FINALLY! You have to believe us…

Why do I have to believe you?

Because it is true.

Okay. I want to hear more, and I want to love you well. I'm sorry for not believing you. But I know that sometimes parts can lie to keep the programming intact.

What would we gain by lying to you about this?

Attention-getting?

This is not the attention we want. Remember the picture (brief flash of torture)

Okay. I see… Please have grace with me as I process this.

True FAMILY, I need help with this. Is this true?

Yes, it is. Facing your own programming is key. You don't want to remember. You don't want to break programming. Feel the confusion coming in and the trying to reason away from it. We have grace for this, and We so deeply love you. We have a way through. It is okay. Can you hold this loosely until We show you more?

Okay. I am willing to face this. Please help me.

(parts cheering)

Darling daughter We see, and We care. This is a difficult road, and it will get harder. We will not sugar-coat this for you. But it does lead to a fuller and more fulfilling life. You've been trapped for a long time and even though you have a measure of freedom now, there is so much more that We want to bring to you. Do not be afraid. We will take you step by step and moment by moment. You are safe in Our love.

Okay. I do see this is the path before me – help me to endure it.

The Struggle

I don't want to deal with my parts, and You know why. They seem agitated that I sent my journaling to Jo.

Yes, it is time to face that. Don't be afraid. We will help you.

But I can't. It's too hard.

We know it feels that way. It feels too hard and too big, but when you bring everything into the light, We can help you walk it out.

Okay, I want that, it's just hard. I'm afraid.

What are you afraid of?

Of memories being true. Can't I go back to fantasyland? Can't I go back to "the good life?"

It is a life of compromise and falsehood because you were not operating from the real you. You can go back, but it is not what you really want.

I know that. It is just hard.

Do you think it is too hard for Us?

No. I know it isn't, but I'm afraid.

We can give you the strength to walk through this. Just ask.

Okay. I need Your help to walk through this. I can't do this alone.

We aren't asking you to do it alone. We've provided for you all that you need. You have the courage to face this.

Okay, I say yes to You and Your timing for all of this. I choose to not back off, but to face this with Your love and with Your joy. You have a way through for me. I can breathe.

Yes, beautiful, Adena. It is as simple as…

I know, putting my hand in Yours and taking the next step.

Dear parts, I am sorry I haven't believed you. I am willing to listen. I know we can work through this together with the True FAMILY.

You betrayed us! Why did you share those things! Now we will be in trouble.

I'm sorry, I didn't realize that. I believe that True Jesus can help protect us from any retaliation. Jo will help us through it too.

Little good that will do! You don't understand what you are up against. You are so naïve and dumb. We hate you. You don't follow the plan.

Yes, I am choosing not to follow the cult's plan for my life anymore, because I believe True Jesus has a better way that will be a blessing for all of us.

You are so naïve. How could you! He is a traitor and powerless.

I understand that is what you've been told, but I know Him differently. He has been faithful and so very good to me. I trust Him.

You are deceived. We have to stick to the plan. There are big consequences if we don't.

I hear you, but I believe that True Jesus is able to help us through this into a new freedom for all of us and blessing to others around us.

You don't get it. Torture is for those around us, bad things will happen. We can't stop that. There are always consequences.

Would you be willing to let True Jesus manage this? He is a really good Protector, and He cares deeply for all of us, including you.

If He cared, then He would know we have to stick to the plan. Let it go and get in line.

True Jesus, we need your help. I don't know how to respond. Please show us the way.

I am here for you all. Do not be afraid. I do see it all and the intended consequences, but I have a way through if you are willing to trust Me.

I am, but I don't know if they are.

It is okay. We don't force. You will continue to work this out with Jo today. Trust and rest.

Okay. Thank you so much.

Don't Rock the Boat!

Thank you so much, True FAMILY, for all that You are doing for me. I choose to trust You today for all things. You will sustain me and not overwhelm me.

Yes, We are delighted to walk through this day with you. Do not let fear gain a foothold but trust Us to show you the way.

Thank you. Keep me steady in You and that I would not enter into self-justification but stay calm and even with explaining and not taking any bait of the enemy. Please give me words to say. *

We are glad to stand with you. Take responsibility for what is yours.

Okay. Thank you. And I repent for being unwilling to face things about the Jesuits. I know if it is not true You will show me in time, but that there is enough evidence to press forward and to believe my parts.

Yes, We are glad to lead you gently in this. Do not be afraid. We will help you. There is a way through.

You are my truth, True Jesus. To my inner realm, I am so sorry for not believing you and struggling to face this. Please forgive me. I want to be sensitive to what you are sharing and to not push it away or to accuse you of lying. I want to hear what you have to say. We can get through this with the True FAMILY. I know it may take some time to build trust, but please know I am willing to hear when you are ready to share, and I honor what you have to share.

It's too late. We aren't saying anything.

I honor that and I won't push you. When you are ready, I am ready to talk about this.

It's too hard.

I know that it feels that way, but I believe that we can face anything with the True Jesus.

We are so confused, there's so many "Jesuses," so we reject them all.

I can understand that. It isn't easy for me. But I'm learning to discern the differences and to know that the One True Jesus is worth following. I would guess that True Father God is challenging as well.

Yes, too many fathers… some are good, and some are not. We hate them. They do bad things, but we also need them.

Again, I'm learning about True Father God who is gentle and kind and who loves us unconditionally. How about Holy Spirit?

Too many spirits. That's why it is easier to just do it ourselves.

To keep safe?

Yes. Too much pain. Bad things. Close down. Stay away forever. Block. Forget. Shame. Pain. Bad things.

I can see why that would make talking about any of this challenging.

Yes, better to be silent. It just gets us in trouble when we talk.

Okay, I understand. I would like to talk soon to any internal programmers who may be reinforcing a lot of things.

Not a good idea. We have to stay in line and keep the rules. Stay safe. Not talk. Or bad things happen.

We can wait and do this with Jo, but I want us to be prepared and ready so that we can have some breakthrough.

That's all you care about. You want to break us. We are trying to help you. Don't you get it?

I know this is difficult, but I do believe there is a way through to find true love and unity, peace and grace for all and to come into wholeness.

You don't realize how dangerous this is. You need to stop now. Get away and just pretend everything is good. Keep your good life. Don't rock the boat. Just go along with things. We will help you keep in line. You will be in trouble if you don't.

I hear you and I understand from your perspective how this is, but I do believe there is another way. But we can take this slow and process gently for all of us. Okay?

You are crazy.

True Jesus, I need You.

We are here. We see and know. You are doing well. Don't be discouraged. Take it one step at a time. Nothing is impossible. Rest and trust.

Okay, thank you. I fix my eyes on You today and I trust You to walk me through this day in love.

Yes, Our delight. Do not be afraid.

*I was dealing with a conflict with a friend at the time

Crazy Feeling

This journaling occurred while working on another book on Paradoxes which will be coming out next. Parts discuss writing for the cult system and learn how to work with True FAMILY in the writing process. It also references my first two books, "3 Easy Steps to Revival" and "The Inheritance" which are available on Amazon and were written before I knew anything about my survivor history.

We are here in your pain. We know this is hard for you to face. The clues are little ones, but they add up. Don't be afraid to look at them.

But I feel crazy when I do.

The Truth will set you free. When you resist, it makes it harder. When you trust Us with everything, We will help you through and help you to see the connecting points.

I don't want to resist. But it is hard to believe. What if I am making it all up (my memories) or making connections that aren't there?

What if you are? Do you trust Us to lead and guide you? That is the true question.

I don't know. Can I trust You? I want to…. but what if You are the programming?

It is a fair question and one you need to resolve.

There are times of clarity when I know that I know it is You and You are TRUE and Truth. But then there are other times when it feels all muddled and I don't know about any of it and confusion comes. I know that True Jesus is not the author of confusion. Please help me and keep me steady.

We are here and We care. The confusion is part of the programming.

How do I stay steady in You, True Jesus?

Take it one step at a time. You don't need to figure it all out now. We are gently revealing things as you are able to handle them. We are patient. We are not in a hurry. You can give Us these little puzzle pieces from this trip, and you can trust Us to work it all out for good. You had some good revelations about yourself through this. That is beneficial, though hard. Don't be afraid of that.

Okay, I release all of this to You. I don't need to understand it all but can trust You. You will confirm these things in Your timing and way.

Yes, that's it! Know that We are holding you through all of this. Enjoy your time here and let the river of Our delight flow through you. Take some time for worship to refresh and stabilize you. We've got you!

Can you phrase that differently? Did you do that on purpose? *

Yes, We did. Yes, you are safe in Our hands, and We are tenderly caring for you. That is what We mean when We say We've got you. We want to reframe your perspective of that.

Okay. I give all of this to You. Why do You purposely trigger me?

We allow and will trigger at times to help you reframe it – to see from Our perspective and to overcome the programming.

Okay.

To my inner realm: I'm sorry I didn't discuss the book writing with you. I understand you have some things to say.

We do. You have to be more careful. You put too much stuff out there and they will come and get you.

I understand your fears. Thank you for letting me know. This is important to me, and I do feel commissioned by God to do it and so I am trusting He will protect me.

Did you ask Him?

No, I didn't. True Jesus, is this writing assignment from You or was this a good idea from Strong Girl? Or someone else?

It is a big step, and it is from Us. We love your creativity and love to work with you on these projects. Your previous books are still valid too. There will be a time to do some re-writes and to republish them with your current understanding.

Thank you. Will You protect us?

Yes, that is what We love to do. This doesn't mean that difficult things won't occur but instead that We are always with you and will see you through. We do work all things together for good.

Maybe, but that isn't a guarantee. We want a guarantee. If it gets in the wrong hands…

I don't think the content is that radical and I have already been very public on Testimony Mountain.

Yes, we know, and we don't like it. You are exposing us.

Again, I am sorry, and I want to be more careful, at the same time I am choosing to trust True Jesus to protect us, and I understand how it works with Him. It is not a guarantee that hard times won't come but that it will be for good.

Who's good?

For all who put their trust in God. He runs the universe and does a really good job.

I don't know about that. He lets the bad guys do bad things. That makes Him bad.

I know it can look that way, but He has a really good plan that is going to be amazing when we see it all put together.

I don't know if we can trust Him.

It is okay to just try. He is willing for you to experience His goodness. His love is real and genuine and unending.

Yes, but they made us do certain things to it we didn't like (in the writing process).

Okay, the good news is we aren't going to do that. With True FAMILY it is not about Them making us do certain things, but about us having fun creating with Them. Is that okay?

As long as They don't force us.

Yes, and They will help us to make sure that there isn't any cult system stuff in there. We don't want to do that.

Okay, but what if they (the cult) tell us to?

We do not need to obey them anymore. We get to make our own decisions. It is okay. You don't need to answer to them or report what we are doing.

It's still happening.

Reporting? **

Yes.

True Jesus, would You help us?

Yes, of course.

I don't know what to do about the reporting. I don't want any more reporting. How do I stop this?

Why are they reporting?

I don't know.

Ask.

Okay, If anyone is still reporting, why are you doing it?

We have to.

Why?

Because that is what we do.

There are other things you can do, and Jesus would love to give you a different job if you are willing.

Is He going to force us and do bad things like they do?

No, He is kind and gentle.

They will punish us if we don't do our jobs.

I understand but it feels very violating to me for you to be reporting what we are doing. Can you see how that hurts me?

Well, you just don't understand how it works.

Okay, then tell me.

It was a deal you made to keep others safe. You have to keep the deal.

We don't have to keep any deals with the cult. They forced us to do those deals with threats. True Jesus can help us break those agreements and be free.

(In the spirit, I see a girl with dark hair and a yellow dress being captured and she is screaming)

See how they are in control.

We are choosing to entrust everything to True Jesus. He will help us, and He will protect her.

Jesus, can You help this girl in the yellow dress?

Yes, she is precious to Me.

Can You set her free?

Yes, I can.

Prove it!

Watch. (Jesus walks over to the cage where they've put her and gently leads her away…)

Wow! Did You really do that or did Adena make that up because she wanted to?

It is real. I can set people free. This is why I came and endured torture and death and rose again, so I could set captives free. It is My specialty.

Okay. Can You set us free? We don't want to report anymore. But we don't want bad things to happen to others. We are very careful to be good.

I know your heart is to care and that is how they controlled and manipulated you. See the tethers they have on you (lines connecting them to others). You can be free.

What will happen to them?

Do you trust Me to work that out and set them free?

Can You really do it?

Yes. Not maybe in the timing you desire, but I do have a plan for them all. I see the big picture and I help them step by step, just like I am helping you.

Why can't You do it faster? Why does it take so long?

We work within free will with Our sovereignty in beautiful ways that are ultimately for good for so many. That is what the

paradox book is about. That is why Adena is passionate to write about it because it has to do with her freedom. This is why she wants to get the good news out. Are you willing to cooperate?

Hmmm…that is a lot to think about. Yes, I guess we can help. The reporters will need some help, so they aren't afraid.

Jesus, can You help them?

Yes. Do not be afraid. I am here.

Is the girl safe?

Yes. She is free.

Did You do that just for us?

It was always my intention to do so, but I also knew that it would be needed to help you to understand who I am and what I can do. I don't have a problem showing you.

Thank you.

*The phrase "We've got you" felt like being trapped, not feeling safe

**About Reporting: Some parts have the job of reporting back to the cult what the presenter person is doing. This is usually done in a way that the presenter or host does not know that this reporting is going on and is completely oblivious to it. Until reporter parts are helped to obtain new jobs and connection with True FAMILY, the cult can know all the details of what is going on in the survivor's life without much effort (surveillance, etc.). Dealing with reporter parts is an important part of the recovery process.

Nobody

I'm scared. I would rather be a nobody.

You've never been a nobody.

I know that nobody is a nobody with You, but I would prefer to be normal, obscure, hidden. Can You erase me?

That is not what this is about. You can only be who you are. Who We created you to be.

But it feels like "they" (i.e. the system) created me.

You know the truth. Do not be afraid.

Can I pretend this is not true?

You can try, but facing it is part of healing and freedom.

What if it is just system propaganda? All lies?

You get to choose whether you will believe or not. What do you know in your heart?

Okay. I give this to. I trust You. Keep me safe in Your arms.

Our delight to do so.

Deceiving Myself?

Please help me today! Thank you for being with me through the night and holding me gently. I choose You today.

See you are stronger today than before. This is how relational skills work. * A crisis can help to strengthen you when you stay relational. Do you see this?

Okay, I get it, but it wasn't fun.

You are in training, and it won't always be fun. We know what you need to do to walk this out. Keep moving forward.

But what if I am just writing to myself and deceiving myself? This is the question. Then everything is a sham. And I am crazy.

You know the truth in your heart, and We are so very proud of you. Don't be discouraged but trust.

Okay. I am asking for strength for today. Please help me.

We see and know. Remember We are making a way.

Okay. I am grateful.

*See the book *Transforming Fellowship: 19 Brain Skills that Build Joyful Community* by Chris Coursey

Section V

Sabotage

Sabotage among parts is common for survivors. This might seem counterintuitive, but programmers program parts to keep internal conflict going to keep the survivor in turmoil and under control. Many of the parts are doing this because they've been programmed to believe that they are doing good and keeping the host safe. It takes time and care to help them see there is a better way. Neither of the examples below resulted in immediate change, however, with time, they were able to make the transition from their jobs of sabotage.

Keeping You Safe

True Jesus, who is sabotaging the work inside?

There are different ones who are doing this to try to protect you.

I want You alone to be my Protector, so how do I deal with this?

Have the conversation.

Okay, all those involved in sabotage, would you be interested in coming forward. We'd like to talk.

No way. We don't want to get into trouble. We are only following orders.

Who's orders?

The top dog's orders, dummy.

Okay. What else are you doing?

Why are you prying? You sound creepy.

It is okay, we just want to know you better and what your role is in the system.

More than you know. I am very important. I approve or disapprove of things. I get to punish those who don't fall into the category of "liking them." It is fun. We love to terrorize others.

Do you really enjoy that? Jesus can share with you a better option that I believe you would like more.

No, got to keep up the appearances. Lots of trouble if we don't ... Where do you think the stomachaches are coming from?

Oh, that's you?

Yes, I'm pretty proud of what I can do.

I see. It really isn't in our best interest for that.

Why not? It works. You will eventually get the message.

I understand that, but there are better ways of doing it. The best is for both of us to accept Jesus as our Lord and Savior.

Yeah, when hell freezes over. Not going to. Never. End of story.

I'm sorry you feel that there is no alternative. But actually, there are many. We are not under the same torture as before, so you can relax.

Right.... You know nothing. There is quite a lot going on and we are making it possible to survive. Without us you'd be nothing.

I hear you and I will take this under serious advisement. Thank you for all you've done for me throughout my life.

Patterns

I knew there was a pattern for most of my life of not living in one home longer than three years and often much less than that. Although I longed for security and longevity in one place, circumstances kept happening to keep us on the move. I didn't realize until more recently this was a cover for shifting relationships and therapy (which was also in a 3-year pattern but dispersed enough that it wasn't obvious).

Okay. Anyone inside willing to talk about this? We get to bring everything into the light of the True FAMILY's love so that we can walk in a new way.

Keep to the pattern. Keep to the script. Programming is important for survival. Obey and live. You aren't supposed to see.

Well, the moving is plain to see.

Yes, meant to be so you wouldn't see the other or blame it on the moves instead of the plan.

What is the plan?

We can't tell you.

Okay. I desire long lasting relationships and stability with True FAMILY.

Can't. Keep moving is safer.

Do some of you intentionally sabotage relationships?

We do what we have to. Follow orders. Can't get too close. Dangerous. Hide.

I recognize my tendency to rigidity and sameness for safety and the other person's extreme risk taking. Both of these are a distortion of the true flow with True FAMILY. I want that paradox of relational flow with Them where there's freedom, not bondage.

Not the way we do things. Have to keep to the pattern. Safest.

I am seeing how the safest way is this relational flow with True FAMILY. They know the end from the beginning and have a clear path for me. Although it is not quite clear to me yet, I know it is a path that is good. They help us through the "step by step" of the journey, so we don't have to figure it out or follow the patterns of programming. I believe this is the best way.

We can't agree. All we know is the script and following orders. Safest. Best. Follow orders and live. Don't and die. It is as simple as that.

I know we've lived our life that way and it makes sense from what we've experienced, but we are discovering a new way that I do believe is worth pursuing. I'm finding much more joy and peace in it.

But it is also causing problems with your family, and it is bringing up all kinds of things you'd be better off not knowing. Better to just forget it all again.

I'm choosing to face these things and even though it is hard, when I process them with True FAMILY, They have restorative things that bring much joy. I don't have to live in constant fear anymore.

You didn't feel it all that much because we kept it from you.

Yes, but it still impacts me. I appreciate what you've done to hold the pain, fear, anxiety, despair, etc. for me so I wasn't aware, but now I'm willing to face it with True FAMILY and deal with it.

Too much pain. Better this way. Remember how easy life is when you "don't go there?"

Yes, in many ways, but I am choosing to face it. I don't want to live a lie anymore.

Section VI

Dealing With Emotions

Walking out our healing has more to do with facing and processing difficult emotions than the actual memories. How we handle emotions will determine our progress. I was a 'stuffer', and this caused great suffering to my body. With mind-control, parts are assigned to carry the pain and different emotions. This can initially make the emotions feel like a million miles away which isn't half bad! But healing comes when we can face the pain with True FAMILY and see restoration.

Emotions are a gift. They communicate important information about what is going on. There are low energy emotions like sadness and despair as well as high energy emotions like anger and fear. The cult system uses our emotions to fuel their purposes. This looks sort of like a grid system where the energy of emotions is syphoned off and channeled in ways they want to cause disruptions, even fueling big, global things like war. Many survivors, me included, gave permission for them to use our emotions because we couldn't face the pain. The good news is that Jesus has a way to transfer that from the kingdom of darkness into the kingdom of His love according to Colossians 1:13!

Anger to Joy

You are more than everything to me, True FAMILY. Show me the way. I want to walk this out with joy. How do I return to joy?

We will help you but there are some things you need to address. The anger.

How do I deal with the anger without running? I am happy to give the anger to You, but I don't know if that is "handling it."

What does it feel like?

A big ball of rage, hate, disgust. They did lots of bad things to us. So many I don't know how to handle it. I don't want to bury it anymore. I do want to face it, but it is more than I can handle.

You can do all things through Christ who is strengthening you.

I want to believe that deep inside. I'm terrified of doing bad things and being used by the enemy. I don't want any of that anymore. Please set me free.

We are setting you free and it is a process. We have such compassion for you, precious Adena. We see and know the anger and the pain... All of your emotions are safe with Us.

How do I disconnect all of me from the grid systems? I really want to be free in every way. I don't want the enemy to triumph over me. Please help me.

Acknowledging the pain and anger are the first steps. Release this all to Us. Give Us the red planet of rage. Know that it is not too much for Us. We can handle it.

There's a fierce part hanging on. Fierce one, it is okay to let go of this to the True FAMILY. They will transfer into the kingdom of Their love and into positive energy for change. This is way better than just holding on to it or using it on the grid system. This takes it out of the enemy's hands and brings restoration. Are you willing to let go and give this to the True FAMILY?

It will destroy everyone! It is that big! You don't understand. Everyone will die. I have to protect you.

I understand and I am grateful to you for how you've kept me alive all these years and taken this huge burden on. However, you don't need to keep doing this. It is only harming you and I and not helping at this time. We get to give this to the True FAMILY and to see Them resolve it peacefully.

NO! I will not allow this. It is my job, and I am not backing down.

Are they threatening you?

Yes.

We don't need to be afraid of threats anymore. They are lies. True Jesus is way stronger, and He has promised to help us. We can receive true help from Them. Only They can do this. If we try to do it on our own strength, yes, there would be bad consequences. But the True FAMILY is willing to protect, eager to be our Protector. So, we can lay aside these jobs and lies that we've believed.

I had to do it. Don't blame me.

We are not blaming you. You did what you had to do for survival. No one is blaming you. It is just now we have a new way to process things and to be much more protected. Would you cooperate with us and True FAMILY?

I don't know what to do if I am not doing this.

The True Family can give you another job that is healing and helpful. You can let go and receive from the True Lord Jesus Christ of Nazareth. He will help you walk this out. Come and let go of this huge burden. And find rest and peace with the FAMILY.

Okay. I am willing. I'm tired of this anyway.

True FAMILY, we give all of this red planet to You. We are tired of carrying this and for it being used by the enemy. We are asking for all of it to be brought into Your kingdom realm. The rage is great on the other side. I am asking for You to rescue the fragment of humanity connected to this red planet and to bring it rest and healing. It is in constant torment, isn't it?

Yes, it is, and it is Our great joy to rescue it and to restore it to wholeness. We are also turning this energy into passion for the kingdom, for righteousness and for true justice! This is Our joy.

I can feel it! That is amazing! I love this! What joy! Thank you so much, True FAMILY! I release this passion with You in roaring for restoration! I want to see this restoration You have for everything that was done to me and everything that I did. You are the God of Restoration, and I celebrate You today! Thank you so very much! Let Your kingdom come, Your will be done on earth as it is in the True heaven of heavens. I rejoice in You! With great joy, I sing Your praises. Thank you for lifting this heavy burden! What yet remains for today?

Let Us handle your day and see it flow with Our goodness. We love you and have beautiful plans for you in every way. Trust and rest in Our love. All things are coming together. Do not be afraid. Take courage and love well today.

Torrent of Emotions

I'm really angry and upset and agitated and I don't know why. The ringing in my ears is worse. What do I do, True Jesus? Please help me. I feel like I'm going crazy… suffocating, drowning, panic. This is not usual for me. What is going on?

I am here, precious Adena. Center your focus on Me. I will help you.

No, no go away! We don't want You. We can handle this on our own. Get away.

Why? Can you tell me what is going on?

No. You wouldn't understand.

I want to understand. I can only understand if you tell me what is happening and how you feel.

It is terrible. Yuck. Pain and darkness. I can't get away. They're coming. It is bad. We can't hide. They always find us. They always find us. We hate this. Bad things. Run away.

Were you triggered by the book?

Yes, and more.

I don't need to finish the book if it triggers you. I thought it would be something relaxing to do that wasn't focused on the healing journey, but I can see how it would trigger.

You don't know what they did to us.

I am willing to listen and find out. I am willing to hear.

No, you are not. You are afraid of it and don't really want to know or the people involved.

Yes, it is scary, but I am learning to trust Jesus to help me process these memories. I am willing to hear anything you are ready to tell me.

You will think we are making it up.

It may be difficult for me to process, but I am willing. It will help us all if we can face the truth, because it will set us free.

Are you trying to quote the Bible? (sarcastically)

It is the truth whether you believe it or not. I am choosing to face the truth.

We'll see.

I'm so sorry you are hurting. I'm here. I am listening, even if you don't want to say anything. I can feel you and I want you to know I care.

Thank you. *

*Not every situation ends with resolution, but the important part is attunement: for the parts to be seen, heard, understood and to know there are solutions available.

Raw Emotions

You have several pieces of the puzzle but not all. Are you willing to trust Us?

I am willing and I do want to face the truth. So, I am willing for more revelation, but I need to know it is from You and not my imagination or programming. I want evidence, but You aren't going to give it to me, are You?

I know you are disappointed, frustrated, and angry. I see the deep pain. We want to address this first because it is a heart issue.

No! Just tell me and get it over with!

That's not how We work. We work with you gently and tenderly because We see and know the deep pain. You can trust Us with your heartache and pain. You do not need to be strong, tough, self-reliant, self-protective and perfect. We want you to live freely from the tender heart that is in there covered over with much pain.

It's too much! I can't handle this pain! Stop it! It can't be true. We will die if it is true!

Shut up!

It's okay, both of you. We see and know your pain.

I'm just fine.

It is okay to be real and honest. It is okay to feel. We've got this and We will help you through the pain and disappointment and anger. There is a way through safely. Are you interested?

No.

Maybe.

Who cares?

I know those of you who want to give up, those who are angry and those who deeply feel pain. There are solutions for all of you. There is a way safely through, although it involves risk – the risk of being loved and receiving love.

Nope. Not going there.

It's okay. We understand why you feel that way. We are just letting you know there are options.

The only option is to be tough, strong, and to not feel. Feeling makes us weak. The weak die. We are going to survive come hell or high water. We can do it.

You've done well to survive, and We understand. We honor your determination, and We have a better way if you are interested.

We have to stay safe.

Yes, We agree, and We have ways of staying safe that are really good and healthy.

Maybe, we'll see. We are done for today.

Okay, We honor that. We are here and care for all of you. There is a way safely through and We are happy to show it to you.

Another time.

Baby Steps

Is there any work with my parts that I need to do? I feel a little bit shut down.

They are overwhelmed, but We will minister to them today in love.

All of them?

All that are willing to receive.

I just am saying to all of you, the True FAMILY is good. They are not the baddies, they are here to love and help and restore. Please open up to connect with Them. It is really good.

We don't trust Them, sorry. Just isn't going to happen.

I hear you and I honor that. I know there's a lot of pain and hurt. Is there anything you want to tell me?

It is worse than you know. It is chaos and pain, terror multiplied. You can't handle it.

I understand that and I am grateful for those of you who have helped by handling it for me so I could survive, but there is a better way that is opening up with the True FAMILY because They are able to bring healing and rest.

Nope. Not going there. Too much bad family. Don't like that word and not interested in relationships with anyone. We are best alone. We do our job and that is all that is needed.

I am grateful that you have kept me alive through all of this. I honor that. Do you have more you can share with me?

Nope. You don't need the gory details. We clean up all the bad stuff, tuck it away nicely. Keep you safe.

Thank you. I appreciate that. I don't know if you've noticed but I am growing in capacity to know what happened. I actually want to know so that I can heal.

Heal is a bad word. Won't work. Not going there. Shut down.

What about the word freedom?

Nope. Too dangerous.

True Jesus, I need help…what do I say or do?

Keep relational. What is the unmet need?

I don't know.

Then ask.

Okay. What is the unmet need?

What? They take good care of us. We are rewarded for our work. No unmet need.

Okay, thanks for letting me know.

Jesus, help.

It is okay. You made progress and opened a door of communication. Now you know some words not to use with these ones.

I don't like it. This is hard.

Yes, but there is a way through. Are you willing to trust Us?

Yes, please help.

Okay. Leave this in Our hands for now. Let Us have your fears and doubts. Remember We work it all for good. Do you want to see the triumph of Our love?

I do.

Okay, patiently watch and see how We will work this out. You will grow through this and be able to help others.

Okay.

Confusion

There is nothing that We can't straighten out, but it will take time, precious Adena. Do not do this in your own strength.

Bring it all before Us and petition for Our mercy and grace and help in your time of need.

I really need you now. I don't know what to think or feel. There's so much confusion.

You know how to walk this out.

I guess so...I am putting my hand in Yours and I am taking the next step. Please show me the way. What do I do with all the voices?

Give them to Me and I will help you sort it out. They are scared and terrified. They don't feel safe.

Can You help them, True FAMILY? I don't know what to do.

Yes, We are on it. Remember love. Remember what it feels like to be safe and secure in Our love.

I can't feel it right now. I just feel the blackness. Chaos. Pain. Hurt. Terror. But I choose to give this all to You and I ask You to help all the parts of me to know You.

I'm afraid. Where are You?

We are always here even when you can't see, sense or feel Us. Take a step back. There are things that are happening for a purpose. Can you rest in Our love?

I need to know it is really You. How do I know. They say we can't prove anything. I hate that. I hate the doubt and confusion they put into me that they think is wisdom and right. But if it is me that is wrong, I bring this to You… Their accusations are that I have a religious spirit and always have to be right. This always confuses me and puts me in darkness.

This is gaslighting. And projection. They are wise in their own eyes. Step into true fear of the Lord.

I don't know what that is. I want to know, and I want to learn. Please help me.

It is more than awe and reverence. It is knowing the depths of Our love and power. Nothing is impossible. There are many things that they teach that is short-circuiting Our love.

I feel that but I don't know what to do. I don't know how to work through this. You said, "wheat and tares." Isn't there a way through?

There is always a way through. What are the conditions for healthy growth? There will always be some tares, blind spots, etc., so that you stay in relationship to receive. It is a safeguard. Can you see that?

Hmm…I hadn't thought of it that way. I'm sorry I haven't spent the time and investment in You. I'm sorry I numb out and get unfocused.

I know your weaknesses and I do not fear them or despise them. I came that you might have life and life more abundantly.

Please help me out of this mess… Please show me the way.

Trust and rest.

Leading By Example

Can you deal with the underlying current and let me rest in Your true shalom?

Yes, give Us your fears.

I don't want to…

Who is that? Why do you want to hang on to the fears?

Fear protects us. Keeps us from doing things we shouldn't.

I can see that there is a better way.

You always say that. We are tired of that. Just accept us for who we are.

Ok, I'm sorry. I do accept you and I don't want fear to control us anymore.

That is the only way to live. You don't understand.

Then please help me understand you. Please share how fear protects us.

It keeps you in line, so we don't get into trouble. You don't understand the dangers you put us all in.

Like what?

Torture, rape, programming, death, you name it… You are so naïve and oblivious!

I don't want to be anymore. I need your help to understand more about what is happening. Would you help me?

Maybe, if you will believe us.

I want to. Just please understand it is a whole new view of my life that has been blocked out. It takes some time to adjust. Please be patient with me.

Okay. The more you consciously know and talk about, the more pressure we experience, and the more things happen. We don't like Testimony Mountain. Shut it down!

I don't want to make it harder for you. I want to work through this. Fear doesn't ultimately help us because it affects our body and takes a toll.

So does torture and programming.

What if there's a way to not experience either?

Pipe dream. Not reality. Not possible. You've seen the bloodline… No way out.

What if that is just their way of keeping us in the system? Jo knows people who are out of the system.

Not like you.

True Jesus, what do You say?

There is always a way. We make a way where there seems to be no way.

You going to trust Him?

Yes, I am choosing to trust True Jesus. He is not like the others. He is really helping us.

You can keep your delusions but keep us out of it. Go back to Oblivion, you will be safer.*

Please True Jesus help!

I am here and there is a way through and there will come a time when they see it and trust in Me. Be patient with yourself and keep your eyes on Us.

Why do You bring these parts forward if I can't help them come to You?

This isn't about you doing anything in your strength or power. It has and always will be Our work. The results are not for you to decide, but to trust and rest in Us and to have patience with yourself. You received more information today that is helpful.

But You are the one who commissioned me to do Testimony Mountain. Is it time to shut it down?

What will that accomplish?

The enemy wins.

Is that what you want?

No!

Okay, then take the next step until We show you differently.

Okay. I put my trust in You. Please strengthen me today to do Your will, True and living God.

It is Our delight to walk this journey with you. Give your fears to Us and We will help you. Many parts are not yet ready to give up their fear, but you can show the way.

Not through oblivion but through facing hard things anyway?

Yes, take courage.

See SECTION XVIII for more on Oblivion

When It Feels Like Too Much

True Jesus, I need You.

We are here. Facing truth is hard.

What truth?

The truth of the chaos inside.

What do I do?

Can you trust Us with timing and how this is walked out? Can you trust who We bring into your life for help? Can you trust Us to see you through? Do you believe that I am the Author and Finisher of your faith?

Cognitively, yes, but all of these parts…. I'm scared and I don't know what to do. I feel stuck.

It is okay. We will see you through. Are you willing to give the fear to Us?

It is so big…

It is not too big for Us. We can handle this.

Okay. Please help me to believe.

Gladly. Keep your eyes on Us.

I can't handle the parts right now… Can You help them?

Yes, We hold all of you safe in Our arms.

Thank you!

Fears Around Provision

Can you trust Us to provide for you financially so that you can continue?

I know You are my Provider and all of that, but… There are so many areas to trust…Can at least *some* things be stable?

Your stability is in Us and nothing else. We provide the rest.

I know that in my head, but my heart is really struggling.

There is no shame in that. We understand. This is why We are taking you step by step. If you can trust Us for today, that is a step. Don't try to figure out all the rest of the steps. If We can sustain Elijah with ravens, We can take care of you.

Are You trying to trigger me with the ravens' reference? (A part of my cult history)

You get to face the twisted version so you can enjoy our true creation. We created the true version. You can face your history and bloodline and overcome.

I don't feel like I can do anything right now.

On your own, that is true, but We are here, and We have provided you with support for this journey and We won't take that away from you.

Okay, thank you. I so appreciate that. I'm still scared.

Do you see the littles ones crying? We have tender compassion for them. We will not leave them orphans.

Please hold me and take care of me today.

Our delight! Why did you stop journaling when the tears started and go to something else?

I couldn't receive. I don't know how.

It is okay. Stay present with Us. We can help you with the pain. Parts of you are trying to go in many different directions to avoid this. We see and know. Can you stay present a little longer?

Okay, but You are the one who abandoned these littles ones. You are the one that didn't help them or save them. They had to do it themselves. You hate me. You abandoned me. I can't stand You. You weren't there.

There we go. That is better. The real pain.

Why do You torture me?

It is how you feel and that is valid, but it is time for truth. We have always been there. We cried with you. We held you. We sustained you. We kept you alive because We knew this day would come when We could walk you through healing and freedom and you could see the triumph of Our love and the good plan that We have for you and others. Can you see it?

Barely. But it hurts. Really bad. I don't want to exist. I don't want to feel this.

We know. We feel your pain too and We can help you process and take it for you. The treasure behind the pain is worth it. It is worth living.

Please help me bear this pain. It's overwhelming.

We are here. We will gladly help you through it.

Okay. Thank you.

Overcoming Rage

Here I am, True FAMILY – I really need Your help! Where is this rage coming from? I feel so discombobulated in all of this. I give these emotions to You. I want to learn to love. How do I walk this out?

Do not be afraid, precious Adena. We see and know all about you and how you are feeling. There is victory and

overcoming. There is restoration. You are on the verge of some great breakthrough. Journal your feelings.

Someone did something that shouldn't have been an issue. It seems silly but it brought out all these feelings of rage, anger, hatred, probably associated with sleep programming. I do want to overcome this. I am so very angry! I could do something really bad. I hate this. Why won't they leave me alone! I just want to sleep! I hate it here! I hate that I have no control. I am freaking out. I'm feeling like I'm going insane. I need help. Jesus, are You here?

Dearest Adena, I have never left you or forsaken you.

Why did this happen?

It is part of the process of restoration.

I don't know how I feel about this. Can You help me?

Yes, We are here to help you.

What do I do with this rage? With this anger? With this hatred?

Acknowledge it. You were violated in horrendous ways that words cannot tell or adequately describe. This was done on purpose. For their purposes.

I hate them so much. I want to do to them what they did me. I want to tear them limb from limb. I want them blotted out of the Book of Life. Is there a Book of Life?

There is. Whose sins you retain are retained.

I know that is not what I want ultimately. I don't want to be stuck in my pain and unforgiveness. But I do want to camp here for a bit.

You can. Just know that it doesn't help you to hold on to this. You know the details of this.

How do I get free? How do I release them, so they have the chance of restoration? Am I jumping too soon to restoration?

Listen to your heart and to your littles. This is bigger than you know.

I don't want all this yuck. I do want to overcome. I'm furious. But it is dissipating. Is this because of stuffing or is it letting go of it to You?

It is a little bit of both. It is important that you deal with your littles too.

Little ones, how are you?

We are enraged! They did this to us again and again and again and again and again. We hate them. We had no control.

Is there a defense system that, in order to survive, forced out these emotions?

Yes. It was the only way.

I want to let you know that we have a new way of operating. We are not going to stuff anymore. We are going to deal with our emotions. I am grateful for you saving my life. But True FAMILY is in charge now and they are good to us. They won't wake us up every hour of the night. They are good and kind and loving. They won't rape us. They won't harm us in any way. They want to help us. So, you can stand down. We can face these emotions with True FAMILY. They are here for us. We don't have to be afraid anymore. Anger, sadness, hatred, rage, you can all find love and release. You don't have to hold these emotions any longer for me. I release you from this burden. You are free to be you. Any yuckies associated with this, you are now pushed away by True FAMILY. I renounce you. I repent for the agreements, covenants, contracts, vows and oaths that I have made, or my family bloodlines have made. I choose to receive the blood of the Lord Jesus Christ of Nazareth to overcome in every way. All yuckies must go. Jesus, can You help me?

Yes, darling Daughter of Zion. I am here and I heard your request and your repentance. Anyone with yuckies, bring them to Me now. This is for healing. You don't need these anymore

to protect you or to help you. They only brought more pain. You know this. It is time for freedom and for love to reign here. Bring your pain, anger, rage, hatred and sadness. I paid for it all. You don't have to carry this anymore. Hypervigilance, you can stand down.

But what if something bad happens?

We will handle it. We work all things for your good. Nothing can happen that We won't turn for glory. Do you believe this?

Yes, I do. Does this justify allowing it?

No. I only allow what is part of the agreements that you and your ancestors have made. This is a delicate walk for you and for them. But I do have a plan to bring it all together for good in ways that you can't even imagine. Do you know the joy that will come to your programmers when you release them?

Wow! I want to do that, but I'm not quite ready.

We know this. It is okay. You've suffered greatly at their hands.

True FAMILY, I don't want anything to block ministry and flow today. How do I handle this? I don't want to spiritually bypass, but I also don't want to miss anything You have for me and others today. Can You help me?

We can take all of this and hold it until you are ready to deal with it.

Thank you so much. I give to You all this hatred, rage, anger and sadness. I choose to let go of self-pity and any attention-getting desires. I want to walk in purity. How do I receive Your love today? How do I help my body, soul, and spirit to rest? I want to enter Your rest. Please help me.

Enter in, darling Daughter of Zion, to Our love. You can do this in the ocean of love or in your inner realm.

I can't yet seem to find peace there, but I can hopefully more in the ocean of love. Why is it there for me?

It is there to set you free. This ocean of love you can enter at any time. Let it soak you as much as you are able to handle. And for the other things that are stressing you that makes it so you can't trust and doesn't feel safe to you. This is your stuff. I can deal with all of it. I don't need you to expose this without the heart of love.

Please forgive me. I acknowledge this and I do not want to expose anything unless I have the heart of love. Can You help me?

Yes, We'd be delighted to do so.

I do want that heart of love. Why is it not there?

You know some things that you are holding on to. There is resentment and hatred for the lies that were spoken.

I repent on behalf of myself and my family bloodlines for our judgments, fears, and resentments. I let go of these and ask for the blood of the True Lord Jesus Christ to wash away all of this from me. I do not want to carry this. I want to have genuine love for others.

We honor this. It is a journey of walking it out. Receive Our love for you and let go of this other stuff that only holds you back.

I choose the path of love.

Do you feel any judgment here?

No, I do not. I want to stay here always.

You may. This is what We've prepared for you.

How do I overcome this stuff?

We will give you grace as you are able.

Letting Go

Where's all my emotion going? Why don't I feel?

There is programming and deeply buried parts and emotions syphoned off for other purposes.

Since I haven't experienced them all my life, how will I handle them now?

You are not doing this alone. You know Our presence is with you. We will help you every step of the way. Your part is to trust and rest. You are afraid of going non-functional. This is a valid concern, but worrying about it will not help you. This is where leaning not on your own understanding is important. You will learn keys through this to help others. Let Us lead the way.

Okay, I choose to trust You with my emotions, and I am willing to feel what it is time for me to feel and that I can trust You with this. Anyone inside have anything to say?

We don't want to feel. It is too complicated and slows things down. It is better this way. You won't survive it if you feel everything.

I hear you and I am trusting True FAMILY for this journey, step by step. They won't overwhelm me but will help me to manage the emotions.

How do you know you can trust Them?

They have been faithful to me, and They keep Their word.

It doesn't feel like it.

I know. But I do believe it is true.

Good for you. We want to keep things the way they are.

I understand that it has worked well for us not feeling things, but we won't be fully free unless we do.

Who needs to be free? We are good. No need to rock the boat.

I believe it is worth it. Having our emotions muted means we don't feel love or joy in the same way others do. We can't really enjoy life without the full range of emotions that God created for us.

You don't know how painful that will be. You can't handle it.

I know that I can't, but I believe with True FAMILY we can. I am willing to face the pain.

You say that now, but just wait and see…

I don't want to run from pain anymore.

You have suppressed it so much; you have no idea.

I am trusting True FAMILY to help us all through this. They have a way through. It will be easier if we work together with Them and with each other. We can do this.

You are crazy. You don't understand. You won't make it. (Mockingly)

True Jesus, can You help us? Do You have a way through?

Yes, We do. It is not an easy way. This part is right in some ways. Apart from Me you cannot do this, but I am with you and that changes the equation. I will help you through.

Okay, did you hear that?

Baloney. Fake stuff. Not real. Imagination. Fantasy. Go back to sleep.

I am awake and intend to stay awake with True Jesus' help.

Just die. It is easier. This is too hard. Forget about it.

I choose life with True FAMILY. I choose to remember.

Don't say we didn't warn you! There will be consequences!

I am trusting True FAMILY to protect me as I walk this out. And this will be a testimony of Their faithfulness and goodness to me and Their power to protect me.

Okay, have it your way.

I'm choosing True FAMILY's way. It is best.

Whatever.

I invite you to participate with us. You can try it out and see. You don't have to commit.

Right, like I would help you. Just go away.

You are part of me, and I care about you.

With what feelings?

That's why I want them back and not muted, so I can feel more deeply and express it. I do care. Please consider.

Maybe. Will see. Can't commit. Watching.

Thank you. I understand.

Emotional Grid System

Today I'm seeing an emotional grid system and though I've asked to be removed from the anchor point, I haven't seen a major shift until now. I trust You with this True Jesus. Please safely remove me from this grid system.

There are consequences to this. You had parts who were crying out ...That it would mean the deaths of many. Are you ready for this?

Is that true? Are we so tied into the grid that death is the result?

Anchor points are significant and removing yourself from it has ramifications. It is not impossible, just a little more difficult. We are here to walk you through this and to mitigate a lot of the consequences that they [parts] believe will happen. You also need to listen to the parts who are fearful and terrified. There are consequences.

Okay, thank you for letting me know. Those who are afraid about this, I would like to hear from you.

You can't do this. It will ruin everything. We can't survive. It affects so many. You are foolish to do this.

I hear you and I'm trusting True FAMILY to help us safely be removed from this system. It is not healthy for us, and we give away our power and resources to stay here.

It protects us. We don't have to feel emotion as long as we agree to this position. Others are affected if you leave it. Very disruptive. Death. Pain. Misery.

I believe there is a way through with the least amount of damage and what will ultimately be a blessing and freedom for all involved. We are not here because we want to be.

That's where you are wrong. We want to be here. It protects us from pain.

That is the lie we've been told. When we face pain with True FAMILY, we find healing and restoration. They give us the strength to face the pain and overcome. This is what we are invited into.

Death and destruction.

I hear your fears. I'm learning to trust True FAMILY and Their ways. They have proven faithful to us and have helped us in so many ways.

You feel the pain in your brain. It will only get worse. You don't know what you are doing.

No, I don't but I am willing to trust True FAMILY. The more we cooperate the better. This is the gentle invitation into love and not fear.

Why today? There's so much going on. This is stupid. Concentrate on packing up (for the trip). You have other things to do.

This is important to me to take care of before we leave.

No, we need the grid system to handle the painful stuff coming. You are crazy to do this now.

True FAMILY, what do You say? I am trusting You.

This is the time, and it does not have to be so bad. We do have a way through. It will be uncomfortable but as long as you

are putting your hand in Ours, We will show you the way. Preach to those on the grid system.

I want to let all those on the grid system know that I have really good news for you. We were tricked and lied to about this grid system. It has kept us in bondage and fear and numbness, and we've missed out on real relational joy and freedom. True Jesus offers us a way of new life. I have been experiencing this and it is so, so good! They give me the freedom to choose, even to choose to walk away. I've never been so free. They are taking me gently step by step and this is another one of those steps. This grid system has kept us alive and I'm grateful for that, but it is not true life and freedom. I am inviting all who would like to also receive this joy and freedom.

What do we have to do?

It is simply asking True Jesus to help you. He is very glad to do this and there's no condemnation or shame. He is not like the fake Jesuses that we've encountered. He doesn't hurt us or do bad things. He loves us.

So do the fathers (Jesuits).

Yes, but they also manipulate and control us and make us do bad things. They don't know any better. I don't blame them, but we have the opportunity to walk it out in new ways. You can try it and then come back to the grid if you want.

But there would be terrible tribulations. We can't.

That is the other good news. True Jesus is the strongest. He is the best Protector. He can do so much more than you can ask or think. (Some littles show interest but are still hesitant.)

We don't want to cause trouble.

The more of us who leave at the same time the better.

It will be disruptive.

Yes, but True FAMILY is with us and will help us through. You are welcome to give it a try. True Jesus, are You here?

Yes, I am. I love this day of freedom.

Are there more grid systems?

Yes, there are. Don't be overwhelmed, just know that We have held these things in Our hands until you are ready. We've mitigated what they (those in the system) can do, and they are furious.

I am trusting You to do this safely and for anyone else who is ready.

Yes, We do not force. Everyone here can freely choose. You can try it out.

(Another little pipes up…)

We've been warned about You.

Yes. They do not want to lose their slaves. You get to choose for your freedom.

It's scary to make decisions. It is easier for them to just be made for us and not care.

Yes, I know that is how we've functioned, but we *do* care. We are coming alive, and we want to face things. God created us with emotions and there are purposes for them. We don't want them stolen away.

It is more convenient. Just wait until you feel more. It's embarrassing. Painful. Too much.

I am trusting True FAMILY with this. Moment by moment. Step by step. They alone can help me. All who are ready, the time is now. This is not to pressure you, just that we could talk about this all day long. This invitation is always open. We do not want to cause harm to anyone. See the bright light of True Jesus. He is here with us, and He will help us to gently disentangle from the grid. It will not be easy, but it will be so good. You can always come back if you want, but I love the freedom Jesus brings. It is worth it. Are there any other parts who would like to testify? (A few parts talk at once…)

Yes, we love True FAMILY. They give us security.

It is much better with Them. We are loved and cared for.

It can still hurt, but They comfort us and help us.

Thank you so much for sharing. Anyone who is ready, True FAMILY is excited to help us!

There are guardians. We are afraid of them.

True Jesus knows the ones who are demons, and He can easily take care of those. Others are humans and hybrids, and He also knows how to help them. He can do wondrous things even for hybrids. Nothing is impossible with Him. This invitation is for them as well and for all human guardians.

Really?

Yes. He has good things for all of us. We get to choose.

But what if this is just more manipulation?

No, it is freedom. They love us no matter if we choose to disconnect or not. They have been keeping me safe since I asked Them to do so. Do you see how I have been surrounded by light all this time?

Yes, we wondered about that. The grid didn't work properly. They tried to cover it up.

So, you see how powerful True FAMILY is?

Yes, we do. But we are still scared. It's risky.

It is and I have found True FAMILY to be so very trustworthy in every situation. They have never let me down.

You haven't gotten everything you wanted. You are getting a divorce. You've got a lot of challenges going on.

Yes, I do, and They are helping me step by step. It is not about everything instantly being perfect but walking the journey out gently with Love.

Sounds nice.

It is available to all. I won't be here anymore. True FAMILY is removing all of me from this system and I invite as many of you (others on the grid) as are ready to do so. You can also ask them to shield you like they did for me until I was ready.

Really?

Yes, that is available to you too.

We'd like that.

True Jesus, you see the ones who are ready. Thank you for disentangling me from this grid system and setting me completely free.

It is Our great joy to do so. And for anyone else who is ready.

We want help. Thank you.

It is Our great pleasure.

Section VII

Safety, Guardians and Protectors

Because so much was unsafe, for survivors, protection is uppermost in our minds and with our parts. How do we stay safe? We are hypervigilant and have protector parts whose job is to keep watch and be alert. Because this is so central to survival, it takes time and patience for our parts to learn that True Jesus is safe and the best Protector we can have. This is a frustrating area for the presenter because we so want everything to be done quickly. Learning to patiently care for our parts, understand their desperate need to be in control to try to protect, and gently lead them to the One alone who is our safety is key in the healing journey.

Lockdown and Perfection

I see those of you who are guarding the rooms. I appreciate you working hard to protect the littles. But there is another way.

Nope. Not interested. We know what we are doing better than you. We've been doing this a very long time, and we are the ones who have to keep you safe. No one else will.

I understand how you feel that way and I do appreciate all that you have done. However, living in lockdown for much of my system doesn't sound like freedom.

Freedom is too costly. Better to be on lockdown. This is safer for everyone.

I hear you. I am finding that freedom is a real joy, to be able to make my own decisions and to not be under the control of others. I'm learning how to walk this out. I'm not doing it perfectly but I'm exploring this, and I invite you to explore as well.

Well, there you said it, you aren't doing it perfectly. There's no margin for error. Not getting it perfectly means death, so we are not interested in anything that isn't perfect, and we are doing a good job at that.

I am learning that it isn't fatal to be less than perfect. It is a lie I believed from the cult system. I worked very hard at it for so many years. I am finding joy at just being able to be myself and that it is okay to make mistakes.

Well, we don't tolerate mistakes. They are fatal. You are risking a lot. Besides, we get punished if we don't do our jobs.

What if I told you that you could be protected from being punished and could do different jobs?

Not getting punished sounds good, but we don't think that is possible. And we like to protect. It's a good job.

I believe it is possible. And I honor your care for the littles ones. It's just that the way things are right now there's a lot of control and punishing and there is a better way. How would you like to be able to do your job without control and punishment?

Hmmm... Again, we don't think it is possible.

True Jesus has a way that is possible to experience love, nurture, and care for our inner realm and to enjoy what we do.

Don't say "Jesus." They are bad... so many of them. They are the punishers. They will hurt us if we don't do things perfectly. You should know this!

Those are false Jesuses and I agree with you that they are bad. The True Jesus does not punish like that. He gives loving correction that brings life. This is the One I've given my life to, and He has proved to be a great Protector and gives tender care to me. He is very powerful but doesn't use it to hurt me.

We've been tricked before.

I know and I'm sorry. I understand that it is hard to trust when we've been betrayed over and over and over again. But True Jesus has proved Himself to me to be faithful. He is the reason we are still alive.

We still think it is a trick. The same way of doing things that has worked is best.

I understand that. True Jesus doesn't force us to choose Him. He gives us choices. You can ask Him to protect you from retribution and to test it out if He is faithful and good or not. He is here if you'd like to talk with Him. You can choose. It can be your idea.

Can we negotiate?

Yes, He is willing to work with you.

Jesus, we don't believe You. We know You have some tricks up Your sleeve. But we are reasonable. What do You have to say?

I come in peace, and I understand your reluctance. I thank you for coming and being willing to negotiate. What are your terms?

We need to see if You can really do a better job of protection. This guard is willing to take the risk. Can You protect him from backlash?

Yes, I can.

What are Your terms? What do we have to do in exchange?

It is paid in full. There are no terms. If you say yes, that is enough – for you to agree.

No payment/sacrifice?

That's right. It has been paid in full.

That seems too good to be true.

It is the truth. You get to choose to believe it or not.

We will put You to the test.

Thank you for being willing to try this. It is My delight to help you and to protect you from any punishers. We can let the littles out, too. They get scared locked up like that.

Don't push too far! We've got to keep them safe no matter what.

It is okay. We will go at the pace you are ready. Step by step.

Okay, we agree.

Not Good Enough

You can deal with some guardians at this time since they are in the forefront. Find your place of rest in Us.

Thank you. I choose to rest in You. Is there anyone on the inside who is a part of me who would like to speak or share anything?

It's about time…

I'm sorry I don't make more time for you. I am here to listen.

Why do you make it so hard for yourself?

What do you mean by that?

Why are you trying so hard?

That is a good question. Am I stressing you out?

Yes.

What kind of information can you give me? Who are you and what is your job?

I'm not good enough.

Is that your name or job or both?

Both.

Are there any memories you want to share with me? (After a few minutes, some images about this part came into focus)

Thank you for sharing with me in picture form why you feel that way and what your role is. Most of my life I wasn't aware of your presence because I worked so hard to be perfect. I'm sorry for not being aware of your presence. I have some really good news for you. You don't need to be perfect or feel like you are a failure, not enough. Through True Jesus, we have everything we need. He is not like the fake Jesus. Do you know them?

Yes, very well. We took the brunt of it… not being enough.

Oh, I am so very sorry. Thank you for taking the brunt for me. And shielding me from feeling that I wasn't enough. That must be a lot of pain.

It is.

You don't have to carry it so much, there are other options.

Why would you want to stop me from protecting you?

For us to be whole, we need to know about each other and learn to work together and eventually to integrate as one.

That is scary.

Yes, I know. But it is the best way to heal. So, I am glad to get to know you a little. I'm willing to hear more. Do you help to keep me up at night?

No, but there are others who do.

Okay, thank you for that. Do you know about the false Jesus?

Yes, they punish me for my own good because I'm not good enough. The more they do it, the more I atone for not being good enough.

Thank you for sharing that, and I have good news for you that you don't have to atone for yourself anymore, because True Jesus, the perfect Son of God, came and lived a sinless life for us and died in our place so that we could live. You can learn a new way of living that is about being enough because of what Jesus did for us. There is so much joy and gratitude when we know this. It sounds better than letting fake Jesus beat you up.

I deserve it. I really do.

Yes, I understand that we all deserve it, but True Jesus in His great love for us did what we could not do. You and I cannot atone for our sin. We were lost completely, but He found us.

I don't like that language.

I understand. I'm sorry for using it.

You just don't understand. You got to feel special and chosen while I carried the "not enough" parts.

I am sorry about that and that is why I am working to understand you and get to know all of my parts so that we can learn to work together and to truly live instead of hiding from one another.

Isn't hide and seek part of a game?

Yes, but it was twisted in the cult. I'm feeling uncomfortable and scared. Terrified. True Jesus where is this coming from?

I sense it too, precious Daughter of Zion. We see and know. Distraction is kicking in. Be aware of what that tells you.

Can I just go to bed? I'm tired now.

Yes, you can. You've done well.

I don't feel I resolved anything.

Remember it is Us doing the work, so you can rest and trust. We love when you cooperate with Us through the journaling with your parts, but you are not responsible to work it out on your own. I, True Jesus, am the Author and Finisher of your faith journey. I have done it and will do it. This is the joyful journey of us together.

Okay, I receive.

Self-Protection

I want to grow in love. Teach me Your ways. I want to understand better. I so appreciate You. I put my trust in You.

We will give you grace to walk this out... Victory is possible. Trust and rest.

Is there anything else I need to do or know for today? How do I connect relationally with You and with my parts?

We are always with you and always open for conversation. You often block Us out as this has been your coping mechanism in all relationships.

Yes, You are right. I am so sorry I do that. Can You help me to undo this? I really want to be connected with You and others and not disconnect through dissociation.

Yes, it is the next step in the journey. We know you are wanting to deal with the Jesuit issue, but this comes first.

Okay. I am willing. I know You know the best order to work through things. How do I proceed?

You can repent for dissociating relationally.

I gladly repent for this coping mechanism of dissociating relationally to survive. I am grateful True Jesus that You have a new way for me to walk out. I say to my parts who are involved in this defense system, we are wanting to learn a new way. Can you cooperate with me? Why do you dissociate relationally to survive? I'm curious. I'm not mad at you. I know you do this to help us to survive. I honor that.

It is the only way. We could cope with just who was in front of us if we dissociated all the rest. It works.

Yes, I understand that. But I would like to be able to feel again and not cut off people who are not present "in my present".

Do you know how overwhelming that would be? Nope. Too hard. We can't handle that.

I know that we can't, but the True FAMILY can help us with that. They can show us how to heal and have Them as our Protectors so that They are the Ones shielding us from the negative effects and allowing the positive ones. That is the flaw of what we've been doing. We cut off everything.

Hmm. I guess maybe that could work. But we don't like to try new things. It is scary and could cause destabilization of everything and everyone. We've got to keep everyone safe. This is most important.

I agree with you that keeping safe is a high priority and so is being relational. The current way is keeping us from having genuine relationships because if the person is not present, they don't exist to us. The True FAMILY is very good at protection and can keep out the bad or help us overcome it while enjoying the good. I think it is worth trying. Would you be willing to talk with Them about it? They can help you with your concerns.

Let us process a bit. We will consider. We've spent decades building such thick walls of protection. It would be a shame to just knock those down. We've invested a lot into this. And we are safe with this method.

I hear you. I really appreciate you and how you kept me alive all these years. But I want you to know that I really desire full relationships and not to blank out people in my life who aren't regularly in it.

But then we'd have to remember. It is too hard to do that. There's so many who hurt us so badly. We can't face that.

I understand. That is hard. I am learning to face hard things with the True FAMILY. They have a way through the pain to healing and freedom and true genuine relationships. To me, this is worth it, and you can have other jobs that are more meaningful than maintaining walls.

We are good wall builders. We don't want to learn something new.

Yes, you are good at it, but doesn't it get kind of boring? Wouldn't you like to try something new that might actually be a whole lot better for all of us?

We want to say yes, but there are repercussions. You don't understand.

I am willing to hear about those repercussions. The True FAMILY can protect us from retaliations. I know you might have been programmed that you have to do this, or bad things happen, but I believe most of those are lies and what might be true, the True FAMILY can protect us. To me, this is a risk worth taking.

Well, we don't. We will have to consider this more.

You can just try it out and see if it is worth it. We don't have to take down all the walls today. We could experiment and try a different way with True Jesus. You could always go back.

We'll see.

Okay. Thank you for considering. I really appreciate you and look forward to working together towards better things.

We'll see.

Exploring Being on the Same Team

In a session with my prayer minister, Jo, we encountered two burly guys (parts of me) who had kept me in lockdown as a result of a "tripwire" that emerged at a retreat I attended. We sat down with them and True Jesus to "negotiate terms." They were expecting a power struggle, but True Jesus agreed with them that safety was needed and validated them. True Jesus showed His "weapons", and they showed theirs. They were impressed with what True Jesus had to offer and were invited by Him to explore being on the same team.

They were willing to give it a try, giving up their codes to True Jesus, but not yet ready to fully disarm at this time.

To those parts, thank you so much for cooperating today with Jesus! I appreciate you and I would love for lockdown to be lifted as you feel safer with True Jesus.

Yeah, His stuff is cool. We like it. But we aren't ready to let go of lockdown. Remember it is for your own good. You don't really need to feel anything anyway. It's better this way. Too overwhelming.

I get it and I appreciate you being concerned for me. And I am learning to trust True Jesus to protect me and to help me with overwhelming memories.

These are too bad. No one will love you if they know how bad. We are protecting you. Suicide programming installed.

Thanks for letting me know that. I'm discovering that I can bring everything into the light of True Jesus' love and still be loved and forgiven, no matter how bad.

That may be true for some people, but not you.

Why do you think that?

It just is. We know. Orders. Keep you safe.

Okay. The problem is that locking the memories away also keeps feelings locked away. Even though it is hard at times, I prefer to have feelings. Lockdown locks out both the good and the bad. I would rather face both with True Jesus' help.

Well, He does seem capable, but we are taking it slow. Trust us.

Okay. Are you in the male form so I would obey you? *

Yes, of course. We know your training. This works. You know to do whatever we say.

I just want to let you know that when you are ready, we can talk more about this. I'm learning I don't have to follow that programming anymore and you can be the real you.

We don't know what you are talking about.

Okay.

*"Do whatever the man says" was a program within me relating to men.

Section VIII

Hate Defense Systems

This defense system of hate was probably one of the hardest for me to deal with. I felt it was so different from who I am, and I couldn't understand it. For the first year or so, I just pushed away any communication from this defense system. I didn't want to face it. But when I realized that these parts were trying to protect me and that they really have a good heart, I began to reach out to them.

Safety in Hatred

I hate this! Get it over with. Just let go and …

To the ones filled with hate. I see you and I understand. I don't hate you. I'm learning new ways of walking out this journey and there is hope.

Nope. Hate is our best defense. It keeps us safe.

What do you need?

We don't need anything, we are good. Hate is a great defense.

I'm not sure I really understand that, can you give me more information?

Well, if you knew all about what was done, it is our way of getting back. Really bad shitty things happened. That is not okay. We hate them. That is our best defense.

I am so very sorry for what happened, and I would like to know more. I'm getting stronger and able to handle more. Can you share with me anything about what happened?

Too gross. We don't talk about it. We just do our job.

I want you to know that I am here and willing to talk more when you are ready. I believe there are new ways we can approach this together that will be more helpful.

Not really interested. This has worked and you could be oblivious. That is better. Oblivious. That's the goal.

I understand that, but I don't want to be oblivious anymore. I would like to know.

Not yet. Too soon. Too much. Go away.

Okay. I understand. Just know that I would like to talk more in the future.

Maybe. Go away.

True Jesus, this is hard. Nobody wants to talk.

Patience, darling daughter. This was good. We are proud of you. Little by little. You've done more than you know.

What Do I Do with This Hate?

I want to be secure in Your love. Help me to receive Your love today. How can I stay grounded in Your love today?

Keep focused on Our presence with you. We are here and you can receive from Us. We sustain you moment by moment. Open your eyes to see. Open your ears to hear. You are Our beloved daughter in whom We are well pleased. This is truth. You are seen and known by Us. We get you. We know the inner workings of your heart and all your parts, and We are not

ashamed to call you Our own. Rest and trust deeply in Our evaluation of you, not your own. You are called for such a time as this.

How do I walk in this? I feel I can barely receive Your love.

Step by step. You are receiving more than you know. We are here. Remember who you are.

Thank you! Please help me True FAMILY. You know all the angry parts and hate parts stirred up. I give all of them to You. I don't know what to do.

Stay steady in Our love. See from Our perspective. Trust and rest.

I can cognitively force myself to do that, but I know that is not what You mean. I don't know how to deal with the pain. There's a lot of it. Rage. Hate. Blame. Terror. Death. I don't know how to navigate this. Please show me or send some help.

Help is on the way. Trust and rest.

I give all of this to You. I don't know how I am going to be able to sleep tonight. All I can say is please help.

Do you trust that We can?

Yes, You can, but will You? I feel all alone. Change is scary.

It is as simple as putting your hand in Ours and taking the next step.

I choose that. But I feel like I'm going crazy. Inside.

There is a lot of pressure right now. You've been suppressing them.

I wasn't trying to.

It's okay. Just ask.

But I'm afraid to. What if …The storm was scary this morning … the rain was coming down so hard it hurt and the child with me was so scared.

Did We see you through?

Yes.

Okay. There's a storm all around you. You have people who love you and are there for you. We are here. You are not alone. Ask.

Okay. Who inside has anything you'd like to share. I am sorry if I haven't been listening and I'm sorry that I'm afraid right now.

We are, too. There's a lot going on. Open doors. Floodgates. Torrents. Pain. Evil. Bad. We can't stop. It's bad.

The True FAMILY is our only hope. They say They will help us. I know it is hard. I'm struggling.

If you can't stabilize then there's no hope for us.

There is always hope in the True FAMILY. No matter how bad it gets, They can bring us through. This morning, They gave me some time to worship and praise Them and release glory and restoration…I forgot about that. It was wonderful until the rain started so hard. I think we can find enough parts to stabilize with True FAMILY. We can do this together. I'm sorry I shut you out. Sometimes it is easier that way.

We know. It won't always be this way.

Yes. Thank you for hanging in there with me. I am sorry for the parts that feel so much hate. Do you want to share anything?

It is our way of getting your attention. We hurt bad. We feel abandoned.

I know. I'm sorry. It isn't fully true, but I know it feels that way. There are many people who care and love us. True FAMILY is here to help us with the pain. Would you be interested in giving some of it to them?

Against the rules. Hate protects from pain.

Doesn't seem like it. Is it specific people or generalized or me?

Some of all of the above.

True FAMILY, I feel disconnected and not really going anywhere with this. What's going on? You feel far away. It feels weird. Like I can't connect. I want to run away and hide. And never journal again. I hate this. What's going on?

We are here and We hold you gently through this. Don't be discouraged. Work through some prayers and if you feel up to it you can come back.

Never.

Who is saying that?

We don't want to do this anymore. We want to die. We are done. It's not worth it. Lots of pain. I hate everyone.

True Jesus, I need You.

I am here.

Hate Protects

Are there any parts who need anything from me? Do you have anything to say? I know there was a lot of activity last night.

You shut us down.

I'm sorry it felt like that. I didn't mean to do that.

We were upset and have a right to be. You are afraid of us.

You are right. I am. I don't want to be that way. I want to learn to work together and to love you.

We protect you and you don't appreciate it. See you got distracted because you don't want to deal with us.

I can't allow you to harm others if you think doing it protects me. I am learning a new way to walk this out. We don't harm others.

Sometimes it is necessary to get attention and to protect you.

I am choosing to operate differently with the True FAMILY. We don't need to do those things anymore.

It is what we've always done.

I know that. But it isn't helpful at this time. There's a better way. We are learning to love others, even our enemies.

That's going too far. If they hurt us, we hurt them back. It is the only way.

There are other options. I know you've done that to protect me, but I am choosing True Jesus.

He's just another fake. He will betray you, just wait and see.

He hasn't so far, and I believe Him. You can try Him too.

Nah! We are good the way we are.

Are you happy? It seems you are always in enemy mode. *

The only way to keep safe.

It doesn't sound very fun.

We like it.

But do you feel loved?

No. But what has that got to do with us? Protection is the only thing.

There is much more to life than being safe. I know that is all you know, but this is an opportunity to be loved. I love to receive love when I am able to. It feels much better than hate.

Hate protects us. Keeps the walls up. We have to maintain the walls. Have to keep them out. Safety is priority.

I understand that, but I've found that True Jesus is a great Protector, much better than hate. He is effective and it keeps love and hope alive.

Who needs those? Protection and safety are the only things.

Well, if that is all you want, True Jesus is very good at that. You can be free to do other jobs that are much more pleasant.

Maybe but the walls cannot come down.

Why?

There's so much bad stuff in there you can't handle it.

I am choosing to trust True Jesus for what I can or cannot handle. He is really good at it. He isn't overwhelming me and is here to help me process everything. I desire to be truly free, and it is the TRUTH that sets us free in True Jesus.

Why would you want to know all this yucky stuff? I'd just throw it away, keep it buried. Never think about it again.

If that were really able to happen that would be one thing, but behind those walls it is still affecting me daily. The only way for it to be truly gone is through the Blood of True Jesus. He redeems and restores.

I don't know…

It is okay, we can take this step by step. Jesus won't take the walls down all at once because that would be damaging, but He knows the pace I need, and I am learning to be patient and go with His timing.

If you want to have it your way…

It is His way… He is gentle and kind.

That's the trick they always use. You should know that. Over and over again…

He is the One True One who has not betrayed or abandoned me. Getting out of enemy mode and learning to trust His love is a really good thing.

Maybe.

You can try it out and see for yourself. He doesn't force you.

We've got to keep the walls up.

How about letting Him do that?

Hmmm…no.

It must be a lot of work to do that. Wouldn't you like just a little break? You can always come back if you want to. Is anyone willing to let Jesus have their wall? (a few raised their hand)

Okay, thank you to those of you who are willing to give True Jesus a try…

*If you'd like to explore more about what "enemy mode" is, check out the book, *Escaping Enemy Mode: How Our Brain Divides or Unites Us* By Dr. James Wilder

Revisiting Boarding School

I recently returned to the boarding school I attended for one year in High School. A friend went with me to process any memories that might surface. Before going, I spent some time journaling with my parts. I wasn't prepared for their reactions. I have left some names of places and people blank.

I hate them! They did bad things! Stay away.

It is okay. We will be safe with the True FAMILY. The reason to go is to get more information that might be helpful for this journey and even to be able to bless and bring restoration. Don't you want to see what they are doing stopped? The only One who can stop it is True Jesus and He will be with us.

That's a bunch of crap.

You might think so, but I do believe.

They all need to be destroyed. They should not exist.

I do understand why you feel this way and I want to know more about what happened there because I don't remember.

How convenient for you!

I am getting stronger with True Jesus, and I can face things now that I couldn't face before. Is this my Hate Defense System?

Yes. We are here for a reason, and you should respect that.

I do. I am grateful for how you've tried to keep me safe and from knowing what really happened there. But it is a new season, and I am ready to know so that it can be fully healed.

Did you feel safe there?

Not really, but maybe safer than what was going on at ________.

Yeah, thought so. But they were brutal too. Bad things. You should be glad not to remember.

_________was kind to me.

Yes, until the sessions. You don't remember.

They went too far, didn't they, and that is why I broke down. (i.e. got sick)

Yes. They weren't supposed to do that. It was the trafficking.

I didn't know about that.

You are so dumb and naïve. It was easier when you were sick because you blanked out more. You don't remember what really happened. You weren't there a lot of the time, but the "sickness" covered it. Drugs kept you in different states for different uses.

Thank you for letting me know. Would you be willing to cooperate with me today so I can learn more?

What good is it? Who cares? What was done is done. You can't go back in time.

I know you don't understand, but it would be helpful, because you know things I don't and working together we can get free of the past.

I don't think it is a good idea.

I get that, but we can go with True FAMILY and They will help us.

Whatever. Sure. It won't make a difference. But I will cooperate for now.

I really appreciate that. Thank you!

Why do you care?

I care about you and about all of us and how we can be restored to wholeness. I didn't know about this before, otherwise I would have wanted to connect sooner. I believe there's hope.

Okay. Sounds delusional, but I will cooperate.

(Later…)

We are so very proud of you, darling daughter! That was not easy. But you got more info, and We will continue to show you as you are ready. This is how you triumph over the enemy.

It didn't feel like that but thank you. I'm grateful. Does anyone need to share anything?

We don't like it there, but you didn't explode about the information so maybe you can handle it with True Jesus.

Yes, we can face difficult things now with True FAMILY. Thank you for cooperating with us. We can do this more. I know that we will need to address ____ (another school) at some point.

Not ready for that yet.

That is okay. We only face it as the True FAMILY shows us it is time.

We want to rest for a while.

Yes, totally understand. Hopefully the rest of our time here can be peaceful. We are safe with the True FAMILY.

We don't quite believe that, but we are willing to try.

Thank you. I appreciate that. We are learning together to trust and rest.

You sound optimistic, but there's still a lot to go. You've just barely scratched the surface.

Yes, I am aware of that, but with True FAMILY we can get through.

Okay. Peace out.

Hate Defense System

Here I am True FAMILY – help me to walk this out. I want to receive Your love today and flow with You. I don't want to and can't do this on my own. Please help me. Please work through me in love to reach these precious ones. I know I have nothing, and I don't want to do harm. Please help it to be all You.

We love to flow through you, and We aren't bothered by mistakes. We are here for you no matter what. Receive Our unconditional love.

Why do You love me? I'm so full of hate.

We know why you are full of hate, and it doesn't bother us because We have the solution. Look, little one, see the scars. They did bad things to Me too. I forgave them and it set Me free, and it set them free to find Me. Not all of them did, but they will. It is only a matter of time. Our hearts are open to you.

I bring all of this hate to You, True Jesus. Come girls, it doesn't do us any good to hang on to hate. It destroys us. It helped for a season to keep us alive and to fuel us, but I'm tired of it and I think you are too. When we forgive, we allow healing to come. Let's give all of our hatred to True FAMILY. They will help us process the pain. I want to hear about it because I don't know a lot of what happened. You've held the emotions and the memories for me, and I am grateful, but now is the season to remember and to heal. You can let True FAMILY come and help us.

We don't like the word "family." *

I understand why at least a little, but I want to hear more.

They did bad things, and they hurt us.

I want to close that door and for all of us to be healed. Are you willing to cooperate with us? I know that the word "family" triggers, but it is the best word to describe the Trinity in a way that is relational.

We want to come to the place where we love this word because, in the True FAMILY, we are held and loved and cared for and protected. It is so key for us to let go of our hatred and defenses and let love in. I'm ready. Are you?

We are willing to start working towards that but listen to us when we have something to say. Don't shut us out.

Yes, I don't want to shut you out anymore, but please also have grace for me. Let's walk this out together with our precious True FAMILY.

We are here to help you and for you to know that We never leave you nor forsake you and We don't do bad things.

What about the Old Testament? Also, even Jesus yelled at people....

We can help you to reframe everything in love. This is possible. We don't need to water it down. The Bible is powerful, and it is enough for you to find your way. Tuck into Our love and try it out. Know that We care for you moment by moment. You can give up your defenses and let Us protect you. Father is a tower of strength. Jesus is a rock, solid and immovable from His purposes to love and restore you. I, Holy Spirit, am soft and gentle – a Comforter to you to gently lead you into Truth. Do not be afraid but enter into this day with joy!

*The word "family" is often used in different cult groups to describe the cult. This is why I differentiate by adding "True FAMILY."

Exchange Program

Why do I have all these parts that just keep talking about hate? I don't like it. I don't want to hate anyone. Can You help me?

Yes, bring them all to Me.

Dearest littles who hate and big ones who hate, Jesus is inviting you to come. He has things to share with you to help you get rid of all that hate. It isn't good for you or for me. He has an exchange program and has something much better to give you. Are you willing?

Yes, we are willing, but we still hate.

I know. This is just a time to be able to process and to be set free. Do you want to be free?

Yes, we do. It is a heavy burden. We'd like to be free. We keep screaming about hate to get your attention.

I'm sorry for not paying attention to you. Sometimes it is overwhelming for me, and I don't feel like I can handle the feelings or the many parts. But I still value you and want you to know I care about you.

You can't say it, can you? You can't say that you love us.

I want to and I want to be genuine. I don't want to lie. I'm frustrated because I want to sleep, and it seems like you are preventing that.

Why do you think we are doing that? There's many more who are sneaky and are doing things to sabotage you.

Jesus, I bring before you those who are sneaky and sabotaging me. Will You help me?

Yes, darling Daughter of Zion, the true Zion. We are here for you. We see and We know. It is not easy what you are walking through. It is also a significant day and an anniversary.

I want to run away-- far, far away. I don't want to see anyone or know anyone. Will I be safe then?

The only place of safety is within Us and in trusting Us. You can run and run, but We are always there. You can't run away from Us. We understand why you are feeling that way, and We have solutions for you to feel safe and loved.

How can I feel safe and loved here?

All things are possible. Do you believe that We can help you through this and that We can redeem all things?

Yes, I do believe it cognitively, but my parts are having trouble. Something is wrong. Really wrong. How do I walk this out? I don't want to be taken. Or used. How do I stay with You, True FAMILY?

We are watching over you tenderly. Our heart is for you and for your restoration. Do you trust Us?

I am willing to trust You. How do I get to sleep?

We will help you, but it will take a little bit of time. There are some factors and some of it is about getting some things out. Reframe everything and choose to trust. More is happening than you know. We love to partner with you and to see many people's lives changed.

I give all of this to you. It feels heavy right now. I just want to be me.

Yes, you just get to be you and that is what We love.

(later) Should I run away?

Where would you go?

I don't know.

Why do you want to run away?

I'm scared. Very scared. What if bad things happen?

Are you willing to trust True FAMILY?

Well, sort of. What if They let us down?

They promised to always be with us and to see us through. I want to trust Them.

I want to too, but it is hard.

Yes, I know. They understand and They are not mad at us.

But I'm mad at me.

Why are you mad?

I can't do anything right.

What do you mean?

I hate and I hate, and I hate. I can't stop it. I hate them and what they did to us.

A lot happened. I know we opened up some things when we went back to visit the boarding school. Is that what is bothering you?

That's it and more. Those bad sisters. They are witches. They hurt us. They got money from the CIA. They did bad things, but they got found out. They had to leave. The whole family was involved.

Who else was involved? High level stuff?

Yes, but hidden.

Jesus, can you take all of this and put it somewhere safe? I really need to get some sleep. Is there more?

There is more. Stay up just a little longer.

Can You lift this burden?

Yes, We are happy to do so, but you have to let go of it.

Why am I hanging on to it?

Guilt and shame.

I didn't think I had any of that. Where has it been hiding?

It has been hiding and it is time for it to come out for healing.

Really? Tonight?

Do you want healing?

Yes, I do. I choose to let go and give You this shame and guilt. It's all my fault, isn't it?

No, it isn't. You were forced into more than you know. It started early and stayed. You were the star of the program. You were brought there specifically for some extra special work. It

was unexpected for you to get sick, but they chose to use it in their plans.

I choose to forgive them and everyone else involved-- those who knew and those who didn't. There is a path of restoration for you. I choose to release you from my judgment. I'm sure these things happened to you too. Or did you just do it for the money?

Both.

I release all the pain and trauma to You, True FAMILY. I don't want to carry this anymore. I don't want to carry shame and guilt. I did bad things, and I take responsibility for them. I don't want to do anything like that anymore. Please help me. I renounce and repent for all bad things I've done, and I cry out to You, True FAMILY, for mercy. Will You forgive me?

It has all been washed away at the cross. You were crucified with Me and buried and rose again.

Section IX

Strong Girl and Good Girl

Strong girl appears throughout this volume and is one of my primary identities. I'm grateful for her as she has kept me alive and allowed me to be functional. In the beginning, I would think that her suggestions were actually from God because they sounded reasonable and good. It has taken time to recognize the difference between her and True FAMILY and to understand her motivation and heart of love for me, that though misguided, is true. She also had a lot to do with managing my body, keeping me healthy and my routine. When I began to learn to flow with True FAMILY with my schedule, she had quite a difficult time adjusting, but now is able to work together with True FAMILY in powerful ways.

Good Girl sometimes works in cooperation with Strong Girl and other times opposes her. She kept up the "perfection" appearance and needed to always be right and do the right thing. She is discovering True Jesus as the only One who is truly good and to trust in His righteousness alone.

My Strong Girl

Okay, is there anyone else? I would especially like to talk with Strong Girl.

I'm here.

I know you've kind of taken over, so I won't feel pain. I am grateful for that, but you don't have to hold my emotions anymore. I am learning to give them to True Jesus to process and it is good.

Nope my way is best. You've survived this long because of me. I keep you alive and functional.

Do you work for the cult or on your own?

Sometimes I help them out, but mostly for you.

I don't want to cooperate anymore with the cult. They are not for us.

Well, sometimes it is to our advantage.

I believe that is a trick. I don't believe that they are able to help us in any way that doesn't come with a price.

But I'm a good negotiator. Sometimes it is necessary for survival.

I understand how you believe that, but I'm learning a new way of walking this out. Only True Jesus can help us. I am choosing to surrender fully to Him. I feel the pent-up rage…

See, you can't handle it…

No, that is not what I am sensing. I can handle this with True Jesus. He will only allow what I can handle.

But I've been doing that job. I've been keeping you safe and now you don't appreciate it! How ungrateful! I hate you. You need me.

I'm not trying to pick a fight. I am grateful that I am still alive and for how you've helped me in the past. I am believing for a new way to function. It seems like a big job you have and a lot of responsibility. It must get tiring. Are there some things you'd rather do?

Of course, but I can't stop now, or you will die. I have to keep you alive and functioning. They will kill me if I don't.

I'm so sorry for the threats they've made. That doesn't sound very safe or loving. I do believe in a new and better way that we can try and that is with True Jesus.

Nope! We've been warned about Him. He cannot be trusted. He might be nice for a little bit but then He will trick you and you will die. He even says to His followers in the Bible to die. Stay away!

I am so very sorry for the lies that you were told. This is not true. If you think about it, they are actually the mean ones… Didn't they do a lot of torture and painful things?

Yes, but they did it for our good. They were making us strong. They know what we need.

But even now they are still tormenting you, aren't they, with the threats? True Jesus doesn't threaten. He treats us with respect and gives us choices and He love us no matter what we've done. This is really good news.

Nope, fake news…

I understand how you might believe that, but I am telling you, He is good. This is a season of new beginnings for all of us. I want to invite you to try this out. We've been doing the same thing over and over and it has kept us alive, but we've not really had or experienced love and true joy and true safety. Can we at least give this a try?

Maybe, but they will hurt us bad if we do anything different.

I understand, but we can ask True Jesus to protect us. He is very good at this. Can I ask Him? True Jesus, can You protect us against them? Can You help us to get free?

Yes, it is My delight to prove Myself to you. Not a hair on your head will be harmed…

Wow! Thank you, True Jesus. I receive Your protection today! Thank you so much! This is good news, Strong Girl!

Well, maybe, we will see.

Thank you for being willing to try. True Jesus has given us a good promise and we can trust Him. I don't need to be afraid anymore.

Cooperating with Strong Girl

I don't like that. I want it to go away.

We know, but if you want to get full freedom, you must face this.

Okay, I leave this in Your hands. Please help me.

We are so proud of you, precious daughter. We know this is not easy and We love your courage to say yes to the process. Stay steady. Good things are coming.

What about the parts agitated about that stuff?

Jo will be able to help.

I want to do it all now.

Is that you Strong Girl or someone else?

Yes, it's me.

We get to learn patience with True FAMILY on this one.

I can take over and solve all of this if you let me.

I know you are strong, but it would just be covering over things we need to face. I thank you for your offer, but I am choosing to do it the way True Jesus leads, and I would love your cooperation.

I can make things go away so you don't have to feel the pain.

I know that you can, but it isn't the best for me right now, because I need to face these things. It is time for us all to heal and find more freedom. I appreciate how you've kept me from this for so long. But now is the time.

Are you saying you don't need me anymore?

No, I need your strength to help me be patient and in other ways. I'm not trying to get rid of you, but that we learn a new way to work together.

I don't know how to do that. That is weakness.

Actually, I have been finding that it is better together. Have you been seeing how working on the book together and with True FAMILY and others is working out better?

Maybe, but we could have done it on our own.

I know we've been used to isolating everything so we can manage it, but I really believe this is going to be much better. So, will you help me be patient?

Okay.

Processing

I feel horrible like something bad is going to happen and Jo will hate me. Why is this coming up now? I feel so scattered and crazy.

Let Us stabilize you. Focus in on Our love. We are here for you.

What if You are the bad guys too? What is real? I don't know.

It is okay, Adena. Remember love.

I need to stop this.

Would you like Us to handle this or are you letting Strong Girl take over?

But she helps us stabilize.

She does, but usually in the way the cult wants her to. Is that what you want?

No, I don't. Please help me…

Good Girl and Strong Girl, it is okay, you can stand down and let the True FAMILY handle this. I will be okay with them. Jesus is the Way, the TRUTH, and the life. It is only as we embrace the TRUTH that is Jesus can we find healing and rest. Anyone interested? (I see internally that some reporters come forward. As they do, I feel like running away.)

Stay steady and keep looking at Us. We have the way to life.

True Jesus, I need to know if that is truly You. Do You get tired of that question?

No, as often as you need to ask it, I am happy to reassure you. The morning and evening prayers* help in this too.

Yes, I usually do them, but I don't want it to become routine. I want to mean every word. But it's not easy.

There are some things in the way and some more to learn. Don't be in a hurry. We will help you walk it out.

*From *Prayer Warriors* by Jo Getzinger

No Doctors, Please!

What about the doctor appointment on Monday? I didn't really ask You about it.

You always have a choice.

I do need to get the bloodwork done so it made logical sense.

Yes, it does.

She is nice and I am sort of comfortable going, but it feels like old stuff. I feel like when I am there, I go into a different part.

Yes, that is true.

Is it dangerous for me to go? Is she part of the system? Did I choose her because of that?

You can go safely with Us with your hand in Ours. We will protect you. Be aware of what is going on inside and prepare your parts. This is part of training in trust. One step at a time.

Will You protect me?

Yes, We will protect you.

Can I be fully conscious with no switching so nothing bad happens?

You are seeing images of past experiences with doctors, and this freaks you out. Injections of drugs, etc. Transport. Those are real. This is why it is important to help your parts before going.

I don't think I'm ready.

They are bad. They hurt us. We comply because we have to. Fear, panic. Terror. Bad things. More bad things.

Can you trust Us?

NO! We aren't going.

You can choose that, or it can be an opportunity to overcome.

It hurts too much.

Take a deep breath. Where is your hand?

In Yours.

You get to choose. You can give the pain, fear and memory glimpses to Me. I will keep them safe until you are ready to process what was done.

Why does building trust have to do with hard things? Why can't it be easy?

There's no reason to trust when everything is easy and going the way you want it to.

Okay, I say yes as long as You are with me.

Let Us settle your inner realm a bit and then you can have a conversation with them.

Why the resistance? This is so dumb. I've gone many times. Why the nausea?

Is that you, Strong girl?

Yes. Of course. You need me to give you some backbone. Get over this. Just do what is needed. You will survive.

Yes, I appreciate your strength and am glad for it and looking at approaching it a bit differently this time.

Why?

Because there are scared parts who had bad experiences with doctors and don't want to go. We want to be gentle with them and to have the True FAMILY help us with safety.

They are just weak and need to get with the program.

That's kind of it. We are choosing to not go with the programming this time around.

Why not? It works. It gets you through hard times.

Yes, but at what cost?

What matters is getting the job done. Keep everyone in line.

True Jesus, I need help with the nausea. And with Strong girl. Please help.

Look where your hand is. Feel Our strength. Choose to step out of the programming and see it as it is.

Can you see this Strong girl?

Yes, but that programming is helpful.

I don't think so. It might have gotten results, but the cost is too high.

But the consequences when we step out are worse.

True Jesus is here to help and protect us from those consequences and to help us walk out a new way of doing things. You've seen some of this?

Yes, but you need me in charge when you get overwhelmed.

Did you see yesterday when I shared with a friend how well it went?

Yes, but I can do a better job. Then you don't need to cry or need anyone else. You can get rid of Jo and save money.

I appreciate what you've been able to do in keeping me alive, however, I am learning a new way, and I am inviting you to try it out.

Old way is best.

True Jesus, can You help us? Can You show her what it really looks like to do it the old way?

I don't want to see that!

It was just a brief glimpse to help you see why we are making changes. You, too, can step out of that programming and try a new way with True FAMILY. They can help keep us safe and protect us at the doctor's office without all of those consequences. You and I and True FAMILY can partner in new ways.

Maybe…

Thank you for considering. Anyone else need to express how you feel about going to the doctor?

I can put them in lockdown, so they don't have to feel anything.

I know that is how you've handled them in the past, but like I said, we are looking at doing things differently.

Can't we just not go?

The True FAMILY want to take us on an adventure of learning a new way, a trust-building opportunity. We can say no, but I would like to do this and would appreciate your cooperation.

Ah, what the heck. Sure, do whatever you want. But I will lockdown if True Jesus doesn't come through.

Let's work toward cooperation and communication.

Whatever.

Thank you!

True Jesus, can this be easier? I feel like I'm going in loops.

Be patient and tender.

Can You just break all the programming?

It would not accomplish true freedom and healing. I know this is slower, but it will bring so much more and the true transformation you desire for everyone.

Okay. I know I also need to address the parts who are afraid to go. Do I do that now or wait until tomorrow?

You can choose, but you don't have as much time tomorrow.

Okay, anyone else want to share?

We don't like the doctors. They do bad things.

Yes, I am so sorry for what has happened in the past. I am choosing to trust True Jesus to protect us this time and that we will be safe. You can bring your fears to Him and He can help you with them, so you aren't overwhelmed.

Can we go into the cages? It is safer there.

We are learning how not to go to the cages as safety, but instead to trust True Jesus. He can keep us safe anywhere we go so that we don't have to use the cages anymore.

But it is better that way. Keeps us safe and keeps everyone else safe.

I know that is what you've been told, but in reality, it just keeps us in prison. We were created by True God to be free and whole. They are restoring us to that. Doesn't that sound better?

Too hard. We are afraid. Can't do it. Bad…

True Jesus, how can You meet these precious ones?

I care for them tenderly. I have a much better plan for them than the cages. What do they need?

What do you need?

Confined.

Why do you need that?

Safety.

What about having safety without being confined?

It's the only way.

I do know there is another way and actually many ways for True FAMILY to protect us without being confined. They also have a safe place that is comfortable and gentle and peaceful. It is not a cage but is where you will feel safe and secure. Would you be interested?

A blanket in the cage would be enough.

If that is as far as you are willing to go today, the True FAMILY are happy to supply the blanket, but there is more available.

No, not today.

Okay. True Jesus, can You provide them blankets?

Yes, gladly. It is okay. Don't be discouraged by this. Each step is important, and We honor that.

Okay. I would have liked more, but I will trust You. Please help me with today. I give my schedule to You and am open for any re-arranging. Help me to love myself and my parts and to receive self-care.

Gladly. Listen for what We are doing and walk it out step by step. Don't be discouraged. We aren't. Enjoy this day with Us. We are delighted to walk it through with you.

Okay.

Adventures with Strong Girl

Where are You God? Why have You forsaken me? I hate You. You left me all alone. I had to do everything. I keep her safe. Stop torturing us. Leave us alone. We can't stand this. Leave us alone.

Precious Strong Girl, We so deeply love you and care. We've always been there.

No, You haven't! I hate You! Get away! Leave us alone!

We are so very sorry for the abandonment you feel. Although it doesn't feel like it, We've always been there, crying with you, holding you tenderly through it all.

Then why didn't You do anything.

We did more than you know. We've been guiding Adena's steps all along, waiting for the day when We could begin to bring full healing and freedom. We know it hasn't felt that way

and that you couldn't see Us, but I know you did feel Us at times. Can you remember? There are times when We prevented or stopped things. Remember.

Okay. But why didn't You do more? If You are powerful, then why?

Remember Our love is not forced. Otherwise, it is not love. We don't control through reward or punishment.

But you do use reward and punishment.

Not in the way you've been trained. Only in love and with freedom to choose. There are natural consequences built into the world, Our creation. You've been seeing Us work with Adena and the changes that are coming. What do you think?

Not fast enough and not enough. You could do more.

Can you see everything?

No.

We can. We understand it all. Adena has asked for the most restoration possible. She (and you) is very courageous. We've agreed to this and so it limits what We will do at this time because We have a plan that is far better than anything you can come up with. You only see now and your limited past. We see it all and We have a way through. We tenderly care for you and Adena and all of the parts. We know the timing and the layers and the things to address along the way. We've perfectly calculated how to bring her through for the most restoration and glory and love. We invite you to participate with Us in this. We value who you are and your role with Adena. She needs you. Can you see this?

But what about the pain? She is not able to handle it.

And neither are you although you try. We have a way through for that as well. True Jesus took all of that and paid for it. He is the man of sorrows and acquainted with grief. He is willing to take the pain and to help turn it into joy and triumph.

It isn't easy, but it is good. You do not need to handle things the way you have in the past. You did that to survive, and We honor that. But now things can be different. You don't need to carry this heavy load. You don't have to compartmentalize all the pain. We can help you step by step. It isn't instant, but it is good. We can give you clarity for this journey.

We have to help her by doing whatever it takes.

I understand that is how you've managed to this point, but there is another way. We are here and can manage things much better if you are willing to trust Us.

What will happen if we do?

The weight is lifted from you, and you can learn a new job or just rest and play. You never got a chance to be a child, to laugh, and to receive love.

That sounds very scary.

Yes, but it is so much better than the way you've lived to this point.

Can You really protect us and keep us safe?

Yes, We can. It is Our delight to do so. It is not a burden for Us.

Why would You do that for us?

Because We deeply love and care. We created Adena and We have plans to bring her into the fullness of Our delight and design. This is what We love to do.

We can't give up.

We aren't asking you to. This is letting Us help to carry the burden and show you a better way. You have a good heart and have done well to keep Adena alive. Now We are showing you other options.

Okay. We will consider.

Thank you.

I just remembered I heard a part say last night "we like blood." At first, I was horrified but tried to quickly turn to compassion. I interacted with the part briefly. I give this to you, True Jesus. I don't know how to handle this.

We will help you step by step. Release this to Us. Well done.

I didn't do anything.

You did. You didn't run. You stayed present and you chose compassion. That is a lot.

It seems like we are doing little things. There's so much more.

Yes, and it is the little things that matter and make a difference. Don't be discouraged by this. It is step by step. Baby steps count. Enjoy and celebrate.

Okay, thank you.

Learning Flexibility

I repent for making my routine my safety instead of You. I didn't see that. I want to flow in my days with You and not make an idol of my routine.

It is good for you to see this and also to work with your parts because this is important to them. They feel safest that way and We aren't wanting to harm them, but to work with them. Small adjustments in the beginning and then We can go from there. Be tender with them.

Okay. Does anyone want to talk about our routines?

We need them. It helps us to feel safe. You are making so many changes in other areas, this at least keeps us grounded.

Okay, I understand that. I do like our routines too, but I also want to learn to flow more with True FAMILY. They are our safety, not the routine.

We get that, but we aren't ready for that. We need stability in something. We want to go slowly. We need routine.

Okay. I am good with that. We are learning to trust True FAMILY and to let Them be our safety. Body, what do you need today?

Rest.

I want to provide that for you with True FAMILY. I do have a full day, but I am submitting this day to Them and They will help us to manage. I want to experience rest even when I am active doing things.

Yes, we'd like that. There's a lot of stress.

Can you tell me more?

No.

Okay. I am willing to listen when you are ready. True FAMILY, I ask for You to help strengthen my body today and that I would be more aware and to flow together.

We understand and We are here to help. Take it slow. There are windows of time in your schedule, and We will help you to be more efficient during this time. And also, times of rest. Enjoy this time. Savor the moments and rejoice! Flow with Us and enjoy. We are so pleased with you. Receive Our love and delight.

I'm still afraid of the fathers (Jesuits).

It's okay. We are holding you gently through this season. We will get there.

Okay. I give all of this to You today. Please keep me safe. What if I don't exercise today?

You don't have to.

But it is good for me.

Yes, and you can learn to flow. You don't have to every day.

But I feel like I should.

That is the part that We encourage you to let go of. You can make a choice not to.

I do need the exercise. I'm afraid. I like the routine.

Remember you get to choose. We aren't making you do it or not.

It is hard to switch up the routine. It is easier just to keep to the schedule. It feels safer.

Do you see the hold this has on you?

Yes.

It is like the cages. We don't force you. You get to try change. Even for breakfast, you can make a different choice.

I don't know…

Just take it step by step with Us. We are here and We delight in you. We give you the freedom to choose. This isn't just about the exercise or the sauna or eating. This is about freedom to choose. This is about taking little steps to flow instead of rigidity. Yes, We know you don't demonstrate it on the outside, but it is there on the inside. We are helping you to be aware of this.

Okay. Thank you. I give this to You. Help me to flow with You. Strong Girl, are you on board with this?

Not really. It is easier to keep to the routine. We don't have to think about it. We just do it.

It helps us work on developing our "choice" muscle.

You don't understand how dangerous that is.

Then please tell me.

We have to keep the order. It brings order. And safety. Personal choice is dangerous. Must follow the order.

I give this to You, True Jesus. Please help me.

We are here. We see and know. We take this step by step with you.

Am I wasting my time doing this?

No. This is important. We are glad to be with you in this.

I don't like this.

There is a flow in community that is different than the order. We want you to understand this.

Okay, I feel like I have done that to a certain extent.

Yes, and what We are exposing are the parts who are still struggling with this, especially Strong Girl and her relationship to your body. This is where this is the strongest. Your body is asking for rest, but the Order is preventing that. Strong Girl is driving that. If you want rest, it is important to walk this out.

Okay. Please help me with this. I hear the word "compulsive." Is this the issue?

It is part of it. Obedience to the Order is the other part.

I don't want that. I don't want to talk about it either. I hear sub-routines. Programs running in the background.

Yes, We are here.

I don't want any of that. I don't want any of it to be true.

If you want full freedom, you will have to look at this. It is the way they can still access and control.

Please help me.

We are here.

I give this to You.

Flow with Us today. Know that you are loved, and We are pleased with you. You are safe in Our love. We will help you through this. Nothing is impossible with Us.

Strong Girl and True FAMILY

We were addressing the parts who were scared. Don't push them away. They need tender care daily. Let the littles come.

Okay, so staying relational and not pushing them away is how we walk this out?

Yes, Strong Girl, pushing them away and putting them in lockdown isn't our way.

But it does the job. They don't whine and cry so much when they are in lockdown.

Yes, but it is not Our way. Instead of lockdown, they can be held and loved by Us. We are available 24/7.

You are too busy with other people.

No, We are able to be with you 24/7 and to minister to others at the same time. This is who We are.

Oh. Okay. But lockdown is easier.

Maybe for you if you are in control, but if you would let Us manage things, then it would not be necessary, and they would actual get what they need.

Okay. We can try that. It makes sense.

You will need to let go of control.

Nope. Can't do that.

Why not?

It is life and death to keep control.

It doesn't have to be that way.

Too risky to try anything else.

I am the resurrection and the life. Your life is in My hands. I hold you gently. No one can snatch you from My hand.

So, You want me to trust You?

Yes.

I don't know. I need to be responsible. These little ones depend on me.

You've done a good job, and We are proud of you in keeping Adena alive, but now she is learning a new way and to trust Us with her inner realm, with all of you.

You could force us, but You don't.

That's right! True love doesn't force, control or manipulate.

Ah, so You are saying I don't really love these parts?

You do, but it is twisted. Do you think locking them in cages is good?

Well, it does keep them safe.

Yes, that was the only option you thought you had, but now there is a different option you can consider. We have ways to keep you all safe that are way better. You like improving things?

Yes, I do.

Okay, then would you be willing to explore this with Us? Lockdown doesn't have to happen.

Well, this time it did otherwise Adena would not be able to handle this stuff.

She is learning new ways too. This is an adventure to trust and rest.

She said it was nice that we did this.

Yes, she was being honest that it is easier in some ways to go into lockdown, but it doesn't solve problems, and it makes more problems ultimately.

Oh.

We can help her to handle anything. She is learning to stay present and to not run away from pain. This is incredibly valuable. You can help her with this. She needs your strength not to hide away, but to face the pain and overcome.

Hmmm… maybe.

We've got this! Come and learn how We do things. You are a valuable part of Adena. She needs you.

Okay. I will consider.

Thank you!

Section X

Reckless

Reckless is a newer part I've come across who just wants to get things done. She is frustrated with other parts who are "too slow" and is the driver behind workaholism. Focusing on work kept out the pain and reaped people pleasing rewards. She is learning to cooperate with True FAMILY in the flow of life.... slowly.

Working with Reckless

You know my impatience to hurry up this process. I repent for that and ask for Your grace to go at the pace You have for me.

We know this and it is a good opportunity to have grace for yourself and your parts. You've asked for the "least damage" and that includes you.

Why do I have this reckless part that just wants to do damage?

It is okay. It is the one who wants to just "fix" it all at any cost. She is desperate. Treat her tenderly.

Okay. Reckless, I hear you and feel you. I know you want clarity and direction now that this present place feels unbearable.

You've got that right! I'm done!

I feel that too, and I heard you on Thursday with Jo. Why do you feel this way?

We have to get completely free! Now! Run away and get it over with.

We could do that, but it would cause damage to a lot of people, including us and other parts who are not ready.

Who cares! Just do it. It is more important to get away than to worry about who gets hurt.

I understand how you feel and also want to let you know that if we don't do this carefully, we will just go right back into another situation where we are potentially handled by someone else. The True FAMILY has a path for us that is the least damaging for the most people and is truly freeing. Their path means that we don't have to go right back into another situation that seems better but is just as bad or worse. They know the end from the beginning, and They will help us. They are our best hope and so I am choosing to trust Them and rest.

No! It is too much! We've got to go now! They are just drawing the noose tighter around your neck and it will be harder the longer you wait. You just need to break free.

I hear you and know that there are many of you who want this now, but we are learning to work together with True FAMILY and to do all things in Their timing. I am asking for us all to work together for true freedom. There is a way through.

You're just getting into more trouble. Get out now.

Can you tell me more?

You saw how you are controlled.

But even on the trips alone, they accessed me… The only safe place is with the True FAMILY.

That's crap. We know best. We know more of what is going on than you do.

Yes, and I would like to know more of what is going on. I am willing to listen and to hear what you have to say. You have keys that I need. I don't remember but I am willing to remember now with the True FAMILY.

It's pointless. You won't listen.

I'm here, aren't I?

Yes, but you don't really care.

I am learning to care with the help of the True FAMILY. I used to completely block you out.

Yes, I guess so. At least we are talking.

Yes. It is good. True Jesus, I need Your help today. Please strengthen me in every way and help me to love well. I give all of this to You.

We are so proud of you, Adena! Keep moving forward with Us and We will help you. You are an overcomer. Don't be discouraged with your progress. It is Our work, not yours. Your part is simply to cooperate as We show you the next steps.

Okay. I choose You today.

The Driver

Reckless, are you pushing this through? (re. writing this book)

Yes, the sooner the better.

I have been driven the last few days. True FAMILY has a better way of doing this. It is in flow with Them.

But we are excited. We want to do this.

Why?

It's a good thing. It will help others.

It feels like you are just parroting that. What is underneath?

Well… There are other things too. Let's just get things over with. I'm a driver. What do you expect?

I am learning that flow is better with True FAMILY. I am tired of the drivenness. I am willing to take this at Their pace. They know the end from the beginning, so They know what is best for me.

Don't you trust me?

I appreciate you as part of me and you've gotten a lot done in the past, but now I'm learning to trust and rest in True FAMILY.

That's okay for a little bit, but we are the ones who get things done. You need us.

I do need you, but I don't want to be driven anymore. I want to rest and trust and flow with True FAMILY.

It gets on our nerves. We just need to get things done.

I know how you've operated in my life. It is very familiar. And we did get a lot accomplished. But there's more than just getting things done. Relationships are more important.

Yuck. Who needs those?

We all do.

I'm done with that. Too dangerous. Better to just get things done.

Are you the driver for workaholism?

Yes, it's me. Doing a good job.

I do appreciate how you've gotten me through, but I prefer flow. It is much more peaceful.

Suit yourself, but we've got to keep the pedal to the metal baby! We get things done.

What did you do when I got sick? *

That was hard. We went underground. But we got back in the game. We always come out on top. We can do great things together.

I'm choosing to partner with True FAMILY and to flow with Them. You can learn a new way that doesn't involve all the pressure. Aren't you tired of the pressure?

We know how to keep everyone in line and get things done. That is what is important. Get things done. If you didn't have me, you'd never have accomplished so much.

I hear you and it hurts my heart. You are quite the driver. I didn't realize how strong you operate in my life. Do you see the changes over the last year or two?

Yes, that has been hard on us too. You've put on the brakes and do things with True FAMILY instead of me.

It is more peaceful, and the results are better. I would prefer us learning from True FAMILY how to work together in a way that is not stepping on the gas and brake at the same time.

But we get things done.

I know you do. And there is a better way that is restful for all of us. The last few days, you've been driving and, although we got a lot accomplished, it was probably too much for our body and for parts of us who just shut down when you take over.

Well, it is good for them to get out of the way.

We are learning how to cooperate and work together. Each part has a gift that is needed for the whole. When we are all working together, that is the real sweet spot! We know when to step on the gas and flow and when to stop and rest. The goal is relationship, not results.

But we get things done.

I know. There is benefit to that, but so much more when we do it in relationship. I do want to get this book done, but not at the cost of the rest of me. Can we take a step back and take it a little slower with True FAMILY?

But…

It is okay. We will get to it, and we will work on it today, just at a different pace. The True FAMILY said we could worship in between sections and that will make it more enjoyable. It is also healthier for our body to move and dance. We will have more inspiration and creativity instead of "just pushing through." Can we work together on this?

I guess so.

Can we invite those you locked down to come out? They may have some good things to contribute as well.

As long as they stay out of the way.

How does that feel?

Hmmm… okay, we can take it a little slower. I will try to be patient.

True FAMILY really wants to help you and show you the benefits of working together.

It's a waste of time! Plowing through is so much better.

But do you see the damage it causes? Especially to relationships? True FAMILY can help you reorient to relational ways of doing things.

Come on, you are going to slow me down.

It is okay. It isn't bad. Why the hurry?

You know.

I'd like to hear it from you.

We've got to get things done. Make up for it all. Keep safe. Keep going so we don't have to face the pain. We don't want to face the pain.

Okay, there it is. True FAMILY wants to help us face the pain in Their love and to receive healing and relief. Then we can do things with joy instead of drivenness.

Don't. Want. To. Face. The. Pain.

Yes, I know but we are learning to face it with True FAMILY. They help to make it better. We can face it in Their love that never fails. It is so much better this way. Better than the drivenness and the running.

That is all we've known.

Yes, and I understand it. But it is probably why we broke down and got sick.

Yeah, I might have gone overboard on that…

It was costly for us, but true FMAILY works all things for good. We don't regret things in the past because we see how They bring good out of even our messy mistakes and failures. We get to be loved and known for who we really are, beloved of the Lord. Cherished. Cared for. Isn't that much better?

Okay, maybe. Will consider. Thank you. Will slow down.

Thank you!

Are you going to put me in the book?

You are already in it, but yes, you contributed to it!

Cool!

*I spent many years bedridden when I was a teenager

Section XI

When It Feels Too Hard

Facing our pain and memories is not easy. The only safe way to do it is with the True FAMILY. Even with Their help, it can still be overwhelming. Yet They meet us step by step! There is the temptation when going through challenging times to fall back into old ways of coping and skills that the cult equipped us with, including "theta power." This is a combination of psychic ability and demonic power. It takes persistence, unconditional love and the power of God to overcome.

Theta Powers

Remember, it is step by step, trusting and resting. Enjoy these next few days. It has been heavy. So, take time to enter into joy and rest. Don't push away love. Or punish yourself. Live the life We've given you. No martyrs.

At the end of the session (with Jo), the thought came up about exploring my theta powers. Maybe I could kill myself. It would look natural. I give these thoughts to You. I give any skills I have to You for safe keeping. I don't want to self-harm or harm anyone else. (I hear, *"but better me than anyone else")*. I bring this into the light of Your unconditional love. Will You help me?

I never say no to that request.

Okay. I give all of this to You. I rest in Your care. Why do I feel such despair? I don't like this.

It isn't an easy journey, precious Adena. If you just focus on the hard stuff, there is more suffering.

I don't want to spiritually bypass.

I'm not asking you to. But you do need to take time to rest and refresh and focus on restoration and the bigger picture. You are focused on certain things that you do not even know are true instead of trusting Us. You want to be in control and that does not have the best outcome. We understand why. You don't want to hurt anyone, but it actually prevents you from what We have for you. Releasing this to Us, even if it is moment by moment, will help you to see that We've got this and there is a beautiful pathway of restoration. Let Us work it out.

I choose to give this to You and in the next moment and the next. I don't want to control the process. I do want to trust but teach me how. I don't know how. It is very scary. It is terrifying.

Let Us hold you through the night. Rest and trust.

Thank you. I do feel better. The despair is not so bad.

See! This is the way. You do not need to feel despair as self-punishment.

Oh, I didn't see that. Okay, I choose to see through Your eyes of love. Thank you!

Facing My Jesuit Past

When memories come for a survivor, sometimes it is a "flood" and other times, it is more like "one puzzle piece at a time." Most of mine have come in the form of puzzle pieces, making it more difficult to see the whole picture. They are little clues, one by one. The Lord is so gracious to share what we can handle step by step. This is some of my ponderings in facing the possibility of having been trained in the Jesuit order.

Well done, Adena. We are here to help you on this journey, step by step. Don't be discouraged. You are gaining ground. Stand firm.

How does the programming from the "god machine"* get broken? I know You have a way through. I don't like the technology programming me.

Yes, We have a way through. True Jesus' blood is more than enough even with technology. Nothing can stand in its way.

I want the full freedom You paid for, True Jesus. Please help me to walk this out today to whatever degree I am able, by Your grace. Thank you for yesterday. What is needed for today?

Continue to surrender it all to Us. We will take you step by step. Nothing can stand against Jesus' blood. His sacrifice is enough.

How do I communicate this to all of me? What about all the trapped parts?

There is freedom for them too. No one needs to be left behind. Freedom for all.

How do I walk this out today?

Stay faithful in prayer. Don't let despair have a foothold. Remember who you are in Us. We will not fail you. You can trust Us.

Why am I struggling this morning to know for sure that this is You?

That is the resistance and "hold outs." Pray for them.

True FAMILY, I give You all of these holdouts. Meet them where they are and minister Your love and grace as needed. I'm avoiding the "fathers" stuff.

Yes, and that slows things down.

Why can't I face it?

You don't want it to be true. But deep inside, you know it is.

The resistance is strong, very strong.

Does that give you clues?

Yes, but…

You can face this with Us. You don't need to go into the "what if's" unless you want to. You know the answer inside. This is deflection.

Okay, I give all of this to You and all of the resistance too. I only want the truth. The clues do add up.

Yes.

Please help me with this.

We are here and We are helping you step by step. What would it look like to face this?

I would have to face the reality of things I did.

Can you face that and also know that Our love never fails?

Only by Your grace and through the blood of True Jesus.

Well said! We know this is very painful.

Yes, it is overwhelming.

Let Us carry it for you step by step and just focus on what We've given you for today. This will be much easier.

Okay, I choose to remember the joy set before and that Your plan is for restoration. I bless the fathers and release Your love to them and ask for their freedom, too. My heart aches. And yet they feel far away… Is that the wall I've built?

Yes, it is. The wall will not serve you for freedom.

But it feels better. Keep them on that side and me on this side. Block. Block. Block.

That blocks your freedom and theirs.

I can't face this alone.

You are not alone, but if you want to wait and do this with Jo you can.

I'm afraid I'm making things up or will get it wrong. Things scatter when I try to face this.

Do you trust Our timing and way?

Okay, yes, I will. I want to run away. Hide. Curl up and die. Please help me.

We are here. Remember the joy set before you and nothing is impossible. We will see you through. This is Our promise. You can get to the other side of this, and We are so proud of you for pressing in this far. Don't be discouraged.

Okay, I give all of this to you. Thank you for helping me.

*See *Never Give Up Part 2 The Struggle* by Svali for more on the "god machine"

Stepping Out of the Programming

During prayers for cleansing, I saw an image of being baptized in blood. Some nausea. Feels like some of the blood was from people I loved. I don't like this, True Jesus. Is this a real memory?

Yes, it is. You can give this to Us until you are ready to process. We know you are overwhelmed by other things. This was intended by the enemy as a distraction from working on the other things and to overwhelm you to stop…

Okay, I give this to You until I am ready to look at it. But it keeps coming.

Keep your focus on Us. Can you see Us?

Okay.

Feel Our hand in yours.

Are You really here or is it my imagination?

We are here for you. See Our hand outstretched to you. This is a gentle invitation, not force.

I'm afraid.

It is okay to be afraid and We can help you with that. If you want.

Why do I feel like running, hiding, etc.

It is the programming, and you can press through that. You can take Our hand and allow Us to help you with this. It is your choice.

Why is the internal response always "I don't want to?"

It is the resistance programming. You don't have to obey it.

Okay. Then I will take Your hand if it is really You.

It is.

I'm afraid You will hurt me.

Do you see that We could do this all morning? We are patient. We can do this, but We know that you want to deal with other things.

Can You take care of this programming so I can move on?

We can and it is your choice to move beyond it. It is the illusion of control that you can step out of. "Seeing" things was what triggered it, but it can also be part of disarming it. Can you see yourself stepping out of the programming?

Yes, I can. That was interesting.

Stay steady and focused on Us. Can you feel your hand in Ours?

Yes

Facing Fear and Unbelief

You are a "high-level asset."

No. I don't want that to be true. I'm not high-level anything. Please no.

Do you want the truth?

I do. But maybe I'm just hearing wrong and making it up and all of that. I can be wrong. I want to be wrong in this case. I just feel more confused.

Stay steady in Our love. We do have a way through this. It is the simplicity of your hand in Ours, step by step. This year's travels are significant in this battle for your life. Each one will test you and your trust in Us. There is a way through and there is the triumph of Our love. But it is not an easy path.

Then do I just cancel everything and stay at home?

That is an option, but not the best one. Going through the fire refines and exposes and brings to the surface the truth. This is not an easy year for you, but there will be fruit from it that remains as you trust Us.

I don't know what to think of this. I'm asking for clarity and confirmation. But I want my heart response to be like Mary and not Zachariah.

We know your heart and the pain that is there. Our desire and plans are to prosper you and to give you a future and hope. Don't be discouraged but trust Us to bring you through.

Okay, I give all of this to You and trust You to show me the way through all of this. Show me which trips to take and which to cancel or re-arrange. I want to be in Your timing, and in the right place that You have ordained for overcoming. Please help me.

Gladly. We lead you through the darkness and into the true light of Our love and restoration.

True Jesus, am I being deceived? Am I hearing right? I don't like anything I journaled today and don't want parts of it to be true. I know there's many parts and programming and more than I know…Its overwhelming but deep down I know You are real, and You do have a way through. I believe in restoration. Please help me to hang on.

We are here and We know how hard this is.

But what if this is all fake and I'm just making this up? I just want to be normal.

We didn't create you to be "normal," but to walk the unique journey of overcoming that We have for you. Remember what We've planted in your heart.

But what if it is all programming? What if I'm hurting others now? Then all of this is a mockery…as I'm telling my parts and clients about True Jesus and His safety and protection and goodness and love…

Do you believe what you tell your parts and clients? Do you daily see Me work in your life and others?

Yes, I do. But maybe it is an illusion. Maybe I don't know what is really going on….

It is a trust journey. Are you willing?

I would rather believe You are true and that my hand is in Yours and that You will keep me safe. But is it naivete'? Or Christian programming? But then again, I can second guess everything and everybody. I just want to die. I want to die…

You can spiral or you can look in Our eyes of love and remember. Remember the joy set before you. We are the Author and Finisher of your faith. We do have a good, good plan for you. We see and know the challenges, pain, heartache. We have a way through. Can you believe this?

I choose to believe it and I want to choose life, but it is hard. Please take the pain and questions.

Rest and trust, precious Adena. You are deeply loved and cared for. There is a way through.

Can't Say No

We understand. You have the ability to say no, and it is critical that you learn to do so. Especially with the trips. The "I can't say no to family" is significant and important to find out why.

Okay, I open this up to You. Please show me.

Ask inside.

Okay. Does anyone want to share why I can't say no to my family?

Handlers.

Okay. Thank you for confirming that. Anything else?

Bad. We don't like it. We don't want to do what they say. But we have to otherwise… punishment. Pain. Death.

Thank you for letting me know. I'm afraid of what is ahead. Where are You, True Jesus? Can You protect me? I want to believe.

We are here and We are able. You believing and trusting are keys to walking this out.

How do I stop this? I need to actually know what is going on. I don't have any memory of anything else. I don't want to be amnesic to it. I want the truth. I want the truth at every level, place and part.

Be aware of what you are asking. It might be harder than you know.

I would rather know the truth than to live a lie. I am willing to lose everything.

No, we don't want to. Let's stay comfortable. Peaceable. That is better. We don't know the truth. It hurts. Stay away. Avoid. Keep in the shadows. Not knowing is best. Pretend.

I hear you. We've done well at that my whole life. Now is the time we are waking up to what is actually going on. True Jesus is willing to help us through this.

We have to obey. Otherwise, bad things happen. We don't want them to hurt those we love.

The only way out of this is for us to see and know the truth and for True Jesus to set us free. He has plans to set our whole family free and those who did this to us. Everyone is miserable in it but don't realize they have a choice and can get out, even if it is very painful. I give this all to You, True FAMILY. I do want to know Truth.

You will be tested on this. Are you willing?

I do want fully out, and I know that the only way is full truth, no more amnesia. I know I don't have the strength or power to do this, but You do. You are my only hope. I don't want to be deceived, yet I feel how easy I can be manipulated by others. Why?

Ask inside.

Why do we so easily succumb to manipulation?

Orders.

Orders or the Order?

Both. Fear. Death. Pain. Not good. Keep up appearances.

In the dream, I had the remote, so I could have stopped, but I didn't. I was awake. This means that I can do something about it with True Jesus' help. We don't have to continue.

Safe is best. Safe. Safe. Safe.

Safe is an illusion without True FAMILY. They're the only Ones who can keep us safe. Just going along is a trap.

We have orders.

We don't have to obey anymore. If we all cooperate and trust in True Jesus, we can get completely free. Doesn't that sound good?

Well, yes, but it is very dangerous. Monitored.

Is this because of reading Svali's book?

You don't believe us. Yet you want us to cooperate with you?

I'm sorry, I just needed to check.

That is, you waking up and being willing to face this, not us lying.

Okay, I do want to know. I'm sorry.

You talk about cooperation, but you are the one asleep.

Yes, and I am waking up. I do want to know, and I am sorry. True Jesus, can You help us?

It is okay. We understand the denial and unbelief programs. Are you willing to see the truth?

I am willing. I need concrete information.

Is that trust?

Not really, I guess, but it would be helpful. Many don't believe.

And they won't. But the question is are *you* willing to trust? This is the only way. Remember about stepping out of the program.

Okay. I take a step out of it. Seeing something different (now)… like programming labs. I thought it was just blank white around the square, but when I stepped out there was all kinds of technology…

Okay. Now you can see a little.

I don't like this.

Yes, We didn't think you would, but you are asking for truth.

Then please help me. (I am feeling stabbing chest pain)

We are here. Remember to see where your hand is. We will walk you through, just as you stepped out of the programming, you can step out of this as well.

Is it that easy?

No, but this helps you to see that it is possible. We will not lie to you.

I feel like I'm writing a spy novel and making this all up.

You can trust and believe or not. We give you this freedom. The "easy" route can appear to be amnesia, but it is not ultimately. The way to be free and help others is to continue this path with Us with Our hand in yours.

Can You help the chest pain?

Ask inside.

Who is causing the chest pain? You aren't in trouble; we just want to know the truth.

The truth will get you in trouble.

I know it seems that way, but Jesus is The TRUTH and He's promised to help us through all of this. It takes trust and resting in Him. He is powerful and protective but doesn't force us to do bad things. He gives us the freedom to choose. He can help us.

They say that's not true.

They don't want you to know the truth. They want us to believe all the lies. But we are waking up. We can make different choices. I am asking you if you can let up on the chest pain and let us…

We have to stay compliant.

There is a way through into freedom with the True FAMILY. They are kind and gentle and tender towards us.

Anguish. Pain. Death. Over and over.

Are you talking about the programming labs? VR?

You aren't supposed to know or see that.

It is better for us to know and to share information so we can get fully free with True FAMILY. I need your cooperation. I won't force you. I know the consequences seem overwhelming, but I do believe there is a way through with True Jesus.

He is powerless against them.

It seems like that because He doesn't force us like they do. He gives us a choice.

They do too…

Yes, in the form of this bad thing or that bad thing. That isn't a true choice. Thank you for easing up on the chest pain. Are you willing to try out True Jesus, and see? It is a freewill choice you can make.

Maybe…

Okay, that is a start. Please let the others know that we are seeing truth and working together with True FAMILY for freedom.

They will be mad.

True FAMILY, will You show us what to do. Will You help us learn to work together?

We do this slowly and gently for everyone's sake. Go at the pace We lead. We are gentle with all. I know you are eager for everyone to cooperate, but this is a process.

We don't have a lot of time.

Time belongs to me. Do you trust Me?

Okay, I am sorry for trying to control this. I give this to You completely. Your timing, Your way. You have the best way through. I surrender.

Rest in Our love. This is not about you figuring it out. Just your hand in Ours. Take the next step.

Yes, I'm sorry. I want that. There's just so much.

There is but see how if you stay close and walk with Us, We can keep you from every trap of the enemy.

(In a vision, I am seeing a scene like in a spy movie. Characters are going through different obstacles, knowing when to move, when to wait, etc. in order to avoid "bad stuff".)

Every trap of the enemy?

Yes, it is possible. That doesn't mean no hard things and challenges will ever happen, but We can get you through in triumph.

I really want that, but I don't know how.

We've said it over and over.

Okay, but that is the hard part.

It can also be the beautiful part…receiving Our love and care.

I want to. Please help me. Can You show them all the scene You just showed me? How it is possible?

Yes, We can …

See everyone, it is possible.

But we aren't one, we are many. Too many. Not possible.

What do You say, True Jesus?

It feels like many, but you are all one with Adena. You are her.

We are shattered. Fragmented. Many.

Yes, and you are also one. Learning to cooperate will help on this journey. When you step into Us, We can do great things. We do not force you. It is your choice, but see how it is possible doing this together?

Too hard. Too many consequences.

I get it and I am just asking you to consider this. True Jesus showed you a way that is possible. Please consider.

Okay.

True Jesus, can I go back to sleep now?

Yes, We are so proud of you. Rest and trust.

Encountering the Lion of Judah

Sometimes parts are too afraid of Father, Holy Spirit or Jesus, but are able to connect to the Lion of Judah or the Lamb of God. Although, for me, one part asked if the Lion of Judah would eat them! My suggestion is to take it slow and ask your part(s) who they are comfortable with.

We delight to pour in Our love and grace. The journey is long, and We will sustain you through it. Do not be afraid.

How can I not be afraid? This stuff is hard.

When you are walking with Us and when you see the beauty of what We are doing in you and through you and how We have an effect on others through you, then you can walk with confidence. You can give Us your fears moment by moment. Let the weight go.

I choose Your way. Thank you.

Many will not understand. Many will criticize and worse. There will be things coming from every side, but We created you to stand with Us through the storm and to rejoice in Our love and grace. This is the position We have for you, and We invite you into. Remember who you are.

I say yes. Thank you so much. I ask for grace for this.

It is given. Do not be afraid. Face the hard stuff with curiosity, not fear. You are an overcomer.

I choose to believe.

That's Our girl! Never give up.

I'm sorry everyone is upset. True Jesus, can You help us?

I am here. This is good for you to face this.

I don't want to. Parts are cutting themselves with a knife. Why are you doing this?

We have to.

I believe there is another way. Are you hurting?

Yes.

Why?

You know.

Okay. We haven't heard anything yet. We can have patience with True FAMILY and trust them. You don't need to hurt yourself. *

We have to do something.

She wouldn't want you to do that.

They did it in the Bible.

Yes, but it wasn't the ones who were following True FAMILY, and they did not have a good end.

We want to die instead. Take us. We will hate Him forever if He takes her. We can't handle any more loss.

Cutting won't help.

It helps the pain.

We can give the pain to True Jesus.

No! We can't. He took too many. He is bad. Too many losses.

Are you willing to talk about it?

No! Never. Buried deep. Can't talk. Bad. Pain. Rage. Awful stuff. Black. Black. Black. Darkness.

I am so very sorry. I am here and so is True FAMILY.

We don't want Them.

It's okay. I thank you for sharing a little bit. I want you to know I'm here. I care and when you are ready, I would like to know more about your pain. There are ways to work through it, so you don't have to cut.

Agony. Deep. Hurt. Can't go on. I'm afraid. Everyone leaves.

I'm here and I care. And I am so very sorry for your pain. I feel the pain. Abandonment? Loss? Both?

Both. Can you see me in this darkness?

Just barely. I saw you cutting yourself with the knife. The Lion of Judah is here and if you want you can snuggle up to Him. He cares too.

Who is He?

He knows a lot and He cares. His fur can feel comforting, and you can hear His heart beat. Do you want to come closer? He won't leave.

That's what they all say.

It is true. He is a great comfort if you are willing. You don't have to say anything. Do you see this spot? You can curl up here and just be for a bit and it will help.

Does He purr?

Yes, He does. Listen.

Does He mind the dark? (The part comes closer to the Lion of Judah)

No, He can see perfectly in it. He is not afraid.

I feel His strength.

Good.

Thank you, that lifts the hurt some.

* This hurt had to do with waiting for news and updates about a friend with cancer

Discoveries

I've been surprised on this trip to the ocean. I thought my eye-hand coordination was horrible but, in the water, we've played catch with a football, and I did really well, even with my left hand! Is this from the healing work we've been doing?

It is part of it. You have more ability than you know.

I don't want to talk anymore… How come?

Ask inside.

I don't want to.

You always get to choose.

I'm afraid.

Why?

I don't know. This is also what I am afraid of about doing an intensive with Jo. What if I "lock up" and can't get anywhere? I don't want to waste time and money.

Who does your time and money belong to? Can you trust Us?

I want to. I don't trust me. I may get it wrong. I may lock up. I may get stuck. I might get overwhelmed.

Do you think that We can handle that?

Okay. Back to this. Why don't I want to look at it?

You are afraid of what might come out. Afraid of the abilities you might have that have been exploited by the system.

Are You with me?

Yes, We are here.

Can You help me through this? Can You help me face anything?

Yes, We can.

Okay. What do I need to see today?

You have great skill and accuracy that was bred and programmed into you, but also hidden from your presenter life.

Can't You make all this go away?

You desire truth in the inward parts.

Why all this pain?

You know.

I don't want to face it.

You said the prayer this morning about allowing Us to decide what you can handle. Do you mean it? *

I want to.

Then take Our hand. We have been and are faithful to Our word to see you through. Step by step. Secure in Our love. To be able to face it.

Okay. Please steady me in Your love.

Gladly.

Why did this trigger tears?

There is much pain here, in the training and what you were required to do with that training.

Do You forgive me?

Yes, I have forgiven you. You can stand in My righteousness, My love, My protection, My grace, My strength.

I did bad things.

We know this. Nothing is hidden from Us. We know that is not your heart.

Gina Phillips said the "nicer" survivors actually have the worst programming (most evil cult parts). Maybe I'm doing really bad things. Maybe it is all my fault.

Are you more powerful than Us?

No.

Is the cult system more powerful than Us?

No.

Do We have a good, good plan for restoration and the triumph of Our love?

Yes.

Can you trust Us that even if you have done bad, horrible things that We have a way through to work all things for good?

Yes.

Stay grounded there. More things will be revealed in time, and We are holding you safe and secure. You desire truth and We honor that. We can give you the strength to face things and not run.

I want to run.

We know. We are training you to stay present and to receive Our love. Step by step. We are so very proud of you.

Why?

You continue to say yes. You are learning to stay present. You are facing hard things. You love well.

I don't think so. If I did, then my family…

You aren't responsible for them.

But I did bad things.

Step by step, precious Adena. Receive Our love. Don't push it away. We care.

Okay. Thank you. I choose You. No matter what. Hold me steady in Your love.

With great delight. It is okay to acknowledge that you want to push away from love. We understand the fear and pain. But the only solution is Our love. We alone can protect you and give you the security you long for. We can handle it all. Nothing is hidden from Us. We know the "end from the beginning." The "end" We have for you is glorious in Our love and is the beginning of so much more! Choose love today.

Okay. I choose to receive. Thank you.

*A phrase from the Morning and Evening Prayers from the book *Prayer Warriors* by Jo Getzinger

Difficult Memories and Decoys

I hate you. I hate you! Don't talk about it. We can't...

(I see someone stabbing a blond girl with a knife. There is blood everywhere.)

True Jesus, I give this to You. I am asking for You to stand between all parts and to protect this one. Is this a decoy to stop me from journaling or is this really happening?

Decoy.

I also felt like the scenes I saw in my session with Jo were connected to the black forest in Germany. (I suddenly get the feeling like I want to run away.)

Stay steady in Our love.

(I see a blank room. The walls appear white, although I could see inside them. It is like a honeycomb structure and there are gross insects inside as well as bees.)

I give this to You, True Jesus. I did pray for deliverance, but I feel nauseated now since getting up. I don't want to exist. It's too hard. They are going to destroy me. I just want to stop it now.

Then who wins?

They do.

You can do this as you just put your hand in Our hand. Remember how True Jesus was so bright and shiny yesterday? Remember how He enveloped Strong Girl and light was everywhere and the darkness had to go?

Yes.

We can do that always. The darkness has to go, and you can face really hard things with Us. Remember the glory and joy set before you. You are more courageous than you know.

I'm still scared.

We know. But you keep going.

I'm scared. I'm scared. I'm scared.

Keep looking at that picture of Strong Girl and Our light around her.

What if it is a lie? Made up.

Do you want to believe the programming or be free?

I want to be free.

Okay. We are holding you gently in Our love. We will see you through this. Remember We know the end from the beginning.

Yes.

So, you say.

Do you believe that We can bring you through this?

I choose to believe. Help my unbelief!

Good answer! Gladly! You know how We answered the one who said that. Remember it is Our faith. Our faith is strong enough. Not yours. Yours is enough to say yes to Us and We do the rest.

Okay. I say yes. I trust You to bring me through. Can You make the bad stuff go away?

We are doing this step by step as you are willing to face this stuff with Us. Uncovering the darkness is necessary. There is great triumph on the way.

It doesn't feel like that.

This is where you get to see as We do, the eyes of Our faith. We are enough. You don't have to figure it out.

Can You unravel what this anxiety and nausea is all about? I need Your help. Please get the darkness away from me.

Bugs in the wall?

Yes. When You say it like that, it sounds like something more.

Trust and give this to Us and We can take care of it. Be aware.

Okay. Okay. True Jesus, You are the way, the truth and the life. I yield it all to You.

Well done! Let Us fight this battle so you can go back to sleep.

Strong girl wants to help.

She can, but then you won't sleep. Rest is important.

How come I sleep really well some nights and other nights not so well?

A lot is being exposed right now and there are things going on.

I thought you were standing between all parts and protecting me?

I am and there's some things allowed for you to be aware of. If We shut it off completely, you would not know what needed to be addressed.

Isn't there an easier way? I just want it all to go away.

You know where that is coming from.

Yes. I'm sorry to whine. I want Your way, True Jesus. But it is hard.

Remember the reward. Remember restoration. Remember "for such a time as this." Remember "just put your hand in Ours and take the next step." We do have a way through. There is a line they can't cross and, while We are allowing certain things for your awareness, We are also blocking a lot because We are faithful to Our promises to you. We do have a way through. Will you trust and rest tonight as We are at work?

Yes. I give this anxiety and nausea to You. Please deliver me.

You are safe and secure in Us. Don't let them rattle you. Keep looking at Us. Rest in Our arms as you go back to sleep.

Okay. Thank you for helping me to go back to sleep.

Rest and trust.

Baby Steps

I am so very sorry for what you went through. I don't remember, but I am willing to.

Why would you want to remember such horror? We keep it safe for you.

I appreciate how you've done that through the years so I wouldn't know and be overwhelmed. However, I am learning with True FAMILY that the only way for healing is to face these truths in Their love. They are in charge of our healing. In Their timing, They will help us face these things. I'm not pushing for it. I am just open to what you and others have to say.

It's too hard. Especially with everything else going on. Too many fires.

I understand. True FAMILY is willing to help. They already know all about it and have a solution for the pain. Just something to consider.

Okay. We hurt. It was bad. I want to forget it all. I don't ever want to know anything about it. I hate them. Bad.

I can understand that. I would too. We can give this to True FAMILY until we are strong enough to face it.

They won't make us?

No. They will bring it up in Their timing when They know we are ready.

I don't think so. We need to be in control of this. Lockdown. Keep safe.

True FAMILY are the best security system around. They know all about us. They care, are gentle and loving. We can trust them.

Not possible. Not trusting anyone.

I understand that, with what you've experienced. They won't push themselves on us. We get to freely choose when you are ready.

I don't know…

It's okay. Just consider it. Know that I care and love you and I don't want you to carry this burden alone.

There's no other choice.

Actually, there is. Even talking with me today helps. You are not alone.

It does feel nice.

Yes. Others have experienced this too.

Okay.

Facing Another Day

I want to die.

We are here and We understand.

I want this to end.

Remember the joy set before you. Remember who you are.

It hurts so bad.

We know. We feel it with you. Trust and rest.

Will You provide for me?

There is so much We are excited to pour into you. You have been faithful, daughter, and We delight to give good gifts.

Why is it such a struggle? I can feel both the faith to believe and the joy in what is ahead as well as the rewards of seeing the mass exodus. But also, there is the terror of failure and loss. Can You hold me?

Yes, We are here holding you gently. Even when you can't see or feel, We are here.

I can't do this without You.

We aren't asking you to. This was always and will be Our partnership with you. Remember, it is as simple as putting your hand in Ours and taking the next step.

But these are hard steps.

Yes, and you are not alone. Remember Jo is on one side and True Jesus is on the other. You are not alone. You can do this together with Us. It is possible.

Am I dreaming too big? I can see and feel it and it fills me with joy and delight! Is this from You?

Yes, We've planted this in your heart, and they could not erase it. This is what We planned for you from the beginning.

How is it possible?

Step by step with Us. Remember who you are and let that be bigger than your fears. We will help you step by step. Do not be afraid. It takes courage to do what you are doing. It is not for the faint of heart.

And yet here I am whining.

It is not whining when you are expressing your heart cry. This is what the Psalms are about. Real people crying out to God, processing their pain and experiencing Our love. We are excited for the things We've put on your heart. Take it one step at a time.

Okay, can You help me to sleep?

Yes, lay down snuggled in Our love. We are protecting you day and night. It is intense, but you can sleep in the boat in the middle of the storm. I did. And now I am with you.

Okay, thank you!

Overwhelmed

I'm afraid, like a little child lost in the dark. Where are You?

We are here. Even if you can't see Us at the moment, reach out your hand. We are here.

Okay, I can feel Your hand. But is it enough? I'm overwhelmed by all the "stuff." What to do? I want to die.

Why?

It is all overwhelming.

Can you take it step by step with Us? Can you trust Us to provide all that you need?

So many parts curled up in the fetal position.

We love every one of them so very tenderly. We see and We know. Remember who you are and the destiny We have for you. This is Our joy and delight. Can you cast all your cares on Us? We care for you.

Please show me how.

Can you do anything about all of this?

No.

Can We?

I suppose.

We care for you tenderly and have given you others who are coming alongside to help. Don't resist the help.

That is overwhelming.

See it as Our plan. To care for you tenderly. This is who We are. This is Our great delight. Can you receive?

That is the hard part. I desperately need and want it, but it is hard to receive. I haven't done enough to deserve it. And I know that is wrong. But it is how it feels.

See it from Our perspective. We have all the resources and love you so tenderly. We know every detail of your life. There is nothing hidden. We love you and every part of you. We know why you did things. We had a plan from the beginning for your restoration. Doesn't it make perfect sense for you to trust and rest?

Yes, if I believe all of that. I do intellectually, but many parts don't.

Then isn't this a beautiful opportunity for them to learn it?

Yes, I guess so. I need to sleep.

Yes, but will you if you are carrying all of this?

No. I want to give it to You. Will You really take it?

Yes, it is Our delight to carry you through the night. Nothing is impossible with Us. Can you rest in Our love?

I want to.

That is the start.

Okay. So, this all is way bigger than I can handle. I give it all to You. Thank you for putting a shield around me and protecting me. Keep me safe in Your love. I need Your peace that passes understanding.

Because of Our value of you, you are worth it. It is Our delight to give and to pour out all that you need for this season and to take you step by step. Trust and rest.

Working Through Accusations

We are here. Take some deep breaths and meditate on Me.

I'm really struggling to connect.

This will take you to a deeper place if you are willing. Don't be discouraged, little one. We are so pleased with you. You are doing more than you know. This is exciting! We are rejoicing with you. Do not fear or be afraid.

I choose to say yes, even when I want to say no. I want to be done with all this and just let go.

What does that mean to you?

I don't know. I'm angry. I don't like ministry. People are hurtful. I hurt people.

Do you want to hurt people?

Right now, I do because I'm angry. People are bad.

Not all people are bad.

But these people were supposed to be our friends. Why did they betray us?

People will hurt people. You said you hurt people too. This is not something to be afraid of but to work through.

I want to stay away from everyone.

We know that you do. It seems like it would be easier, but it would be very lonely.

Can't I be lonely?

You can if you want, but there is a better solution.

How do I get into the ocean of love?

Just step in.

I can't.

We can help you. We have you in Our arms. Do not be afraid.

I want to run away.

We know this, precious one. Running away doesn't solve anything. You get to either be part of the solution or part of the problem.

I handled this badly. I should have intervened that night. *

You could have, although it might have been worse. Trust Us and know that We are here for you. We can help you walk through this if you are willing.

I guess I am willing. I know there is no other way but You. So, I choose You, True Lord Jesus Christ of Nazareth. Show me the way.

Take it step by step. Trust Us and the timing. There is more at stake than you know.

What does that mean?

We are working all things for good. It is okay. Remember that We have this. There are parts that are needing to express some things. This is good work, though painful.

True Lord Jesus Christ of Nazareth, are You here for me to engage with?

Yes, I am here along with the rest of the FAMILY. Let go of pettiness and receive the fullness We have for you. Do not spiritually bypass. It has been good to see your littles in action.

True Family, I give this mess to You. I can't fix it. I can't manage it. I want You to manage it. Please show me the way.

Thank you so much, precious Adena. We've got this. You do not need to think or stress about it. Enter into a new place of joy.

Thank you. I choose joy!

(A little while later, a book that I was reading was causing triggering. The littles begin to talk in response…)

We are not Bluebirds, but Butterflies. We don't exist. We don't want to be here. We don't belong. We will fly away and never come back. We fly away. We fly away. We fly away. We fly away. We fly away. Don't touch us. Don't remember. Be silent. Sit still. Don't look that way. Smile for the camera. You don't exist. We don't exist. It is all an illusion. Ying Yang. Topsy turvy. Sit and don't move...

True FAMILY, please come to these littles and help them. They are in such need. Do I stop reading so I don't trigger? Is this helpful or not? I am reading to get insight into sex magick for the class. Will this trigger them?

Take some deep breaths and relax.

Is it all fake?

Relax and breathe.

They're killing again. They are killing again. They are killing again. Help! Will someone help?

We are here, Adena. We have always been here. Through it all, We have been here.

Why didn't You do anything?

Because We had agreed to go to the other side of restoration. You saw the glory and you said yes to this pathway for restoration. It is so key…

I don't want to say yes anymore.

We know. Remember who you are. Remember that it is worth it all. Pull into Our embrace. We will not hurt you.

But You did because You didn't do anything.

We saved you more than you know. What is playing out is amazing.

*"That night" is referring to an incident when there was an accusation against me

Running Away

I want to run away.

What part is this? Why do you want to run away?

Life is just too hard. I feel overwhelmed. I don't want to face today.

We are so grateful for your honesty. You do not need to face this alone. We are with you. Receive Our help to make this easy and light. This is Our promise to you.

I am willing. What does that look like?

It means resting and trusting.

I don't know how to do that. I have to be strong and hypervigilant. There are so many dangers all around.

You can let True FAMILY do that. They are better at keeping us safe than anything or anyone. Let go of this need to be in control and let True FAMILY help us.

NO!

It is okay. We love you deeply, just as you are. We are so sorry that life is so very hard right now. You have a choice to be able to let love win or stay in self-protection mode. You can let True FAMILY handle this.

No.

Are there beings who are making you do this?

I have to do this for Adena's safety.

Let me tell you some good news. Jesus paid for it all and He is wanting to help you. You don't have to carry this weight.

If I let go, the whole house of cards falls down.

Maybe it's time for that. Letting go is not a bad thing or shameful.

But I'm good at holding her together. If I don't do this, she will fall apart and may not survive.

Can you trust the True FAMILY to help? It is a heavy burden to carry this alone. You were never meant to do it for long, only long enough to find True FAMILY. Put your fears aside and open your heart to trust.

I don't want to.

We won't make you, but Adena chose True FAMILY to be in charge, so you can let go and rest.

Section XII

Good Times

I wanted to add a section on the good times, because it is not always painful and hard. It is important for survivors to experience joy. We can only heal at the level of our "joy capacity." The good news is that our brain is wired to be able to continue to expand that joy capacity. Laughter and times of refreshing are desperately needed and just as important as facing the pain. We can't do one without the other. For more on joy capacity check out the book *Joy Starts Here* by Dr. Jim Wilder.

Gift of Grace

I felt a shift last night and more clarity, love, and sound mind! Thank you, True FAMILY, for Your gift of grace and to anyone who was praying for me! Please send abundant blessings back to them – I am so very grateful. Please show me how to bless others this way and to pass on this grace! Sustain me, True FAMILY, by Your power and might and grace!

We love to give good gifts! Enjoy and receive a rest even as you enter into challenging times, knowing that We are here for you, and We will see you through. You do not need to do anything but to stand in Our grace and see Our salvation

manifested for you. Saturate yourself in Our love and care. This will help to buffer you in coming days.

Thank you so very much! I am rejoicing. I'm a little afraid to engage with my inner realm in case that brings things in another direction, but I trust You and that You will help me step by step.

You've done good work, even though you felt you didn't accomplish much in the session. Take a break and just enjoy Our love and practice joy today. This is the path for you today!

Making Progress

True Jesus, what do You want to say?

We have always been here, tenderly loving you and walking you through this journey. We are so pleased with your progress, and We are not ashamed of you. We have what it takes to see you fully restored and overcoming. These obstacles are not a problem for Us and We work with you gently in Our perfect timing for each piece.

Why can't You just make it all better now. It is too hard.

We know that it feels that way, but are you interested in maximum restoration for the most people? This is Our heart.

Yes and no. Just fix it.

Remember the verse about the patience of the saints?

Yes.

Can you trust Us? The system is coming down, and you have a part in it as you are praying and forgiving and healing yourself and helping others. This is glorious.

It doesn't feel like it right now. We just want to run away and hide forever and not exist. Can we just "not be" for a while?

I know. When I faced the hordes of hell at the last, the garden was agony, and I wanted to run away and hide too. I know what it feels like. It is okay. We are here to strengthen you through this. We will help you step by step. You are not alone. I overcame so that you could also overcome. This is the joy that I set My heart on in order to endure the cross. I invite you to this place as well. It is the joy of your own healing and also the joy of so many others whom you will and are influencing. It is worth it all.

Okay, then I need Your strength today and for all of my parts.

It is Our joy to do so. Be encouraged. We know that it seems very slow and the same thing over and over, but you are making more progress than you know. The powers of darkness are in fear because they know their time is short. Hang on to Us and trust. We will see you through.

I don't know how it is possible, but I am willing to trust. Thank you.

You are most welcome! Remember the triumph of Our love. You have spoken on it and, deep down, you believe it even though you have many parts who are terrified. Our love will triumph over all. Receive Our strength and love today.

I need Your grace too.

Of course… there is more than enough. Trust and rest.

Tender Towards Weakness

Trust and rest in Us. Give this time to Us and We will walk with you step by step.

I am willing to see whatever aspect or part of me I am neglecting. What am I not feeding, nurturing and caring for in my life?

You are not ready to see the fullness of this, precious Adena. We give you what you can handle.

I want to handle it now. I want to know.

Hear the desperation and demand. Are you willing to rest and trust?

Why show me if You aren't going to help me?

We are helping you and gently bringing to the surface those things that We desire you to be aware of. It includes these attitudes. You want to fix things now instead of trusting and resting.

Yes, thank you for showing me and for being so tender with me. I release these things to You. I'm sorry.

There is no condemnation. This is where you get to be tender towards your weakness. It is okay. We've got you and We've got this. We are lovingly walking you through and there is beautiful restoration for every aspect of your life as you trust and rest. This is the most important thing for you to learn. This is why it is what We tell you every day. You think you know what it is, but there is more. Come as a little child, letting go of the need to fix, survive, figure it out or make it right. Just come to be loved.

I don't know how.

That is okay, because We want to teach you. Just come.

Okay. Here I am.

Amazing Love

I give this day to You.

We love to honor this and also to challenge you in areas that need challenged, so do not be afraid of the difficulties when they come. Yes, there are things you can do to minimize them, but know that all things are working together for good. It is not about the perfect life, but about living in union with Us.

Is there anything I need to do today to actively position myself to receive Your love?

We are always pouring Our love over you, and it is always accessible. It is your awareness of this or not that is at work in you.

I want to be more aware of Your love and how to receive it. You know the blocks in my life. I want to receive.

We hear your cry, and We are answering. Don't be discouraged, just know that it is here. It is available. Always. We will help you grow in being able to receive both from Us and from others. You are deeply loved. Always and forever.

Thank you so much. I am so very grateful for the beautiful community You've given me and the support system. I know I couldn't do this without You.

Nothing Is Impossible

Thank you, True FAMILY, for more rest and better sleep. I am very grateful. I need You today! Please show me the way.

We are here, precious Adena and nothing is impossible with Us. Don't be discouraged about things but look to Us. We have a way through.

Okay, I choose to trust You today. You know what I need and will guide me as I set my gaze on You. I don't know what to do about yesterday and my parts bringing up the 13th. You know I don't want to look at this, but I am trusting You as the Way, The Truth and the Life. I only want to know what You know I am able to handle today.

Dearest Adena, We hold you gently in Our hands and nothing can harm you as you set your gaze on Us. We will keep you. These things are true and also Our grace and love are truer. If you look at the other too much, you will miss what We have for you. We will reveal what you need to know step by step in Our perfect timing.

Thank you. I don't want to resist the things You are doing. I say yes to You again. I'm afraid of getting it wrong and making stuff up. I only want Your truth for me today.

It is programming and parts that block or distort but We can help you through that. It is possible. What do you need today?

I don't know. My inner realm feels fragile and conflicted. Can You repair and restore anything that happened that I don't know about?

Yes, We can. Remember, We are working out a good, good plan for you, for your restoration and so much more. Rest and trust.

Okay, do I need to address any parts? I am afraid to.

Why are you afraid?

Because I might get it wrong.

Can you trust Us?

I want to. Please help me.

New Mercies Every Morning

Here I am, True FAMILY! I am grateful for all that You are doing. Please keep my heart centered in You today. I choose to receive all that You have for me.

We delight in you, precious Adena! You are Our delight! Stand in confidence in who We created you to be and know that We are daily loading you with blessings and benefits. This is not an easy journey, but We are with you. Stand and sing the salvation of the Lord.

Thank you so very much. I give this day to You and thank you for Your mercies that are new every morning. Anything I need to be aware of?

Know that We are holding you gently and all of your parts. See Our tenderness for them, even the ones who hold so much hatred and pain. Nothing is impossible with Us. We provide the way through as you trust Us. There is so much that We have for you as you are ready to receive.

Please help me to be able to receive. I give it all to You. I am inviting all parts of me who are willing to come and worship the True FAMILY with me.

Overcomer

We are delighted in you today. The changes that you are making will have a ripple effect. Rejoice in what We are doing in you. Watch for overconfidence and stay connected relationally. We will strengthen you through this. Watch where Strong Girl or Good Girl are taking over. Do not run in your own strength.

Okay, thank you. I choose to rest in You and follow You step by step. Show me the way. How do I receive love today?

Remember who you are and take the time to see how We see you.

How do You see me?

You are an overcomer. We've called you to lead in this hour. You are so very precious to Us. We know your heart.

Please cleanse every part of me and help me to stand in Your strength alone. Thank you for not abandoning me. I thank you for being my provision. Keep me steady in Your love.

Powerful Prayers!

I am so very grateful for powerful prayer time this morning! How can You love me so? I am so grateful for Your power to overcome and to stand in this hour. I thank you that nothing is impossible with You. I am asking for that mass exodus from the cult system in Your timing and way. Thank you for allowing me to partner with You in this in any way I can by Your grace. Thank you for setting me free! I choose Your ways and Your timing and Your truth. Thank you!

We delight in you, True Daughter of Zion! We have placed you here for such a time as this and delight in you with all Our heart! Do not be afraid of what is ahead. We will gently carry you through. There will be many more challenges, but you can overcome through the grace We give you as you partner with Us. Receive Our love and affirmation to carry you through.

Please teach me how. I want to engage with this more, to be able to feel Your love and to be secure in it.

You have made much progress and are learning this. We are excited for this adventure with you. Do not be afraid.

Thank you so very much. I give this day to You.

Believing for More

Here I am True FAMILY – I am so very grateful for all that You are doing and for setting me free and continuing to set me free! I give to You all that I am. Thank you! I can't say it enough. Cleanse me and wash me thoroughly that I might walk in Your ways and Your righteousness. I give all that I am to You.

We delight in you, Our precious Daughter! We are the Ones leading and guiding you. Put your trust in Us alone. We have the supply and provision that you need. You just get to ask.

I am asking You, TRUE FAMILY, to be my full provision in every area of life and in Transformations Community! I give You all the glory! I thank you for abundant provision in all areas— the resources, the team, and the other people You are supplying as well as the gifts and financial blessings, the properties and the lands. I am asking too much, aren't I?

Do you believe I can do this?

Yes, You can, but will You?

That is the question. It is Our desire to pour out abundantly above all that you could ask or think. There is no limit to Our resources. Can you believe?

I believe but help my unbelief. It is so big. I so want to have a part in the mass exodus but feel so small and broken myself. I yield this to You. You are my Healer, Protector, Provider. Nothing is impossible with You. Please help me to believe.

It is Our joy to do so. See beyond your limitations to what We can do as you yield to Us. See through Our eyes as to what is possible.

When I let myself dream, I can see it and it so fills my heart with delight!

Don't shrink back. Fight the crazy programming and believe it is possible.

Okay, I choose to believe. I choose to step into what You have for me and for Transformations Community.

Section XIII

Parts Work

Working with our parts is one of the most critical pieces of recovery for survivors. We've been fragmented and programmed in so many ways, often systematically in order to be in constant internal conflict. Working gently with our parts brings cooperation and, eventually, a willingness for parts to work together instead of against each other. The True FAMILY loves to provide all that is needed for our healing as well as to our parts so that we can all come into wholeness. That is the goal.

At the same time, it is important that we do not "rush" to integrate parts into wholeness in Christ. I've found that it tends to happen spontaneously when the time is right. The patience and care required for this process can be frustrating, as you can see. I'm often impatient and just want things to hurry up and be done! This work, however, is helping me to learn patience for myself and my parts and also helping me to trust True FAMILY for Their timing and Their way. Although it may seem slow, this is the best way to bring the most healing. True FAMILY (True Abba, True Holy Spirit, True Jesus) is ultimately responsible for healing our parts and for our overall restoration. Sometimes we decide to take on the role of "healer." When we do, this is just another form of trying to control our parts or "get it right." We get to yield moment by moment to God and His ways!

Reporters

Parts who report back to the cult the activities of the host are called reporters. This is a key issue in "safety." No matter how much physical safety measures you put into place, if there are active reporter parts, the cult knows where you are. Working with True FAMILY, they can be persuaded to stop that activity and to cooperate. True FAMILY is the ONLY safe place for survivors.

Okay, so are there any reporters who are reporting? You aren't in trouble. And Jesus can protect you from any retaliation. Would you be willing to share?

We don't want to.

Why not?

We aren't supposed to. We have to be good and follow the rules. We tell and they reward.

What are the rewards?

We don't get punished.

That doesn't sound like much of a reward. Jesus has much better rewards and He doesn't do torture like they do. His rewards are loving and good and bring delight.

Well, that might be, but we have to follow the rules. Bad things happen when we don't.

Who do you report to?

Those ones you don't want to know about. (The Jesuits)

Okay. Thank you for letting me know. Jesus, can You help us? I don't know what to do.

It is okay. We are here to help and to protect. Reporting doesn't help Adena on her journey. In fact, it makes it much harder. I can protect all parts who desire it and show you a new way that is not so much about rules but about relationship.

We can't do that. We must follow the rules. They will be very mad if we don't.

I understand and I appreciate that you want to be obedient. But we were tricked. They are keeping us in bondage through this. We desire to be free.

We can't ever be free.

Why is that?

Someone has to do these jobs, otherwise bad things happen and lots of people get hurt. We are helping by what we are doing. You must follow the rules.

(I drift off for a moment.)

I'm back.

See you do it too.

Do what?

Dissociate.

Yes, but I am learning that it is not the best way. I am learning that there are better ways of walking this out with True FAMILY, who love us deeply.

The ones we don't talk about love us too. (Jesuit fathers)

It is true, but they also torture us and that is not okay. True love sets us free to be all we were created to be.

They created us.

It might be true that they engineered us in the lab, but God is the one who breathed life into us.

Well, not really. It was the other one.

True Jesus, I need you. Am I making this all up? That is what is so hard. Maybe I've read too much. I know too much and so I just fabricate these conversations from books, etc. I hate this. How do I know what is real?

We will help you step by step. Don't be afraid.

Can You tell me if parts are reporting?

Yes, they are.

I don't want that anymore. Can You help?

We have been protecting you and only allowed minimal information to be reported.

Why not fully cut it off?

We do not force and there are many parts who still think this is valid and that they must do this. You've heard them about following the rules.

And I'm pretty good at it!

Yes, you are! This is a new season where you get to walk it out differently.

Demonstrating Jesus' Power

I'm still nauseated. Can You help me here?

Have the conversation with your parts that you don't want to have.

Okay. Those who are causing the nausea, I'm here to listen.

No, you aren't. You are just saying that. We hate you.

I do mean it and I am willing to slow down my day so I can hear you.

We have to follow orders, or we die. You put us all at risk. If you would just compromise, you wouldn't be experiencing all of this.

Thank you for sharing that. Do you like having to follow their orders?

No, but we must in order to survive.

There is another way. We can be free. True Jesus is making a way for us. And I need your help.

We won't help you. We will resist to the bitter end.

I hear you, but that doesn't seem to be helpful to any of us. When we stay in internal conflict, we are actually just making things worse. Our best path to freedom is working together. I am willing.

That's what you say but you just want us to do what you want to do. You want to control us. You are just like them.

I am learning to bring it all to the True FAMILY. They are showing a way to experience true peace and true love and not to have to do all that other bad stuff. Wouldn't it be nice to be truly free?

That comes only at death…we'll get there sometime.

What if we could have that peace and love sooner?

It's a pipe dream. We've tried to escape before, and it never works. They are too powerful.

I know. I thought that too, but I've found that the True FAMILY is way more powerful and has really good things for us. I know it is hard because we've been deceived and betrayed so many times, but I believe this is true and real. You don't have to make a full commitment, but you can try True Jesus out and see.

No thank you. Been there, done that.

Those were likely false Jesuses. This is different. Are you willing to at least meet Him? He is okay with any safety measures you want. You don't have to get close to Him. You can just talk.

Talk is cheap.

It is a start if you are willing.

Maybe.

Thank you, I appreciate that. It is a start. I don't want to be nauseated this morning. Can you help my body to settle down so we can face this together?

That's not us, that's them.

Parts or demons?

Demons.

Okay, would you like to see how True Jesus handles them? You can see His power.

Okay.

Jesus, I am asking you to remove all demons creating the nausea so I can be free…True Jesus I believe in You and Your power to set me free. Please come and heal me and set me free.

I am here, Precious Adena. I am delivering you. Let it settle into your body. Be free.

Parlor tricks…they will be back tomorrow.

Only if you let them. True Jesus can protect us from them, so they don't come back. Wouldn't that be great?

I suppose, but we've been through this before.

Maybe, but the issue is that parts of me always let them back in through fear. When we trust the True FAMILY, They will help us.

Those prayers you pray do cut down on the harassment.

See! It does make a difference. If we work together, it can be even more.

Okay, we are willing to try this out.

Thank you so very much! Thank you, True FAMILY, for helping us today. We need You. Please protect us. Be our shield. Come and fill us with Your peace and presence. We give this day to you.

(I begin to feel the nausea lifting…)

A Demonstration

Remember to come to Us for everything. When Strong Girl takes control, then We can't help you as much.

Okay, Strong Girl, I know you want to help, but we need True FAMILY to help us.

We hate you so much! Leave us alone.

Who's this? I'm sorry for your pain. I want to hear about it. I want to know how you feel.

We hurt. We've carried all this pain for too long and now you get to feel it.

I understand that. There is a better way. We can give the pain to the True FAMILY and They can help us work through it. I want to know what happened. I'm sorry I've stuffed everything and for how I haven't connected to my body. I want to be available to listen, so you don't need to cause the body to express things.

It's the only way.

I know that is the way it has been, but I'm here now. I am willing to listen.

Bad things. Terrible things. Ripping the flesh, tearing it apart, so much pain. Then fake healing. Well, it works but not really. It is magick and we hate that too. There're always side effects. They patched you up good. But we suffered.

I'm so very sorry. I want to invite all who experienced this to come forward so True Family can help us.

We won't all fit. There's too many of us.

The True FAMILY can make room.

No, there's so many of us. You can't handle it.

Okay, I am willing for all whom the True FAMILY sends. How's that?

Better. You are so dumb.

I'm sorry about that. We are learning to work together. True FAMILY, what do You have for us? How do we deal with the pain?

Precious ones, I see you. I know your pain and I am here to help.

That's what they all say and then they do it all over again.

We are not like that. You have a choice. You don't have to do anything you don't choose to do.

But you will manipulate us. They always find a way to control us. Even Adena does.

I'm sorry! I don't want to anymore.

It is okay. You all are learning healthier ways of communicating. Who wants to share?

Too many reports and Adena can't handle this. Bad things will happen. Death. We've taken a solemn vow.

Did you know that you can break your vows to the cult system? They are illegal according to the True FAMILY. They will keep us safe from retaliation. They will protect us.

Lies! You will get us all into trouble.

It is okay. Let's just talk. You are all deeply loved.

Who cares?

How about a demonstration? What do you need?

Sleep, rest, food, play dominos.

Okay these are all freely provided for those who choose it.

What do we have to do? What is the catch?

There is no catch.

But don't You want us to love on You?

Not like that. That is the system way of doing things. We don't do that. These things are freely given.

We've heard that before.

It is okay. I understand you don't yet trust, but you can try it out and see. We will step back so you are more comfortable.

Thank you.

(I see these parts looking at the yummy food put before them by the True FAMILY)

Is it poisoned?

No. Take as much as you like.

Then what?

Rest and enjoy. There are no expectations. Just a gift.

But then You will want something in return.

No, true relationship is freely given. When you want to have relationship, We are here.

That's the catch.

No, even if you never come back, We care about you, and you can have whatever you need. We want to build trust.

And then break it.

We understand your hesitation. I am so sorry for all that you've been through. There is a way through. You can experience true peace, love, and joy.

Not for us. We are too broken.

We are able to restore when you are ready.

Is that free too?

Yes, it is. I was also broken so I know what it feels like.

Really? You don't look broken.

Yes, look at my hands and side.

(I see Jesus showing them the nail holes on His hands and the wound on His side)

*Oh, we went through that too. **

Yes, I didn't have the use of magick. I felt it all.

Not very smart.

I did it for you. So that you could be set free. I paid the price for your freedom so you could receive it freely.

Why would You do that?

Because I care.

Why would You care?

I created you.

No, It was the petri dish. They did it.

That is what they thought, but I am the One who gave you life.

So, we could suffer like this? Thanks a lot.

No, so you could be restored. There is so much more We have for you than this. But We are taking it slow. Step by step. No hurry, just care.

I like the word care. Thank you for using it instead of love. Love was used for bad things.

Okay, I am glad you like care. It is My heart to tenderly care for you.

When will You abandon us? It always happens.

I won't.

That is what they all say. Words are cheap.

That is why I am willing to demonstrate this to you – as long as it takes.

**Crucifixion rituals*

Controllers

Any parts need to share this morning? Have I shut down? Has something happened? It feels different/weird inside. Is this good or bad? Does anyone feel suppressed?

We are here. It's quiet.

What does that mean?

We can't talk right now.

Why?

We can't tell you.

Okay. True FAMILY, what is this?

Look for the controllers.

I may need help with this. I don't know where they are.

We keep things locked up tight. You are revealing too much. It's time for lockdown. Maintenance on your system. No more talking. It's the rules.

Thank you for letting me know. Do you like being controllers?

Well, it keeps you alive. You are getting too dangerous. Too many people. Too much access. Dangerous. Got to shut down. Tune up the programming.

What if I don't want to run those programs anymore?

Too bad. They are running. Shut down mode commencing. No choice.

I know you believe that, but what if you really did have a choice? Did Jon (a therapist) shut you down or did he trigger it?

Triggered. Done. No more. Too much info. Bad man. Keep us in line.

Is Jon the bad man?

No. The other bad man.

Can you tell me who he is?

Nope. No can do. We hate him but we have no choice. It's time.

I'm choosing to trust True Jesus to help us and to keep us from shutting down. He has a path of freedom for us, and he has healing. We don't have to listen to the bad man anymore. We can freely choose.

Delusions. Must do what we are told. Otherwise, bad things happen.

What kind of bad things?

You know.

Okay. True Jesus can protect us from the bad man. And the others.

Must shut down now.

True Jesus, can you keep me open? Can you prevent this from happening all the way? I don't want to go backwards. I don't want to shut down.

We are able to keep you, precious Adena. Do not be afraid. We've allowed this to surface so you can be aware.

Life in danger. Don't interfere.

I know that is what they've told you. But my life belongs to True Jesus. He can keep me. Jo is showing me a real-life example of this and helping me to have courage. We can trust True Jesus.

Lies and delusions. Must keep programs running. Must not change. Obey the bad man. Must always obey.

True Jesus, I give this controller and controller system to You. I don't know what to do but I am trusting You. Please help me.

We will hold this gently in Our hands until you are ready.

Thank you.

Defense Systems

I feel a bit off tonight. True Jesus, are You there?

We are always here, and We are always delighted to be with you. We know the thoughts and questions on your heart. Don't be afraid. We are holding you tenderly.

Thank you so much. Help me to receive. I thought I was more connected to my body, but in conversation with Nikki (my health coach), I felt the resistance and the whole line of defensive parts "protecting" my body. What is this?

Don't be dismayed by this. We are allowing you to see that more is going on. The attitude you have inside for your body… Regimented. And yet….

I can't hear the words…but there's anger. Burning rage for what has been done to my body.

Stay away! Don't touch! It is ours. High walls. Plastic doors.

Why plastic?

Melts easy. Fake. Plastic. Pretend. Be what they want you to be. Do what they want you to. Kill whom they want you to kill. Don't think. Just do. Compartmentalize.

True FAMILY, am I doing more harm by opening up these places? Or is this good to see? I don't want to destabilize tonight. I do want to move forward safely with You. I give this time to You and these questions.

Step by step. How safe do you feel?

Not very.

Take the time to press into more of feeling and sensing Our love. This is needed.

I do that more in worship than here, but I want to be able to do that here too. Lots of anger tonight. What do You want me to do with this?

Who is holding the anger?

They are mad at father/the fathers.

Hate. Regret. Pain. Self-loathing. For I am one too.

I don't want to write that. Is that true?

You aren't ready for that.

Then why did it come?

Keep steady in Our love.

Lots of anger. Pain. Rage. Death. Destruction. Burial. Stuff. Forget.

Am I supposed to be getting in touch with this? I thought I was supposed to feel Your love.

The anger is in the way. You have been picturing the little one raging at the strong tower (father image) … Hitting it over and over again. She cannot receive Father's love until she deals with the anger.

Oh.

The anger is real. But misdirected. She is raging at True Father, but it really is to herself and to the other fathers.

I want to die. I can't do this anymore.

Remember there is a way through.

I wanted to stop journaling like this …

Until it is worked through, it will be similar. Step by step. Don't be discouraged by this. You know deep inside what is going on.

The agony. Can You help me True Jesus?

What do you want to do with the anger and rage?

I don't know. It is too hard for me to bear. I will kill myself trying to beat down the strong tower.

True Father would not allow you to do that because you are precious. He is allowing this picture so that you can see what is going on deep inside.

Why does she need to work through this?

Ask her.

Little one, I see your anger and rage. Can you tell me about it?

No, not supposed to. Pain.

I am so sorry you are carrying all of this. It is very painful.

No choice.

I understand that it feels that way, but I know Someone who can take that pain and hatred and anger.

What's the price?

There isn't one. It is freely available.

Tricks. Trap. Bad.

No. There is no trick or trap here. There is just love.

Can't forgive.

Who?

Me and fathers. We do bad things.

No matter what you've done, there is forgiveness and rest and peace that is available. True Jesus has a way through. He can take all of the pain for you.

Nope. Too big. Too much. Just waiting to die.

You are loved and cared for. More than you know. That Strong Tower is meant to help you and be your true protection.

Nowhere safe.

I know it feels like that. I feel that way too, but I am learning to trust True Jesus and to receive Their help. They are kind and true. They don't lie to us or go back on Their word or ask us to do horrific things. Do you want a change?

Yes. But we don't know how and that only makes the rage worse. Kill ourselves with it. Can't quite do it.

Are you talking about theta skills?

We aren't going to talk about that.

Okay, you don't have to. I just want you to know that Jesus can help us.

Can He kill us?

He could but He won't.

Even if we want Him to?

No. He is the one who gave us life.

I feel like I'm slipping away.

Can you stay just a few more minutes?

No, pulled under. Going away.

I want you to know that you are loved and there is hope.

Gone.

True Jesus, why? I'm trying to stay present. Why can't they?

Remember it is a process, and We are being gentle. Rest in Our love. Take some time for prayers.

I still have all this anger.

With what you have access to, you can it give to Me on her behalf. Look at how much you can access. She couldn't do it without getting in trouble, but she left some anger behind for you to handle with Us.

Okay. I give you all this anger and rage and hatred and pain and death. You are the resurrection and the life, and I need You to infuse every part of me with new and fresh life. I choose life.

Well done! Can you feel the shift?

Barely, but I want to believe. Please help me to feel more and more of the shift. I want to truly feel Your presence… I'm glad we can talk but I would like to see and experience You more.

We would love that as well. There is more work that We are doing in and through you. Be patient and trust Our timing. There are more levels and parts, and they are all held safely in Our hands.

Can You keep me from doing any bad things?

We keep you moment by moment in Our love. Remember that We only allow what will ultimately lead to freedom for you and so many others. We know you want a fast, instant work, but this is a slower beautiful process in Our love. Our love does not force, but We do find a way. Remember the back door of hope. Remember original agreements to come here. We will keep Our promises. Trust and rest.

Okay. Why can't I stay steady in Your love?

Be patient with yourself. You are doing better than you know. Facing this stuff is hard. We are so very proud of you. We love you deeply and tenderly. We see and We know. Let Us love you.

Sleeper

Yes, it is My delight to bring light on this journey that is often so heavy. We are with you, and you don't need to be afraid

as you keep your hand in Ours. Enjoy this time and let Us show you step by step the things to avoid, when to wait, and when to move forward. We love your desire to plow through anything and everything, but it won't be effective here.

Thanks for the reminder. Anyone inside have anything to share? Everyone seemed pretty quiet… I'm glad for the deeper levels to let me know you are there. You are included. I care about you.

Don't engage those ones. You aren't ready for them.

Is that me trying to plow through? Ha! Thanks for that tip. I just want them to know I know they are there. I want them to know when they are ready or when I am ready, I look forward to connecting.

It is "wait and see" for us. We are taking things in. We have a lot of doubts and questions.

I respect that. I am open to questions and taking them to True Jesus. I care.

Do you really or is it just wanting to "fix us?"

That is a good question. True FAMILY is helping me to see *you* are the priority, not fixing things. I know I don't always get that right and often I do want to just "plow through," so please forgive me for that. I want to learn how to listen better and to work through things together.

Maybe we like captivity. Maybe it is nice not to have to decide or figure things out and to just be told what to do. No responsibility. Just follow orders.

I get it that a lot of you do feel safer in confined places, and I can see how being told what to do can be easier at times. I can see how that feels safer, not having to take responsibility.

Yeah, stay in stasis until orders come. Sleeper. Wake. Sleep.

Why are you up today?

Well, there was a lot of activity and signaling happening.

You felt that too?

Yes, we did. Muddled. Not clear transmission. So, we don't know what to do right now.

Well, I'm glad I get to talk with you.

Not for long.

What did you think of the conversation today?

Not sure. Don't know. Don't really care. Just follow orders.

I hear you. There might come a time when it interests you more and you can see other ways of doing things.

Been trained for this. It works. I don't have to worry about anything else. Just do what we're told. Sleep.

I want you to know that I care.

Whatever. Goodnight.

Jumping Ahead

I'm sorry I sent the journaling to Jo even though you resisted… I should have gotten agreement first. Who inside wants to share anything? Please forgive me.

We do. It's just… Do you have to send things? We get the repercussions.

I want to be more aware of that. Also, I want to say that this was me, not Jo. She doesn't require me to send things. I don't want you to be mad at her. It's me.

Yeah. We get that.

I feel the strong pull to forget everything. Is there a lot of triggering, etc. going on?

More than you know.

I am willing to hear about it.

Nope. Not ready.

Me or you?

You. Not sanctioned.

I do want to work towards more cooperation.

It's better compartmentalized. Safer for everyone. Just keep on keeping on.

That is the way they want us to be. We do have a choice.

Not a good one. Not safe. More trouble. Done.

Do you know there are people who don't live like we do? They have the freedom to choose.

Good for them.

Well, wouldn't it be wonderful not to be forced or have to force others?

It's the way it is.

But it doesn't have to be. Just something to think about and consider. We could explore some options. Others have done it. True Jesus, I feel like we just go round and round with the same thing all the time. Is this making a difference or is there something else I can be doing?

Who's in charge?

Good question. Is this about me trying to do all the work or is this about system controllers or both or more?

You are doing well in communicating and offering something different and you are learning and growing. And you can have the same or similar conversations with many, many parts for a very long time.

I do want You to be in charge. You are the Author and Finisher of my faith. I want to do what You are doing. And You say the same thing to me a lot, but because I need it. Is there a new strategy?

What's going through your mind?

How to get it right. I know that it is wrong.

Because who's in charge?

Okay. Thank you. I thought it was okay to send the journaling to Jo even though I had resistance, but I didn't ask You directly.

It's not about getting it right, but about flowing with Us. You don't have to get permission for everything, but We do like to do things relationally. Sending without cooperation internally doesn't help internal conflict or trust in your inner realm. You do have parts who want to send but it is because they want to feel connected to Jo. Then you have others who are afraid of what is in the journaling and that it might make things worse, or Jo won't like you anymore. So, you get anxious once you start to send something and until you hear back. There is a way to communicate so parts can be in agreement. A lot came out this week. There's a lot of inner turmoil. We can help you. It's scary being this vulnerable.

But I feel like it is the only way. I don't want to hide anything. And because I send them to Jo, I read them over several times which helps me to remember, because otherwise I forget. Even this week, I forgot some of the dreams. This keeps me accountable and remembering.

Yes, and that is good, but doing so together will be helping your inner realm to learn to work together. If they feel you are "blabbing" everything, they may be more reluctant to cooperate. You trust Jo, but many of them don't yet. You still want to be the perfect client. That is not what this is about.

Thank you for exposing so much that is still there…

You desire truth in the inward parts. This is what it is about. Facing yourself in Our love. No condemnation. You don't have to get it right or perfect.

I teach this but I am still working through it.

Yes, and you are not a hypocrite. They all know you are walking this out as well. You tell them that regularly and they love you for it. They are not looking for someone who's got it all figured out, but someone who is walking it with them.

Okay. Thank you. Please help. I want to learn and grow.

You are. Rest and trust.

Okay. I give all of this to You. Help me to walk this out with You.

Gladly. Ask the question coming up.

Okay. Is this just me talking to an inner therapist part or are You True FAMILY?

We are the True FAMILY and We care deeply for you.

What's Happening?

True FAMILY, here I am. I ask for your grace and help! During powerful prayer time, I felt nauseated and also dizzy and sleepy. Please help me. I am glad things are being handled by You, but I also need help in this. Is there any information I need to know?

You did well and We are proud of you. This is helpful for learning things that you can pass on to clients and groups. The victory is assured. It belongs to Us, not the enemy, Satan/Lucifer, etc. Take your stand, precious Adena! You are called at this hour for this-- to be set free yourself and to partner with Us and others to set captives free. This is the time! Rejoice even in this challenge, knowing We are at work.

Thank you so much! How do I work through this?

Ask inside. We are with you.

Anyone inside want to share?

Why did you do that?

Because we are on an incredibly exciting adventure with True FAMILY for full freedom and healing for ourselves and for all those God has called us to.

It hurt us.

I am not meaning to do that. I believe these steps will ultimately be such a blessing. If I am going too fast and beyond what you are ready for, I am trusting True FAMILY to help us sort this out.

We can't do stuff.

What stuff are you referring to?

You know.

Okay. That is stuff that I don't want to be involved with anymore. I am choosing True FAMILY now. This is my heart and my life. I am inviting you to participate in this joyous journey.

Do you know what you are doing?

No, not really, but I am trusting True FAMILY to take us step by step.

Isn't that a mistake? Shouldn't you know what you are doing?

I am trusting True FAMILY to lead and guide me and to help me clean up any messes I've made. If I have done something wrong, They will help me clean this up.

You are so mean. We hate you.

I understand, and I'm sorry. I want you to know that I care, and I am hoping we can work through this together. The True FAMILY deeply loves and cares for you.

No one can but the fathers.

That is a lie we were taught over and over in many set ups, but it is not true. I am finding those who are not part of that system who love and care for me.

You are causing more trouble than you know. We don't like it. We want to stay with what is familiar.

I understand that change is hard. True FAMILY can help us in this process.

We don't want Them. Forbidden.

Why is it forbidden?

You know.

What if the truth was kept from us?

I think you are the one deceived.

True Jesus is the way, the truth and the life. I have chosen Him and Him alone.

We have a Jesus you can follow.

No, I want only the True One. I will not compromise.

Even if you are deceived?

I have found His way so much better than the way we were taught. His love is so much more, and it is unconditional. He sees all that we have done, and He is not ashamed of us and does not love us less for it. I am fully loved and accepted. I know nothing like His love.

Have it your way.

This isn't my way. This True FAMILY's way. I am choosing to trust Them.

Fatal mistake. There are consequences.

I am trusting them step by step and that they will protect me/us and, like Daniel's friends and Esther, if I perish, I perish. If He doesn't rescue, I will still trust Him in the fire.

Foolishness!

I know you see it that way, but I am inviting you to consider.

Never! We hate you.

I understand and I know the fears. There is a way through and the more that we can cooperate, the better. Fighting against each other doesn't help us.

Then just give up. We can offer you a lot more than they can.

I am not interested in fame and fortune.

We are the ones who truly love you. We'll do anything to get you back.

See, this is the thing. True FAMILY gives me freedom to choose, and I really like that. To me that is what love is. Love is not force, control, and manipulation. That is all we knew. I am learning a new way where I can choose True FAMILY or not.

Of course you can, that is their manipulation! Lies and deceit.

Have you been seeing the changes going on inside?

Done.

Okay. I want you to know I care, and I am here when you want to talk. True FAMILY, I hope what I did was okay. I felt the power of the prayers and joy in it, but if I moved too quickly, I'm sorry.

We are with you and delight in your journey. This was needed for this time and for breakthrough. It was not comfortable for many of your parts. Rest in Our care and love.

Am I safe with You?

Yes.

What about those I love?

Yes. They will try retaliation. This journey is not an easy one, but We prevail. Things are shifting. You can trust the plans We have for you and those you love.

Thank you.

Watch for over-confidence and traps that are being set.

I want to stay in step with You. Can You help with the nausea? It has diminished but is still there.

Yes, We will help you.

Anything else I need for today? Please help me with groups and clients to flow with Your timing, Your way, and Your words of life.

It is Our joy to do so. Look for Our joyful surprises and blessings. We are with you!

Thank you so much!

Needs and Wants – Giving and Receiving

I give this (a dream) to you True Jesus. All I can see is that I can't get my needs met. Someone else's need always comes first. This is a pattern in my life. But You brought this up for a reason, So I give this dream to You, and I am open to what You want to say.

Precious Adena, you matter. Your needs matter.

Nobody else sees it that way. I'm the "giver". It's my job. I help people. I receive some, from You, True FAMILY, and from others.

Yes, you are learning, and this goes deeper.

Okay, I am open to more.

Programming to not need. Or want.

So what? It is what it is.

It isn't how I designed you.

It can't be any other way. I can handle it.

I didn't create you or design you to function this way.

But it is the way it must be.

Who says?

Okay, I get it. I know the right answer.

Go deeper.

I don't want to. I can't.

You always get to choose, but you know that We only bring you here for your good.

Yes. Why is there resistance?

This will unlock some deep things.

Yes, You are right.

Bad things. I can't need. I can't want. Pain. Shock. Blank. Rescue.

I repent for myself and my parts for calling on help from the demonic as my only rescue. * And the only way my needs will be met. I am asking for the blood of True Jesus to wash me, cleanse me and set me free. True Jesus, are You here? Can You help me?

Yes, I am here, and it is My delight to meet your needs.

But You won't.

That is what it has felt like and how you were programmed. Have compassion for yourself and know that We are here to help and have always been. You were tricked as the only way to meet needs was through them. Feel that pain.

Why do I need to feel it?

There is more that can be uncovered if you invite those who felt and carry the pain to be here.

They don't want to come.

We don't force them. It is always an invitation to more freedom.

They are afraid. Of You.

Try the Lamb of God.

Will you come?

He's cute. But we can't feel.

Who's carrying the pain?

It is very far away.

See, True Jesus, it isn't possible.

Are distances too hard for me?

No, but …

Would you like help?

Why the wrestle?

You are afraid your needs won't be met and there will be more pain. Better to send the pain far away and to not expect anything.

How can You help me? Can we do something even if I can't feel the pain?

Are you willing to face the pain?

I might explode. Can't need. Can't need. Can't need.

What is the truth of how I created you?

To have needs, so that I can be vulnerable. The key to overcoming shame.

Are needs meant to be met?

Yes, of course, but not mine.

Why?

It's forbidden.

Why?

So, I won't need You.

Yes. Think deeper and beyond the life you know consciously.

It feels like this isn't going anywhere.

Do you trust Me?

Okay. Please help me. I ask that of You all the time.

Go deeper. Ask inside.

Okay. Who wants to share on needs?

Too dangerous. Not allowed. Only they can meet them in the prescribed way. Backwards. Torture. Pain. Bad. Forget. Walk away. Needs hurt. Suppress. Pain. Explosion. Bad. Go blank. Live without. Submit. No other way.

I am sorry for all the pain.

What pain? It's gone.

True Jesus, are You here?

Yes, I am.

Please shine Your light in this darkness. Please help me.

Gladly. You are not alone. It just feels that way.

Spin. Pain. Confusion. Darkness. Pain. Wait forever. Crash. Bright light. Pain. I can't see. I can't know. I don't need. Just die. No hope. Forget. Pretend. Be good. Know nothing.

Thank you for facing this with me. I know it is hard.

But I don't feel much.

It is okay. It will come in time. Being aware and acknowledging is the first step. We will take this step by step. It is in the light of Our love now. It can be healed. Your parts can learn to come to Us when they are ready for their needs to be met.

In the meantime, will You take care of me? Will You provide for me?

It is My delight to meet your needs and to provide. I also provide through others.

No. I can't be a burden.

Remember this is the way I designed you and others. For community. You are uncomfortable with receiving in most cases. It is foreign to you. If you want to receive healing and wholeness, then you get to address this. Remember to go deeper.

Okay. I say yes to Your way, True FAMILY. I have needs. I am willing for You and others to meet those needs. I don't want to receive from other sources that You have not ordained. I reject the help of demons. And again, I repent for believing they and cult members could meet my needs and help me. I choose True FAMILY and invite as many parts as are able to join me.

Don't include us in that. We aren't ready.

I'm glad you let me know. Can you tell me more?

It's just the way it is. We don't have a choice.

You do have options.

Not any that are safe.

Have you noticed True Jesus and how He is safe and good to us?

It's fake. You're deceived. Fraud. Broken beyond repair.

I know that is how it might feel, but I am finding True Jesus reliable and faithful to meet my needs. I can receive from others. My needs can be met. Okay, I need to sleep. True Jesus, can You help me sleep?

We will help You. Be of good courage. Well done. You faced this.

Please deliver me and close all access. I only want You to meet my needs as well as those You choose.

This is a process, and We are at work in you. Don't be discouraged but keep saying yes.

I say yes to You, True Jesus.

*In programming set-ups, children are tortured, and it only stops when they accept demons to "help" them or to take the pain away. It takes patience and unconditional love for parts to be open to a new way of seeing things.

Getting Unstuck

Anything specific or anything I need to do inside?

You can ask.

A lot is going on. Many changes. I am here if anyone wants to talk about it.

We can't do much when you pray like that.

Thanks for letting me know. How do you feel about that?

We are confused. We are supposed to do our jobs, but you are not letting us.

True FAMILY is helping us to learn a new way that is easier. They are powerful and gentle and work with us to work all things for our good. They don't force and program you to do certain jobs but invite you to experience joyful partnership with Them. You get to freely choose.

It sounds nice, but we don't know how to make that transition. We are stuck.

True Jesus is really good at getting us unstuck if we ask Him.

Will it hurt?

Sometimes change is painful, but the results are good, so it is worth it. He does not willingly hurt us, but sometimes it hurts in the process. Does that make sense?

I guess so. I don't want any more hurt.

I understand that. But you are already hurting, and this will ultimately relieve that. You don't need to carry all of the pain.

But what if we get into trouble? They won't like it.

I know. But staying only keeps us and others in pain. As we are healing, it will affect them too. They will have the opportunity to see that there is a different option and that it is safe, and life can be very good.

I'm willing but I'm scared. I don't like change.

I know, me too, but I am finding it very rewarding. Can I take your hand? We can do this together.

Okay.

True Jesus is here to help us. We are not alone. Anyone else who wants to come is also welcome.

We do!

True Jesus, here we are. Can You help me and these ones to receive Your love and protection?

With great joy. Each of you are so very precious to Us.

Sexual Abuse and Shame

So, what do I put as my prayer focus?

Tell the truth.

I don't want to.

We know that. It is okay. It is a safe place. Being vulnerable is important although it is hard.

I want to run away. I wish I had not told you that.

Little one, it is a safe place to share. We can let the True FAMILY comfort us.

We don't want anyone else to know.

I understand and I respect that. Sometimes the way forward is by being honest with a safe group of people. May I share with them? They love all of my parts and care about us. They can help us. If it is too much for the group, I will honor you in this. This is not about exposing you and humiliating you, but about getting help.

You can share with them. Will the group be mad?

No, the group will not be mad. There is no shame in this. You were forced into this. You did not know any differently. You thought every little girl was taught this (i.e. sexual grooming).

They weren't?

No. It is okay how you are feeling. There is no shame, because True Family is here. Jesus paid for it all and we can rest in Their love.

I don't want to. It is too hard.

I understand.

I'm bad. I'm bad. I'm really bad.

(I see the little one banging her head against the floor)

No little one, you are not. Let me hold you.

No, keep away from me. You don't want to be bad too.

Come, let's let True Family hold you.

NO. No more big sticks (i.e. penises). Stay away.

Okay. Know that I love you and that there is a safe place for you. You don't need to hurt yourself. There is love for you.

Stay away.

True FAMILY, can You please help these parts of me?

Yes, We are watching over them and caring for them, though they don't know it. We are sad too about this, but We have a plan for your full restoration so be of good courage. Bring her in to where there is carpet, so she is not hurting herself.

Why does she want to hurt herself?

She does not want to live. The horror of it all is too much.

Okay, little one, I will show you where you can go where it won't hurt so much. There is carpet. You don't need to hurt yourself.

But I do. She must be punished.

She?

All of the bad girls. Must be punished. The ones who bit and screamed must be punished. Everyone must conform. Everyone must be good. They must do what they are told.

No one gets punished here. It is safe and secure with True FAMILY.... True FAMILY, please help me.

I Need Help

Did you ask for help?

No, I didn't.

Why not?

I didn't feel anyone would help me. I'm not sure.

Go deep inside. Where did you feel out of control and not able to accomplish anything?

I couldn't get away from them. I was powerless. I felt powerless to do anything to fix it.

There are parts in you that have given up. This is more than you know. These are also the ones who don't want to live. There is a significant amount of grief that is hanging around in here. Grief and hopelessness.

I don't want to talk about it.

That usually means it is a good idea to do so. We are here to listen. We are not here to judge.

I did bad things. They made me do it. If I didn't do it, they would make me do worse things. They threatened others. I hate them. I want them killed. I don't want to live. Life is hopeless. I don't want to live. I want to not exist. Too many bad things. I can't handle it. Too many demands. I can't do it all. It is overwhelming. I'm trapped. I can't do it. I can't not do it. They demand and push and prod. I don't like it. I want to run away but I can't. I'm restrained. I yell, shout and scream inside because I can't do it on the outside. They hate me. I'm bad. I do bad things. I don't want to live.

I hear you, precious ones, and I am so very sorry these things happened. We learned to freeze, didn't we?

Yes, they don't hurt you as bad if you cooperate and are quiet, although sometimes they like the sounds. Keep it in. Keep it in. Don't give them the pleasure of hearing the screams but sometimes it isn't possible.

Did you put cement down?

Yes, lots of it. Cement me in so that they can't hurt me anymore.

But it is lonely and painful there, isn't it?

Yes, but that is better than what they were doing.

It is time to come out of hiding and find that there is a place of safety where you can just be you. The True FAMILY is here to help you. This is the True FAMILY who never leave you nor forsake you. You can trust them.

I don't trust anyone.

I know. That is okay but it is a miserable life. You want to end it.

Yes, it is and yes, I do.

The best thing we can do is get help from the One who knows it all and is all powerful. He can help us and set you free from this stuff so you can enjoy life. There is love and safety available to you if you would just say yes. I have decided to do this from my core, and it is helping.

We don't trust anyone. The bunker is safer. We prefer the bunker. We will keep ourselves safe.

How many of you are there?

25, 26 or more.

Do you have provisions?

No, but we'd rather be safe than sorry.

The True FAMILY have more than enough provisions for you. Are you planning on starving to death?

That is an idea, but no. We'll figure it out.

You don't need to figure it out. You can ask for help.

That is for sissies! We can do this on our own.

How is that working out for you?

Well, we are still here, aren't we?

Yes, you are, but isn't that a lot of fear and burden to handle?

I guess so. I am working on plans to expand the root cellar. There is more that we can do. We must hide.

Jesus, can You come into the bunker/root cellar and help these parts of mine?

Yes, I would love to.

Will they be frightened?

Yes, but it is okay. I will help calm them.

How come they won't ask for help?

That has been unanswered in the past. They don't want to be disappointed again.

Okay. Dear ones, the True FAMILY can be trusted. It is time to let them handle things instead of trying to do it all on our own.

What's the payment?

There is no payment. Jesus paid for it all on the cross. If you believe in Him, you can join Him.

We don't like to do that.

It is okay. Jesus loves you. True FAMILY, please help these wounded parts in the bunker/root cellar. I don't know if I can reach them.

You are. This will take some time. Do not be afraid of this. Just speaking with them helps them to learn to trust and that it can be safe for them if they can come out of hiding. They will not be judged or harmed. We want to love them and care for them.

They don't know how to be loved.

Processing

I want to run away.

That is a part speaking.

Okay, part of me wants to run away. The best place to be is with True FAMILY. They have a path for us that is good and real and true. Nothing is impossible. We can trust Them step by step. True FAMILY will help us.

But no matter what we do, we keep messing up. We can't be perfect.

I know and we are not meant to be perfect. Jesus is perfect and He did it for us, so we just get to be loved and held and comforted and grow. It comes naturally. It is not forced or based on performance. You can rest and know that True FAMILY is safe and that They are protecting us. We get to rest and not strive.

But I'm scared.

I know you are. What we are doing is not easy. There's a lot of pain that we are still holding on to, but the invitation of True FAMILY is to come and rest and to give Them our burden of guilt and shame and anger and lust and terror and rage. We get to walk this out daily with them. They provide all that we need.

I need help.

I know and we are trusting True FAMILY for this. I don't know what to do either. True Lord Jesus Christ of Nazareth, we come before You for help today. Holy Spirit, are You here to Comfort us?

Yes, We are. True Father is here too, and He delights in you. There is no shame or condemnation here. We are so very proud of you. Come and listen to what is on Our hearts for you.

Okay, we are here. All of me, all parts, listen, all fragments. I am scattered all over, aren't I?

Yes, darling Daughter of Zion, but do not be afraid. This is possible with Us. We can bring you back into wholeness while holding you in Our wholeness. Do not be afraid but trust that We will see you through.

Open my eyes to see You clearly and to know it is You.

This is what We are in the process of doing, precious Adena. There are blocks and filters, but We are making progress. There is more for you than you know. Let Us gather you and bring all that is true into the light. We are being as gentle as We can be. There are lots more to show you and reveal as you are ready.

I don't know if I can handle this. I feel this shutdown happening. I think it has something to do with my inability to cry. How did I think I can help anyone? I'm so messed up.

This is Our glory to do amazing things through a weak and broken vessel, while We are putting you back together. This is a joyful journey for Us and We invite you into seeing it from Our perspective. Are you willing to surrender all to Us?

Yes, I am.

Yes, you are! Trust and rest. We are so pleased with you. There is no striving here. This takes you to a deeper level of trust and truth and overcoming.

What do I do with Testimony Mountain? This has been hard. I don't feel like I have a testimony anymore.

We know and this is why it is good for you to do so. Not from compulsion but because of Our love. You have more to say than you know. Just get in front of the camera and roll. There is a wealth of treasure within you. This is what We see. And all that you have gone through has prepared you for this moment in time.

But this sounds like the crazy stuff they warn about. What if You really are the bad guys convincing me?

We understand and there is no condemnation or judgment, precious Adena. We know it is hard to know what is real, but the promise is that you will hear Our voice and know the difference.

But others can't hear You.

Everyone can if they choose. Now you know why they are struggling. We are here to help you, and We delight in doing so. It is not a burden. We love to show Our love and glory through you. This is Our joy. Let go of what you know and choose to trust Us.

Okay. Can I rest now?

Yes, sleep sweetly and do not be afraid. We are helping you step by step.

Where Are You Jesus?

I hate you! I hate you! I hate you! You are disgusting and bad and mean! Don't touch me! I have to get away. I have to get away. Don't do that to me. Ouch! That hurts. I don't want to be here. Let me go! Let me go! I've got to get away. Help me! Will someone help me! I need to get away! I can't stay here. Bad things are happening. We have to get away. I can't make them stop. They are coming for me. Help me! Help! Someone please help me! Don't you see what is happening? Why won't anyone help me? I need help! I'm screaming but no one can hear me. I go dead inside. I go dead inside. It is the only way. It is the only way. Do you hear me? I'm really struggling. I don't know what is wrong. Something is very wrong. Why won't they stop it? I can't take this anymore. I will fly away. I will go home. Jesus, take me home. They are doing bad things. Where are You, Jesus? Can't You see me? I need help. Where are You? It is all dark. I can't see anything. I can't feel anything. Am I dead? Maybe that is good. Will someone please help me? Why did they turn the lights on? It is very bright, very bright. I can't see anything. It is too bright. Straight into my eyes. They are burning. They put something in my eyes. They make me see. I don't want to see. It is bad things. Very bad things. People are hurting and dying. I can't stop it. I can't help them. Nobody will help us. We are all alone in hell. Bad things all around. Bad things. Bad things. I can't see anything else. But I can't stop seeing. It is bad things. Very bad things. Then there's nothing. Silence. The screams have stopped. Is everyone dead? Am I dead? There's no way to know. But I'm thinking, so maybe I am still alive. Or maybe it is some other form of hell? I can't see anything. I can't feel anything. Life is done. We hate it here. We can't take it anymore. It is so quiet. They haven't come for a very long time, and I am glad. But also, what if they never come and then I am trapped here forever? I don't want to be trapped. I can't see anything. I can't feel anything. Thanks for listening.

Thanks for sharing. I'm so sorry that happened to you. True FAMILY is here to help us. They never left us.

It's too late.

It is never too late. True FAMILY can help us heal and be whole. You aren't in that place anymore. We are safe now. They can't get us.

That is what you think. You think you've always been safe but that isn't true. They did bad things all the time to us, and you didn't even know. How could you?

I'm so sorry. I blocked it out. I'm sorry you had to hold all of that ugliness. True FAMILY is here to help us heal the pain and come into wholeness. Are you interested?

It's too late. We are all dead in here. Only the echo of what happened surfaces from time to time...

You aren't dead and True FAMILY is here to bring resurrection life so you can feel again.

We don't ever want to feel again. It is too painful. They did bad things. Why didn't They help us? If True FAMILY is so strong how come They didn't rescue us?

Jesus, can You answer them?

We were always there with you. We wept and cried with you and held you through it all. We have a plan of restoration and are inviting you to come.

Is this a trick? It is always a trick. We are offered all kinds of things, but there is always a cost. What's the cost?

Jesus already paid for the cost so that you can get it for free.

No, that is too tricky. There's always a price to pay and we've paid heavily. We've been tricked over and over again. We won't let anyone trick us again.

Then you can't be free. Do you want to be free? It will take learning to trust. I can tell you that True FAMILY is trustworthy, and They want to show us how They were with us all the time and good things can come out of the bad things that happened. They want to tell us about the beautiful story that we can walk out together.

We don't want any of that. It is just fantasy. Christianity is just fantasy. Bad Christians did this to us.

Those weren't really Christians. They just pretended to be. But Jesus is real. The True Lord Jesus Christ is good and kind. He does not hurt us. He is very powerful too.

We just want to curl up and die here. No need to worry about us. Forget we said anything.

I can't forget it. I want to hear you, and I want to know what happened.

We aren't talking anymore.

You can choose that, but I want you to know that we can heal together. We can grow together and be whole again. This is what is best for all of us. There can be joy again.

No more tricks!

This isn't a trick. Feel the warmth coming from True FAMILY. Feel their frequency. They are safe and good.

It's a bunch of baloney.

I'm sorry you feel that way. I've found Jesus to be my Savior. He has helped me to experience His love and grace. I'm finding a new way to live that is better than anything I have ever experienced. I invite you to try Him out. He won't force you. You can back out if needed, but I invite you to just come close and see. Talk with Him. He is gentle.

It's a trap. Don't come near us. Leave us alone.

Okay, I just want you to know that I care about you and that I won't leave you. I'm here with Jesus to help you.

Don't call Him Jesus. That is a bad name. We hate that name.

I understand. You were introduced to a false Jesus who did bad things and hurt you. I understand how that hurts. We can call Him Yeshua if you'd prefer.

I won't call Him anything.

That is okay. He is the way the truth and the life. He is everything to me.

Then you are a fool.

I may be, but it is the best life I have ever experienced. I can walk in peace and joy and love, even though knowing some of what we went through. Yeshua has lifted the burden and cleansed me of my sin and guilt and shame. I can now experience joy. You are invited to that joy as well.

I don't know. As long as He stays over there... I will watch You like a hawk. If He pulls anything bad, I will know.

That is just fine. You can do that. He is not offended. He knows what you went through and He's here to earn your trust.

Why would He want to do that?

Because He cares about you and wants to help.

I'll think about it.

Jesus, thank you!

The Three Marys

True FAMILY – I am grateful for the revelations last night, although they were painful. I submit these to You. These parts--sexy Mary, bloody Mary and dirty Mary-- I ask You to keep them safe until we can process. True FAMILY, I don't like the name Mary. Is that from anti-Catholic stuff or is that related to these parts?

It is related to these parts. You loathed these parts of you and what they did. But they are part of you. Are you willing to forgive them and embrace them?

I am willing but I am scared. I don't want to do bad things. I don't really want to remember the bad things I did, but I am willing for healing. Please help me.

We are here and this is part of your healing journey. You cannot be fully healed apart from them. We know this is not easy, but We are here each step of the way. There is more to this, and We will continue to show you in time. We are working with you gently so that you are not overwhelmed. Stay focused on Our heart of love for you and your choice of forgiveness. This will be key as you move forward. Be preparing the rest of your inner realm to receive these lost and broken ones, to forgive them and to learn to love them. This is only accomplished as you spend time in Our presence with the parts. This is healing time. Don't run from it. You want to keep things in your head and not go through the harder parts of this, which is from the heart. You are afraid of the pain and trauma, but only as it is brought into the light of Our love can you receive healing.

Okay, I am willing. I put my trust in You. Keep me safe and secure.

Be Quiet!

Inner realm, how are you doing today? Anyone want to share anything?

Yes, we are insulted.

I'm sorry. What is this about?

Everything. You say too much. Just shut up and be quiet. You're going to get us in trouble.

Why do you think I am getting you in trouble by talking?

You don't know the rules.

You are right. I don't know them because I don't remember. But you do. Would you help me to remember?

But then you are just going to talk more. You will just get us into more trouble. Just pretend it all away. As if it never was.

It is tempting, but I know that the only way for true healing is to know the truth. The truth sets us free.

That's just a dumb Bible verse. It doesn't mean anything.

I understand you feel that way, but I don't.

There you go again. If you keep this up, you will really get us all into trouble.

What kind of trouble?

The deadly kind.

I understand your concerns. But I am choosing to trust the True FAMILY, which includes True Jesus. He is my Protector and He does a really good job.

No, you've got it wrong. We are the ones who have been protecting you and you are so ungrateful.

I'm sorry. You have done a good job of trying to protect me through the years. I honor that and I am grateful. And I am learning a new way.

New ways are dangerous.

I believe this way is the best way. It seems dangerous to you, and I get that. I'd like to offer the opportunity for you to see it from a different perspective.

Nope. Mines the right one.

Jesus is the TRUTH. He is the WAY and the LIFE. I am choosing to trust in Him.

He is a fraud and a fake. You will die believing this.

I'm not afraid to die because He is the resurrection and the life. My life is in His hands. I know I can trust Him no matter what.

You are foolish. Don't say I didn't warn you.

I do hear you and invite you to meet with True Jesus and see a different path. You've had to work very hard to protect me and you've taken a lot on my behalf. But there is a better way. Isn't it logical to explore better ways? At least consider it.

Okay, maybe.

Thank you for sharing today. I really appreciate it. I want you to know that the communication lines are open. I want to hear from you and your concerns.

You are usually too busy.

I don't want to be anymore. I want to take the time to hear you all and know you better. I appreciate you. I believe that as we learn to work together, things will go better for all of us as we explore a new way of doing things.

Suit yourself.

Thank you, Jesus, for this time. I appreciate it and help me to love every part of me.

It is Our joy! Walk in Our blessing throughout this day and receive the grace needed.

Section XIV

Death And Life

For survivors, death can be a daily issue. We saw it, felt it, and contributed to it. Many of us were also brought to death multiple times and then brought back to life. Suicidal programming is common. Life is hard and death can seem like a refuge and a way out. Each person's journey is unique. Don't freak out when someone expresses a desire to not live. Instead, gently attune— "I hear you, I see you, I understand and there are solutions" -- and then evaluate with the Lord if this is a serious threat or is simply an expression of how one feels at the moment. Based on what you read below, please don't think that I am suicidal. I have never attempted to take my life (that I know of) ---and wouldn't in my right mind. These are just the expressions of parts of me and me in despair, being honest about how I feel and receiving the truth and comfort from True FAMILY.

Do I Keep on Going?

I'm really scared. I have a really good life. I could just forget everything and be normal. I could distract myself enough to not feel anything and just pretend. I don't know what scares me more: the option to do that or to keep going. I can't go on. I want to run away to somewhere where I am nothing and nobody. Hide forever. Dig a hole and be buried. Never show my face again. I don't want to live. Help me, Jesus, help me.

I am always here. I deeply care and I see and know the heartache. Nothing is hidden from Me. I see all the parts and their fear, pain, terror. It's going to be okay. I will help you all the way through.

Is any of it real? Are You real? Who am I? I wish this would stop. Can I disappear?

You can choose that. But I know who you are and what I've called you to. While it seems impossible right now, We can help you through. Do not despair. We've got this.

Why?

If you could see the whole picture, you would know and understand and you would rejoice in this journey. It is more than you know.

But what if it is all a deception? Pretend? Made up?

That would be sad, wouldn't it?

Yes.

Because I created you for purpose and for glory and to partner with Me for amazing things, to see the triumph of Our love that is more powerful than anything else.

Can You hear the parts screaming "I hate You?"

Yes, and I know why. I know their pain. I'm not offended. I tenderly love each of them. There is a way through, even though you can't see it.

Okay, I say yes again, but You've got to help me. I can't do this on my own. Please help me. It's so very hard.

I know. I see the tears and I am crying with you. Remember who you really are. Remember the truth.

Can You confirm some things so that I know?

It will come in time. Be patient.

I feel like such a fool. It is all crazy and made up. It means nothing. I'm crazy.

Remember who you are. Stay steady. This takes courage to face this head on when you want to run. I know. The cross was the hardest thing I faced, but I thought of you, and it was worth it. Now think of Me and trust. Put your hand in Mine and just take a step. You always have a choice. Bring it all into the light.

It's bad stuff. It isn't pretty.

I know. But the only healing comes in the light of true, unconditional love.

Why do they care about me? No one should. I've done horrible things. I'm bad. I can't stand to be loved. It hurts too bad. If I let the ugliness out, they would all hate me. I hate Jo. Better she finds out now how bad I am. I want to be the perfect client, but I'm afraid. Very scared. Bad things. Run away. Give up. Hide. Jesus, is this bringing it into the light?

Yes, darling. We are so proud of you. When you try to hide, We can't heal.

Please hurry up and heal!

It is a process, precious one, Our delight. Trust Us step by step. It is okay to be afraid, to need, to feel. We are not ashamed of you.

(The next morning) Thank you for last night, True Jesus. Thank you for meeting me right where I was. I so need You.

It is Our delight, Precious Adena. You delight Our hearts even in your pain because We see the end result and your full restoration. In your weakness, you lead others to Us, and this stirs Our heart with great zeal and love and passion for you. Don't despise the gifts We've given you.

Okay. I don't understand, but I say yes to You again. Please help me today to teach with Your words and power and might. I have nothing.

We love it when you have nothing because We can flow more purely through you. When you think you are great and powerful on your own, We are limited in moving through you. Always remember this.

Okay. Thank you. I put my trust in You today. You alone are my strength. Show me the Way.

Gladly!

Jesus, why is it such a struggle? Can You help me? Is this a coordinated attack?

Yes, much is happening right now. Do not be afraid but choose to trust. We will help you step by step.

I need You Jesus as the Way, the Truth, and the Life. I don't want anything fake or counterfeit. Please expose anything that needs corrected and healed. Please help me.

Always with great joy!

Time Wound

A "Time Wound" is what I felt the Lord speak to me about when there's a traumatic event on a certain date/time. It describes how we can feel powerful emotions every time that date or time comes around. There can be multiple "time wounds" on our timeline. As we process with the Lord, these can be healed, so we don't have repetitive trauma around those events.

I want to learn to feel. I want to process what I need to during this time. I feel like throwing up. What is this?

There's a lot of pain there. Do you want to talk about it?

I'm willing to but what is there? I don't want to know what is there. I don't want to feel like I'm making it up. How do I know if it is real?

Are you willing to trust Us?

I am. I know this is the issue, but until the "false Jesus" issues are cleared up, it is hard. True Father, I didn't know there was a time wound. Oh my. What do I do? I don't know what to do! Please help me! I feel all kinds of things, big emotions. Horrible stuff… Where is this coming from?

It's okay. We know you want to attune with a face-to-face human, but you can attune to Us now.

Who are you? I can't find anyone. It is all darkness and swirl…a swirl of darkness. I can't hear or see. I'm bad. This is what she said. I'm bad. I'm bad. I can't go to school anymore. I'm too bad. They don't like me. My bad. Kicked out. Not good enough. Evil. She said I do bad things. I don't want to do bad things. I tried really hard. I was very good. She told everyone I'm bad. They all think I'm bad. Can anyone see my pain? My shame? I feel so bad. I tried really hard. I really did. No one is safe. There's no place that is safe. It's all bad. Pain everywhere. No matter how hard you try, it will always be bad. Death is the only true friend. Die!

True Jesus, I need You. Please come help these parts. Please speak Your truth. I'm stuck. Please get me out of the time stamp. I can't hear or see You right now, but I know that You are there. Enough of me believes to hang on. Help my unbelief.

We are here, tender Daughter of Zion. We never leave you. We bring life and joy and rest. You are making progress and getting through a lot. We are so very proud of you.

But it hurts really bad.

We know. Just bring the pain to Us.

I can't. It's too much. Please help me. It's crushing me. I can't move. Are You able?

Yes, We are able. Let Us have it all. We turn sorrow into joy. Do you trust Us? It was what was needed to get you on a better path. There was no other way.

If I had listened to You better, would it have happened?

Those questions aren't helpful. What is helpful is to know Our love and to learn trust.

How can I trust anyone after this? They are the tip of the iceberg. They are what I know. You know the rest, right?

Yes, We do. There has been a lot of betrayal, more than you know. But this is not a death sentence. We offer you life.

I can't.

We know that is how it feels.

But I will get hurt again. I'm done. I don't want to do this again. I'm scared of big feelings. I haven't had to face them before. We just stuffed and disassociated.

We know, but this is good that you aren't stuffing, and you aren't dissociating. We are so proud of you.

I just want to die.

You are reliving that day.

Yes.

What would that accomplish?

It would hurt a lot of people. You could just take me and then they would blame You.

Is that what you want?

No, not really. I do want to live. This hurt seems like more pain than I can face.

You are not facing it alone.

Okay, then please take it because I can't.

Let it out.

I don't know how. We have to keep it hidden in small places. But it is everywhere. It's too much. I don't have anyone to synchronize with.

There are those who would be honored to be there for you. You only let in so far.

I can't. It's too painful.

It is okay. We are holding you and We've got this.

I need a place to go where I'm not leading. I can synchronize with Jo, but she is busy, and it is short. I talked too much last week.

But it was important things you needed to hear as well. It is okay. Can You trust Us step by step?

Yes, and I am grateful for all that You have provided…

Let Us hold you tenderly. Let My blood wash over you and your timeline. You do not need to keep reliving this moment. You can move on.

Thank you!

Pain in the Night

We know this is not easy. You always get to choose. We are not forcing you. This is the gentle invitation.

What if something bad happens tonight? I can't sleep. I can't sleep. It might happen.

You either trust that We are bigger and more powerful or not.

I want to believe. Please help my unbelief and fear. I want to believe. I feel like I'm going crazy.

You are not. Remember it is as simple as putting your hand in Ours and taking the next step.

I can't. I just want to die. It's too hard. It is so bad. I can't believe it. Dive into the deep well of pain and never come back. Forget it all.

No. I choose to believe. True Jesus, please help me. I really need You.

We are here. Trust and rest.

Will I make it?

You will. Take courage, precious daughter. So many are cheering you on. You are running a good race. We are proud of you. You are not alone.

Please help me sleep well tonight. I am asking for all.

(Then to parts…)

He won't force you, but our safest place is with Him. Please give it a try. We really need to sleep. True Jesus is a very good True night watchman. He will keep us safe. Have you ever felt safe?

No.

Well, then at least give this a try. Remember insanity is…

Yes, I know… maybe we can try it for tonight…

Thank you so much. I ask all of my parts to cooperate – we really need to rest. True Jesus is putting up a barricade, so we are safe. He is our strong tower, and He will keep us safe. He wants to heal the deep wounds. We can trust Him.

No!

It is okay. True Jesus, can You help us?

Yes, I am here. Don't be afraid. I will keep you through the night.

Quiet Before the Storm

Why can't I seem to journal with parts?

You haven't really tried.

Yes, I'm afraid.

They are also in lockdown with Strong Girl and Good Girl in charge.

It is kind of nice. I sometimes hear the "I hate you" group.

Temporarily, this is okay but you will need to open up soon so you can process fully.

I don't want to.

We understand. We will help you through this. What do you see?

I see myself curled up in the fetal position wanting to die.

Is that who you really are?

No. But it feels better right now to just die. The pain is too hard to face. We are scared of the radical change this brings.

Yes, it is big. And We are here to help you through it. We will continue to hold you and provide for you gently in Our love. Nothing is impossible with Us.

Can I just die?

That is not Our plan for you. We have glorious things ahead that you were designed for that will bring you great joy. It is worth fighting for.

Okay. I give all this to You and put my trust in You. Please help me.

We are here always. Don't be afraid to engage with your parts.

I can't.

You can with Us.

I don't want to.

We know. It is okay. What are you afraid of?

The barrage. I can already feel it.

Ignoring it won't make it go away.

We hate you! You are ruining everything! You can't break the pattern. Stick to the order. You won't recover from this. Everyone will leave you. You know this. Backstabbing idiot. Get in line. Before it is too late.

See True Jesus, it is too much. I'm having a hard enough time as it is. I'm a failure at this.

You can take this step by step with Us. We know about these parts and their distress. See them and understand them. This will help. We are with you.

I hear you and I am so sorry for how hard all this is. I feel and hear your pain.

No, you don't. You have no idea what you are doing. We hate you.

I get that and I am not trying to be difficult or hurt you. This is hard for all of us. I am believing the True FAMILY will see us through and that ultimately it will be better for us. They care and provide protection.

Remember your dream. They will hunt you down. You can't leave. Everyone will die.

I know it feels that way, but I believe that True FAMILY is stronger than the cult system and They have a way through.

Lies and blasphemy! You're an idiot.

What do you need?

Things back the way they were. Better. Safer. Conform. Do what you are told.

We were pretty miserable doing that.

Maybe, but the alternative is worse.

We can try it out with True Jesus and see.

The consequences are too high. You don't understand.

I want to. Can you give me more information on what they plan to do?

No. Can't do that. Against the rules.

Did any of you participate in the attack on Jo?

No, it was them. Higher-ups.

Did you see that they couldn't do any real damage? She is protected by True Jesus.

But she still felt it.

Yes, and possibly part of that was to help me know this is real.

Of course it is real.

Yes, sometimes I struggle with unbelief and denial programming.

It is there for a reason.

I'm learning a new way with the True FAMILY that is so much better. Do you see the changes?

Yes, like breaking up your marriage and your family? You call that good?

I have seen True FAMILY take what is difficult and not good and bring good out of it.

Sure, that is going to happen. You are so deceived. Get in line.

See, True Jesus, this is why I didn't want to do this.

It is okay. Well done facing this. We are here and We can do more than you know. You are planting seeds and there will be fruit from it. Don't be discouraged. Trust and rest. Well done.

Nothing's changed.

You faced the pain.

Okay.

Facing Body Issues

I don't want to. I want it fixed now. I don't want to walk this out. I want this to go away.

We know, but We have a better way. This is releasing your body to Us and trusting Us just as you are learning to trust Us with your soul parts.

NO. My body is off limits. No.

We understand this defense system, and this is what We are after. You desire healing of your body, soul and spirit. That is your true heart. You have parts who are vehemently trying to protect your body, but it is actually causing harm.

I can't trust You with my body. You never helped all those years. No way. I can't.

We understand why you feel that way and We are not offended. We are here to help you step by step.

I don't want any help. I will do it myself.

You can, but you will still have the symptoms. What is going on is multi-faceted and We are the Ones who lovingly created you and know every part of you deeply. We know the solutions and are the only help for you. This rescheduling (of a doctor's appointment) **is a blessing for you and will work for your good. Deep inside you want healing.**

Yes, but this is hard. *NOBODY CAN HAVE OR TOUCH MY BODY.*

We are the safest option for you, precious Adena. Your self-protection hasn't worked and isn't working.

Yes, I know, but I can't give up. This is stupid… why is this so hard? It shouldn't be.

There are definitely reasons, and We honor this. It is not surprising with what you've been through.

Is this all imaginary?

No, it is real. We are real. It is okay. We love you right where you are. This is not a surprise to Us. We are here for you to walk this out.

I feel so out of control.

It is okay. We are asking you to release that to Us so that We can help you manage your life.

No, You just want to use me. No more. Not for anyone.

God, why does this hurt so badly?

It is okay. These parts coming forward are looking for healing even if it doesn't seem like it. They want to be truly loved and cared for, even though they resist it. Trust and rest in Us and find restoration.

Okay, how do I release my body to You?

You can only to the degree that they are willing to cooperate.

But what if they won't? I don't want to be in this place.

We understand the internal conflict. It has always been there. It is just coming to the surface now. We tenderly care for you. This is the time. We hold you all together through the process.

I can't let go.

We know. It is okay. Take it step by step and don't be afraid.

I want to throw up.

We've got this. We are here. We will help you through this.

I want to run away and die, hide. Be gone forever. Not exist.

Yes, We know this very painful part of you. We have plans for your restoration and for every part of you to receive love and healing and care.

I don't think I can handle being loved. It is too much.

We know. It is okay. Take it step by step. We've got this. And We hold you tenderly in Our hands. We've ordained every moment of this process…

I hate them all. Everyone who did this. The hate is too much. The pain is too much. I hate it. It is really bad. Unforgiveable.

Remember again Our goodness to you. Remember both the cross and the resurrection. There is hope. Hang on.

Why did the canceled appointment flip me into this?

Because it is where We wanted to bring you for healing.

This doesn't feel like it.

Yes, but it is the path. You would not have known this if you'd just gone to the appointment today. This was the best place to bring this to the surface. There is much resistance, but Our love is stronger than death. Your body is in need of great healing. We've held you together tenderly and allowed you to function to bring you to this place. But now it is time for you to surrender your body.

NO. Please don't use those words.

We used them intentionally for you to see and to get to the root.

I surrendered my body over and over and I don't want to anymore. I want my body dead so nobody else can do that to me again. Ever.

Are you willing to give Us the pain?

Why?

Because Jesus paid for it on the cross and you do not have to carry it any longer.

I deserve every bit of it.

In some ways yes, but Jesus paid for it, so you don't have to. You can be free. Would you turn away such a beautiful gift?

It hurts too much. It hurts to be loved. I can't let it in. I'm afraid. When I opened up, they took advantage. I have to keep in control. I can't let go. No matter what.

Jesus, I want to give it all to You. You know the struggle.

We do and that is enough. We will continue to work tenderly with you. Take a break and rest. We've got you even with this resistance. It is not about making them surrender but about exposing the pain so that We can heal it in time. This doesn't change your protection or how much We love you, so don't be afraid.

Okay, thanks.

Death Programming

I hate this journey! I wish I didn't exist. It is too hard. I can't do this. I just want to go home to You. Can't You make it easier? Let me go.

You always have choice, precious Adena. This is a part that is really frustrated. Take courage and do not be discouraged.

Dear part, I know how you feel, and I am so very sorry for how hard this is. We can do this with the True FAMILY. We can't do it on our own. So much we've done on our own to try to self-protect and make things happen. We've done pretty well at that, but now we get to learn a new way. I know this journey is hard, but the True FAMILY is willing to make it easier than when we do it ourselves. Can you join me in cooperating with Them for healing?

They can't promise it will be easy. I know this. The Bible is full of suffering and pain. We are so done with that. We don't want any more. We just want to melt away and not exist. It is too hard.

I understand. I know it is hard. True Jesus, I don't know what to do because I feel this too. Please help us.

It is okay. This is some programming designed to stop you from moving forward. See it for what it is and see the lies and programming behind it.

NO! We have to do what they say. You are ruining everything. Now we all will suffer more! Can't you understand! Stop this process.

I hear you and I'm glad you are sharing this. We can do this together. We've been tricked and tortured and lied to, but this is a season where we get to try things differently. We don't have to stay stuck in the programming and pain.

There is no other way.

I know that is what you've been told, but I do believe that there is another way. Jo is helping us to work through those things and she cares. She's helped many other people.

Like who?

That's confidential.

Then she's lying.

No, I believe her.

It's a trick. She is one of them. She's tricking you.

No, I don't believe it.

You are stubborn and programmed, so how do you know that you aren't just falling into another trap?

I hear you. I get that we've been tricked so many times by people we love. It is risky to trust again. But I don't want to live the rest of my life afraid and not trusting. I am willing to take this risk.

No! They will torture us.

They will torture us anyway… This is our best chance to get completely free. We can try and if it doesn't work out, we can always go back. Would you be willing to try?

They say we can't.

Who are "they"?

(I have a sense right away that "they" are the Jesuits, but for a moment I hesitate to express this…)

See, you don't want to type it because you are afraid.

You are right. I don't want to believe it is true.

Then you don't believe us.

I'm sorry. It is hard. You are right that I struggle to believe it is real and that we aren't just making up this conversation, but I'm learning to be honest about these things and to trust True Jesus.

He will let you down in the end.

I know that is what you've been told. I don't believe it. I believe He is my one true hope.

We have to follow the rules. That is our only hope. It is the only way to live. There is no existence apart from that.

I'm sorry, that doesn't sound very fun or loving.

They do care, which is why they do bad things to us. They are trying to make us better.

Is it working?

Not really.

Then would you consider another way?

We can't. The ramifications are too bad. We don't want to be tortured forever. *

I don't believe that is True Jesus' heart. He died so that we could live. All we need to do is accept Him and receive His love. I know that you desperately want to experience true love.

It is a fantasy. It is not possible. Work hard, obey the rules… that is the only way that we might ascend. You should know better.

I am learning a better way that doesn't involve all of that. We do things freely because we love True Jesus. He helps us to learn how to experience joy.

Nope, not going there. We can't break the rules. And you don't believe us.

Okay. I know there's some things I am struggling to face. It is likely some of the programming too. But I do believe that we can work together, and I am glad to be having this conversation. I want you to know that I am open for more.

Okay. When you can believe us, we will talk.

True Jesus, I am sorry I struggle to believe them. You know why I don't want to. It makes it so bad.

Why are you afraid?

I don't know. It is just that if I know, then it makes it more real. I don't want any of it to be real. But I know I need to face it if it is.

What if it is real? How does knowing if it is real or not make a difference?

I don't know. I guess it really doesn't because we are still doing the same thing in working through things step by step. So, You are still holding my hand even if it is real. But I can't stand it. It is too bad.

Don't pull your hand away but instead let Us quiet you inside.

But what if I'm wrong? I don't want to be crazy.

You aren't crazy and it is okay to feel this way.

It feels horrible. Can You help me?

Yes, We can. This is why We take this step by step. When you are ready, We can face what you don't want to see.

Okay, thank you. Do I have to do this?

No, you don't. We don't force you. If you want to be free, then you must face the TRUTH.

I want to hide and run and not exist.

It is okay. We are here for you. We know these big feelings are overwhelming. Rest in Our love.

Okay.

*The littles here are referring to the Jesuit concept and programming around hell.

Guardians and Difficult Memories

Keep me in Your love. Help me to have patience.

We are at work for the greatest redemption and restoration. We deeply love and care for you, even when you are shut down and don't feel. We are here.

Okay. Thank you. But I don't like this. I want to run away. Disappear. Stop being.

We know and We care. It isn't easy, but We can help with that if you are willing. We can make it lighter as you learn to trust.

I can't trust anyone.

In your own strength, yes. We understand that. We are tender and gentle with you because We know what you've been through. There is no condemnation. We are gently inviting you into life. We knew the shutdown would happen.

Why didn't you tell me not to go? *

Even in your weakness, you did some powerful things with Us on that land that had an impact.

But parts of me may be doing bad things too and I can't stand that!

Can you trust that We only allow what is needed for restoration for you and others? You will make mistakes. It is not about being perfect and doing everything perfectly. We've given you choice. And We will work with you step by step along the way.

Why did I "drift" into being in a car in the garage with the engine running? Please help me.

Fortunately, you don't have a garage!

You are right. Thank you. Please help me in this despair.

It is okay to face the truth in Our love. We are here. You shut down with Jo because of the images you saw with her that scared you instead of trusting Us to help you.

I'm too bad. I can't live. I hurt others.

Face it with Our love. We have you safe in Our arms. You do feel.

I don't want to.

Let it come. Let the tears flow. We've got you safe with Us. We can help you through this.

I'm so sorry.

We know. It's going to be okay. Don't let the hardening of bitterness get a hold of you. Choose to keep your soft heart.

Okay, what do I do with the tough ones?

It is all they know to keep you safe and from feeling. Have compassion for them. Talk.

I don't want to.

It is the only way.

Okay. Tough ones, I appreciate you trying to protect me by keeping me from feeling. You've helped me to survive horrendous stuff. You've done well.

We are strong.

Yes, you are. And it must be tiring… keeping all things in lockdown.

Yes, but we rotate and do what needs to be done.

So, you aren't the same ones from yesterday with Jo?

(I see the same burly guys that I described in Section VII)

Nope. We rotated. Keeps you safer.

Did you see what happened yesterday?

We heard about it. Not impressed. Got to keep our jobs. Keep you safe. Keep rotating. Keep blocking.

Are you with the brotherhood?

No. Not with them. Occasionally rotate through but no. Hate them. Keep you safe. Rotate, rotate, rotate. Keep things smooth. Keep order. Keep safe. Best way. Everyone plays their part. Plenty of us.

I look forward to getting to know more of you. I appreciate the intent, but I am also learning a new way of functioning with True FAMILY. They are really good at protection and can give you a break.

We don't need one since we rotate.

What do you do when you aren't in charge?

We lock down. It is easier that way. Just stay in stasis. Rotate. Keep the order. Don't have to know what is going on. Loose lips sink ships.

Then how did you hear about yesterday?

That's the point. They went off the rails. Got tempted. Brought chaos. They shouldn't have given codes. Big breach.

Where are they now?

We can't get to them. Some sort of force field. Bad. Not safe. Compromise.

What if what they experienced was superior protection? The fact that you can't get to them is significant, isn't it?

Well, maybe, but can't be curious. Must do job.

What if you could be curious? Would you like to know more?

Naw. Keep job. Do duty. Keep you safe.

True Jesus, I need help here. Can You stop the rotation and help these ones?

Remember, it is a process, darling daughter. All of these ones are very precious to Us. But We won't force them. They are seeing change, even if they can't yet accept it. You got some freedom from this time with them and Us as well as some new information.

Okay, I choose to trust and stop the complaining about how hard this is.

See, it gets easier when you do. Just put your hand in Ours. Take the next step.

(Later)

I "forgot" that last night I went to sleep around 9:30 and then woke up at 10:15 with severe "sodomy pain." It resolved after maybe 15-20 minutes. It was also the summer solstice. True FAMILY – I don't even want to ask if this was current or body memory.

It is real, if that helps until you are ready to know.

Can't I pretend it isn't?

Not if you want to heal. We are here for you, and I know you feel the edges of the shame and humiliation and rage deep inside. But also, are afraid of it. You can face these things in Our love. It is possible to overcome.

But it was much simpler before because I liked myself, knew very little shame, and overall had a really good life. I hate this. I would like to go back to that reality.

But you desire truth in your "inner man." You asked for this.

I didn't know what I was asking for. How can this be a "good God?" This is horrific.

Yes, and there is a different way to look at it… through Our eyes and the perspective of eternity. You know about the triumph of Our love because you've seen it.

But it is hard to see tonight. The despair pulls under and the rage builds.

And Our love is greater still.

Blanking out is easier.

Temporarily. But it takes great courage to see the great reward. It is worth it. I know.

What do I do with all this pain and rage? I don't want the cult to use this.

I will gladly take it.

Is it that easy?

Yes and no. There is more processing. You are only feeling the edges and the memories are not all here.

I do want confirmation. How can I continue in ministry? I'm afraid of hurting others.

Do you believe We are more powerful?

Yes, I do, but…

You can do more than you know in Our strength. Our love and grace are more than enough. Fear, unbelief, pride, and rebellion limit what We can do because We honor your choice.

That is the scary part. I can feel some strongholds in parts and while I've repented for them, I don't know if that is enough.

Are you willing to trust your life with Us? This is the only way.

Yes, I trust. Help my untrust.

Remember how We answered that prayer? Give what happened last night to Us for now so you can sleep tonight. Rest in Our love for you.

Why did You allow this?

We only allow things to surface for your best good and for restoration. Keep that in sight as you process. This is not an easy one, but the rewards are beautiful. It is worth it.

If You say so. I can't feel that now. But I am willing to trust. Thank you for sending friends and Jo to help. I am very grateful.

*I am referring here to a trip I took that was especially challenging.

Can I Trust Again?

Stay steady with Us, precious Adena. We are taking you gently by the hand. We know what you can handle. Are you willing to trust Us with all of this?

Not really, but I know You've given the invitation today to say yes and I want to say yes to You. Do You really have all of this? I'm afraid I can't handle anything more. I'm afraid of losing it.

This journey requires trust.

But so many bad things have happened. I trusted many and it turned out badly. I'm scared.

We know you are. It is okay. We are here. We care.

Can I just disappear? It is too much responsibility. What if I lose it and let everyone down? They are trusting me with their stories and lives. They are so very precious and also broken like me. We are all so fragile and I'm afraid.

You are not meant to carry it all. It is too much for you. But you can learn deeper trust by releasing all of this to Us. Remember the joy. Remember restoration. Let Us steady you and carry the weight of this. Our yoke is easy, and Our burden is light. Remember this is what you teach as the plumbline. Are you taking on more responsibility than We are asking of you? Can you joyfully let go tonight and enjoy the rest of the evening? You can read Svali's book if you want to.

I guess I'm afraid it might trigger more things and I'm fragile.

Do you trust Us to handle things? We can help you. You can spend time in worship, work through some prayers, and/or read the book. We've got this! Being honest is good, but also you don't have to wallow in fear or the heavy weight of responsibility. You can step into light and joy and Our love. Remember the good things with gratitude and leave the questions with Us. We will provide the answers in the right

time when you are ready. Remember that today was meant to be an exercise in rest and trust.

Well, it definitely is that! Okay, I choose to shift course and trust, even though I don't feel like it. Thank you so much. You will keep me safe. I can trust You. You are helping me day by day.

Let Us hold you. Let Us carry this.

I am tired. Thank you. There's so much responsibility on every side, so many people asking things of me. Please take all of this. I want to help, but I can't do all of this.

You aren't meant to. Rest, darling daughter.

Sea of Forgetfulness

We love to walk out this journey with you, precious Adena. Stand in this and be refreshed by Our love today. Feel your hand in Ours, safe and secure. Take a deep breath and experience Our goodness.

Keep me there! There's so much today. I ask for additional grace to love well and to see things as You do. To all those in the sea of forgetfulness, I want you to know that you are never forgotten, and that True Jesus is always with you. He wants to help you come out into the fullness of light and glory and love. Forgetfulness is no longer our safety, He is. Some of you know this and are willing and I am so glad. Those of you who don't, He is gentle to help you. He knows our fears and He gently leads us in His love. You don't have to forget to be safe anymore. We can face it all in the light of His love.

We like death. It is easier.

I understand and I feel you. It was the way for us to survive and I thank you for helping me to survive.

But life is too painful. This is why we chose this. The sea of forgetfulness is our comfort. Oblivion. We don't have to know anything.

I get it. I know that is all you've known, but there is a better way. Life is meant to be beautiful and active. I'm experiencing joy even though I'm facing hard things. True Jesus is sustaining me. You can experience that too.

Will He really do that?

Yes. He said, "I am the Resurrection and the Life." This means He loves to bring to life those things that are dead, including us.

Seems too easy.

It is different than we've known, but it is good news, isn't it? True Jesus has conquered through His death, burial, and resurrection. We can have freedom, too. This is His heart for us. You don't have to make a commitment. You can just try this life if you want to. I'm not trying to force you. I'm just telling you the good news.

But what about the pain?

True Jesus is willing to help us face the pain in Their love. He is willing to help us process it in the right ways so that we can return to vitality and health in all ways.

It sounds good, but we are sleepy and have no strength to do what needs to be done.

What do you think needs to be done?

Well, it all takes work, and we aren't up for it.

Not with True Jesus. He has done the work. Our part is to receive it. That can sometimes feel like work because we often resist it, but when we just say yes, He does it in us. Give it some thought. He is always available to talk to and to help you understand His ways. He is ready to even transform this dark sea of forgetfulness into a glorious place of His love. This is possible.

Hmmm… We'll consider, take it slowly.

Yes, no problem. I'm not trying to rush you, just to let you know the possibilities that True Jesus offers.

What about the other ones?

Do you mean false Jesuses or other parts?

Well, both. We don't want to get into any trouble.

We don't need to obey false Jesus anymore or be controlled by the lies we believed about who Jesus is. True Jesus is also able to protect us from internal and external handlers, protectors, and fathers. I also want to let those who developed the theta skills to protect us, and our loved ones know that there is a better way for you, too. True Jesus is stronger than any theta skills and any other powers out there. In partnership with Him, He is willing and eager to help us learn new skills that keep us safer and that bring joy, not death.

Killing is what we do.

I know that and I understand why you do it. But there is another way that is full of joy instead of pain.

We don't feel pain. We know how to rule over it.

It might seem that way, but likely it is just dissociated to another part of us or given to demons to hold (it fuels them) instead of really solving the problem. We are being used and that isn't fun. There is an alternative with True Jesus. He would like to show you how He can turn those skills into something way more meaningful, true, and just.

This has worked pretty well for us.

I can understand how you feel that way but think of all of the lives taken to fuel that system. There are so many ways that we were tricked and controlled and manipulated into doing things that hurt others.

We don't care as long as it gets the job done.

I know this is because the true feelings and value for life is "lost" in the sea of forgetfulness, but this doesn't mean it isn't there. True Jesus, can You help them see from a different perspective? Can You shine Your light into the Sea of Forgetfulness so they can see the truth?

Briefly and gently, yes...

Oh! We didn't see that!

True Jesus didn't do that to shame or condemn you, but so you could see the truth. You want the truth, don't you?

Yes, but that is hard. We can't face that right now.

That is okay. He is here and ready at any time to help you walk through this. I hope that gives you perspective so that we can all heal and find freedom. Please don't forget this.

They will just reprogram.

What if there was another option? Jesus is able to protect us from re-programming if we ask Him.

He would do that?

He is for us and for our freedom. He has a way through. Would you like that protection?

Yes, but what do we have to do?

Just ask Him. He takes it from there.

But there is always a price.

Not with Him because He paid the price already and just invites us in to experience His love.

Seems too easy, but okay. We'd like protection.

Thank you so much! True Jesus, you heard that?

Yes, I did, and I am delighted to help all of you on this journey. Rest and trust.

Section XV

Parts Testify

As more of my parts have come to Jesus, at times they give testimony to the rest of my inner realm of His goodness and love. This often encourages me as well, especially when I am struggling. Enjoy!

Fiery Trials

This is a fiery test, darling daughter. Can you stand with Us? We do have a way through, and the truth will become clearer.

I am willing if You are with me. Please burn away anything not of You. I step into the flames and look for You. Please purify all of me and refine me as gold. I know Your purposes are for my good. Lead me step by step. I give to You the losses. You are my Provider, and I know You are more powerful than the enemy. Though You slay me, I will put my trust in You. Help me to be faithful to You. Please strengthen me through this trial.

We are here and We delight to be with you. We are not ashamed of you and gladly stand with you. Do not be afraid. You are not alone. We will take care of you step by step. You have more courage than you know. Let Us strengthen your heart.

Thank you so much, True FAMILY. I trust Your promises to me. If some of this is suffering righteously, I bless that and ask for it to multiply to Your glory. If this is my exposing my own stuff, I bless that and thank you for revealing and if it is a combination, I thank you for Your severe mercy. You alone are my God, and I choose to put my trust in You. Any parts want to testify? This will help us as we face this together.

(Here different parts chime in…)

We feel better when True FAMILY is in charge. They are helping us step by step.

We are finding stability in Them. We aren't so afraid.

We can rest in Them and find peace even in the storm.

We are happier now and less stressed.

They help us through the hard stuff.

They forgive us.

They love us even when we've done bad things.

They know how we feel.

They see us.

They don't hate us.

Thank you all so much. See, doesn't that help? I want to testify to those of you who haven't experienced this yet. The True FAMILY is so good to us and They want to help us all. The more we cooperate together, the more healing comes. This includes being able to talk through anything that is currently going on. If you feel you need to do things to protect me or those I love, we can talk through a better way with the True FAMILY. We can all be set free. Anyone want to talk about this?

We are sorry. We just wanted to scare you into stopping what you are doing. They said it would help you and keep you safe.

Do you see how they lie to us always? Thank you for sharing. True Jesus can help us clean this up. They know your heart is good.

And you've been manipulated into doing things you don't really want to. There is a better way. I forgive you for this.

We are truly sorry.

I know you are. The promise of True Jesus is that He works all things for good and we are going to trust Him in this. We can trust Them to work it out for good for us AND for those who have been affected by this. I forgive you.

Thank you. We were just trying to help by scaring you. How can you forgive us? We've done lots of bad things.

True Jesus is the one who made a way for us to walk in forgiveness and to truly experience healing that lasts. We are trusting Them for this journey. They will help bring good out of this.

We are so proud of you all! Well done! We are happy to work this all out for good. This is the power of Our triumphant love. Nothing is impossible. Do not be discouraged by this. We rejoice in the request and in the repentance. This sets you free in more areas. Learning to testify together helps greatly.

Thank you so much for showing us that. I am so grateful to everyone for working together on this. Doesn't this feel so much better than when we started? Good teamwork! Whenever any of us are afraid or struggle with doubt or unbelief we can remember this, and we can do this again. How does that sound?

Yay!

There's many more who don't know the good news yet, so you are all free to share with others at any time True FAMILY shows you the good news. Isn't this better than sharing fear?

Yes, we agree. We'd rather do this. It helps us feel better.

We don't push anyone or force anything. We don't want to control or manipulate.

We are so very proud of you, Adena. You see the victory from tonight. In your deepest despair, there is light and a way through.

Finding the Way

Does anyone need to share anything?

"Pie in the sky" thinking. Come on, they got us controlled on every front. There's no escape. You've tried this before. Doesn't work. Better to just go along with things.

I hear you and I want you to know I value you and how you've helped to protect me through the years. But I'm learning new ways to walk this out. And I would love your help and cooperation in this. We don't have to be subject to them anymore. There is great freedom that is available to us now. We don't have to wait for death. You've carried a very heavy burden, and True Jesus is inviting us to give those burdens to Him. He is well able to handle it. Anyone who is willing to give up the heavy burden, come! The good news is that True Jesus can also protect us from any backlash. I have asked Him to be between us so that we don't harm each other. I have also asked Him to be between us and anyone in the cult system who threatens our lives. This relieves so much pressure and is a way that we can process our pain and other emotions. I'm so very grateful. We don't need to be afraid anymore. We don't have to be bound by the many contracts.

But they do own us. They created us and that gives them the right.

They cannot create true human life. Only True Jesus gives us life and breath. They thought that they had, but it is not true. He is the one who breathed life into us. They cannot copy this completely, although they try. Everyone, including them, is owned by True Jesus. He died for everyone, not just those who would receive Him. He provided for all. There is hope for us and for them.

This is so different from what we've been told. How do you know it is true?

Because of time spent with True Jesus and His faithfulness to me.

But He's done some really bad things over the ages.

It can appear that way, but when you look deeper, you see His hand of love and mercy through it all. Most of what we've been taught is twisted. We get to learn a new way.

You have almost persuaded me. Much to ponder…

You have freedom and space to work through this. I know there is a lot involved, and it can feel complicated and scary, but when we surrender to True Jesus, He brings all things into simplicity and clarity.

No "thousand steps to enlightenment?"

No, just putting our hand in Theirs and taking the next step.

Okay, will ponder…

You can try Him and experience His strength and protection and if you aren't satisfied, you can go back. He won't force you.

You are trying to take everything from us, the magick...

I may have been trying to move too fast and I am sorry. I just know that I want to do everything with True Jesus and to receive the freedom He has for us. We don't need to use their magick anymore. It always comes with a price tag. But True Jesus paid the price for our freedom and our part is simply to believe and trust in Him and to walk with Him on this journey of love.

It seems too easy. What would we do with all the knowledge we have? We are very skilled.

You can help other parts and other people to see the truth and to be set free. We can participate with True Jesus in dismantling everything we've done in the cult system. Remember what True

Jesus did when we were with Jo on Thursday? He was able to heal even the deep magick of the universe and change what was twisted into wholeness. This is such glory. Wouldn't you rather participate in this than the other that had such a great cost?

Yes, it is very interesting to us. We are baffled by this kind of power. It didn't require a bunch of sacrifices.

Anyone who wants to learn more from True Jesus are welcome. He doesn't want to hurt you, but to set us all free. We can trust Him. He is good. He is not like the false Jesuses. The cult system tries to counterfeit everything that True Jesus does. They twist it and make us think He is powerless and dumb and weak and can't really help us or that He is so mad at us that we can never be forgiven. Yet He gives freely and loves to forgive us. We've done horrible things, and He paid for it all so we that could be free.

That seems pretty radical.

It is. And it is such good news! I am inviting all who are ready to freely come. This is not a trap. You are free to try it out and to go back if you want.

But what about the punishments? They will be very mad.

If True Jesus really has this much power, then He can use it also to protect us from any retribution.

See what I've prepared for you. I am freely giving to you, and I can protect you as you trust in Me.

We've been so shattered. How can we trust again?

In your own strength it is not possible. But you will see that I can strengthen you and, as you receive My love, things will change. No force or coercion. Freely given.

Does anyone who has experienced this want to share?

Yes, I feel much better now.

I'm not so afraid and it is peaceful with True Jesus. He's taken the great weight off.

I don't miss using the magick. I don't really need it anymore.

I feel safer now.

Thank you all for sharing so beautifully. Anyone else?

Yes, I feel more like the true me. I don't have to pretend. I can be me. There's a lot less stress.

The more that we are cooperating with True Jesus and with each other, the more freedom we can experience. We are not truly owned by them. That is all lies. True Jesus can eliminate all those contracts. We don't have to be sex slaves anymore. We don't have to do what they tell us.

But there will be consequences.

There might be challenges, but True Jesus can help us through them all and will protect us.

It sounds too good to be true.

Yes, I know, but you've heard the testimonies. This is real. They offered us a twisted version that has kept us in bondage. We get to experience the true freedom only True Jesus can bring.

What do we have to do?

You don't have to do anything. But come give it a try.

Risk free trial?

Yes. Come experience freedom. True Freedom in True Jesus.

Okay, I am willing to give it a try. But I'm holding you responsible if this turns out to be another trap. Don't trick us.

True Jesus, would You ever trick us?

Not in the way you are talking. That is not the way We do things. We are here to love you and to help you be set free.

How can You love us when we've done so many bad things? We are evil.

My blood is more than enough to cleanse you from all evil. You are not evil to the core like they've said. You have a beautiful heart that I gave you. We get to unbury it and let it shine.

That sounds good.

It is. Come. True Jesus is stronger than anything and anyone. I think some of you know this and have seen Him work before or you've seen the angels He has sent. Is this true?

Yes, but….

True Jesus has been there all along and He cares. But He didn't want to force us like they did. Come all who are thirsty to receive the water of life from Him.

Is it magick?

Not like theirs. It is True and holy and good. It changes us inside and out. It cleanses us and gives us strength. This is our time of freedom.

I'm scared.

I know and He knows. He loves to bring comfort and to take our fears and set us free. Can you show them True Jesus?

Gladly.

Lockdown Again?

Okay, I choose to rest in You. Please increase my joy capacity. What do I need to be doing?

Keep focused on Us and We will guide you. Receive Our love. We know it is not easy. Listen to your parts.

I don't want to.

You don't have to, but if you want to experience more healing and freedom you will need to face things.

Okay. Anyone have anything you want to say? I am willing to hear you.

Lockdown imminent.

I am asking for no lockdown. I'm sorry I triggered you. It isn't helpful when we lockdown. I want to open up and receive God's love for us for healing. I'm limited when you lockdown.

We don't want Him anyway.

I hear you. True Jesus is really good and loving and caring. Are there parts who know Him who would like to testify?

That is just a gimmick. Fake propaganda. He's a charlatan.

I don't believe so and neither do many of us. Please share.

True Jesus is gentle with us. He is kind and we like Him.

He is healing us. I don't feel the pain as much. I can breathe.

He is faithful and hasn't let us down. He cares.

We are finding new life.

Just more programming. Don't you see that? You are crazy. Let this go and come on back. We will show you true love.

No, I have made my choice. I am going with True Jesus. He is the one who is the most powerful of all. There is no one who is like Him. He alone satisfies.

I see you are brainwashed. Controlled by Him. You need reprogramming to know who really loves you.

I know it is hard to know what is true and what is programming and all that, but I have experienced Him and know His love.

I see the doubt. You struggle to believe.

Yes, I do. I also know that only True Jesus makes sense and fills me with hope. I am choosing True Jesus. I do not consent to re-programming. True Jesus has redeemed me and is restoring me. I am safe in Him. He is my Protector.

We'll see.

True Jesus, I don't know if that was helpful. Please help me. I really need You.

We are here. Don't let this part intimidate you. That is its job. It only has the power you give it. It is connected demonically.

Okay, can You handle that? Please separate out the demonic from my humanity and help set me free. True Jesus, stand between all parts and help me.

I am here.

Please show Your power and Your love so my parts can know You are real. Please speak peace to every part of me.

Peace, be still. Know My gracious love for you and care beyond what you can think or imagine. We hold you tenderly. You are not alone. We will help you through this. This was not meaningless. Parts testified. This part heard truth. Don't be discouraged. Every little bit is helpful and effective ultimately, even when you feel there is no change. Trust Us.

A Dream

I had a dream where I was always losing to someone else. This is the conversation that followed.

Does anyone inside want to share about this dream?

Well, it is hopeless. They are always stronger than you and always controlling. You can't get away. Just comply.

Thank you for sharing. I hear you but I see things differently. True FAMILY is helping us make changes and we are finding our voice and moving more in love. It isn't about which one of us "wins," but about the way of love and the ultimate triumph of God's love.

Baloney! It's all hype! Get a grip on reality and stop living in fantasy. Conform or we all die.

I'm sorry you feel that way. I'm not trying to hurt or harm you or anyone else. I do believe the true path to freedom, healing, joy and love is with the True FAMILY. I know this counters how we were programmed and taught to "just go along with what the man says." I'm learning I don't have to conform anymore, and it feels good.

That's the trap! Lull you into sleep and then change the rules and cause great pain.

Yes, that is how the cult works, but not the True FAMILY. They are gentle and kind and They lead us in paths of righteousness. They don't make us do bad things or hurt others.

Crazy talk!

Actually, it is true. I know you've been programmed to believe that the True FAMILY is the enemy, but it was lies. We are learning a new way. Does anyone want to testify?

(Various parts speak up…)

It has been much better.

We like the True FAMILY.

They haven't been mean to us.

They listen to us and don't push us.

(The initial part pipes up…)

See, no discipline. No order. These parts need to be reminded of the way.

They seem pretty happy with what is happening now.

Things will fall apart if you don't have order. And we will all get in trouble for any deviation from the track. This is disaster.

It doesn't have to be. The True FAMILY has a flow and order that is refreshing and much easier. These parts are learning that and experiencing love.

Only the family (i.e. the Jesuits) can give us love. Be loyal. You are ruining this. You are deceived.

I know that is all that you can see right now, but I would encourage you to consider something different.

Who's calling who deceived?

You can try the True FAMILY out and see. You don't have to make a full commitment.

I'm done talking to you. This is useless.

I'm sorry you feel that way. Remember what I've shared, and we can talk again.

Not likely.

Okay. True FAMILY please help this part to see and receive Your love. Is there anything You can do?

We continue to draw them in with Our love. Be patient and don't be discouraged. It might seem like the conversation with parts is the same thing over and over but take a look at how many are coming to know Our love! This is exciting for Us, and We are delighted.

Internal Fathers

With mind control, often programmers will program parts to believe that they are actually an outside person or entity, such as a handler, programmer, demonic, or other being. It can take care and love to help the parts to see that they are not that outside person but are really a part of the survivor. Also, the prayer mentioned below on false identities comes from the book *Prayer Warriors 2* by CARE, Inc., which I highly recommend!

Anyone inside have anything you want to share? I know there's a lot of resistance to the issue of the fathers (i.e. the Jesuits). I am wondering if the part that experienced relief and being held by True Father would be willing to testify?

He is so, so good. He is not like the others. I feel safe with Him.

Thank you so much for sharing. That encourages my heart! I know many of you are struggling with this.

They did bad things and hurt us, and we love them (fathers). It is so hard.

Are there internal fathers?

Yes.

I want them to know they don't have to play those roles anymore. Can they hear me?

Yes, they can. They aren't happy. Trying magick to stop you.

True Father is here. He is protecting us. And we can work through this. I want them to know that I care about them and am sending love.

They don't want it. They hate you. You are ruining everything.

Please let them know that I am sorry they feel that way and I want to work through this. I hope they heard the testimony of the one sharing about True Father.

They don't believe it.

Hopefully someday they will. Can they see how powerful True Father is? Their magick is not working.

Yes, and it frustrates them.

It is not my desire to frustrate them. I want them to know the goodness and true love that is available for all of us. And that there is another way. They do not need to continue to walk in those roles. There are better ones available. (I took a break here and did some prayers on false identities from the *Prayer Warrior 2* book and then came back to journaling.)

Why did you do that?

Do what?

The prayer.

Because I care and want to see us whole.

You stripped us of our power.

That is not the power that we want to operate from anymore. It required much pain and suffering. The power that is now available to us through True FAMILY is so much greater and the price has already been paid. We do not need to do bad things to keep our power.

We will get into so much trouble.

True Father is willing to protect us. He is a strong tower and is more powerful than any other being. We've been tricked.

You can't just do this. We can't function without it. We will die.

I'm sorry that is not true. We can receive true power for overcoming and True Father will protect us. He is gentle and kind. He knows why we've done what we have. He is not ashamed of us. We don't have to earn anything from Him. We just get to come and be.

Unlikely. Just more tricks. You are such a sucker. Listen to you. Crazy. No wonder your family hates you.

I am loved and deeply cared for by True FAMILY. They know me and care for me tenderly and will not forsake me. Those demons run when True Jesus comes. They have no true power, only what they get from our agreements. We can live in a new way.

Not likely. You will be brought back just like before.

I have chosen True FAMILY. No matter how long it takes, I choose to be free. It is the only way. True Jesus, can You help me?

We are here. We see and We know. Rest in Our love. You've done well. This is as far as you can take it for today.

I want so much more.

We know and it is important to follow Our pace. We have the way through.

I give all of this to You. Thank you for leading me step by step and stabilizing me.

It is Our joy, always!

My Weaknesses

We know your weaknesses and how to get you back. We've done it before.

Yes, I do have weaknesses, but True FAMILY is helping me to grow. I am choosing to walk with Them now. I am finding more peace and freedom as well as love and joy. I would love for you to experience all of this too.

Not going to happen. We work hard to open doors and keep them open. We make a way for the "true king." (lucifer) May he reign forever and ever.

I'm sorry for all the hard work you are going through. The cost of the cult system is enormous in all the sacrifices and things you must do. Do you like doing all of that? Do you like to hurt others and take lives?

No, but it is necessary for ushering in the glory of the age to come.

What if I told you there was another way? That you didn't have to do all of that?

Lies and deception. We know the truth. You can't persuade us.

I honor your choice, and I would not want to force anything on you. This is the beauty of the True FAMILY. It is that They don't force us to do things.

That's what you think! They are manipulating you.

That is not how I have experienced Them. They have been so very gracious and merciful through it all and have forgiven me of the bad things I've done. It is really beautiful and a joy to be in relationship with Them. I would love for you to experience what I am experiencing with Them.

Not going to happen. Too difficult. We've chosen this way and always will. We'll get you back in line. You just wait and see.

Any parts willing to testify to the goodness of the True FAMILY?

They don't force us to do bad things. We get to play.

They have food that is good and nourishes us deeply.

We get to experience true love that doesn't involve sex. They don't violate us.

(The resisting parts speak…)

No! We don't want to hear any more. Go away.

We respect that. We want you to know that we care, and we are here when you are ready to talk more.

Forget it. Go away.

True Jesus, I give all of this to you. Would You continue to minister to these parts?

Yes, gladly. Well done. Realize this is step by step. They will come around. You've planted some seeds.

Can I close the doors of access?

Do you trust Us?

I want to, but I would really love for all doors of access to be closed.

There is a timing for all of this in cooperation with your parts in a way that will ultimately bring the fullness of freedom for you and others. You want lockdown. We understand this. We can do this, but it would not result in the fullness of growth and maturity for you. We can provide angelic guards and assistance that will be more beneficial until your system is ready.

Okay. I am choosing to trust You. I give all of this to You, every door or access point. Please post angelic help and only allow what is needed for the fullness of restoration for all.

We love your courage. You will see great fruit from this in yourself and others. It will be a testimony of Our great love. Thank you for trusting Us.

Anything else for today?

Rest and trust in Our love through the storm – worship and rejoice!

Brokenhearted

We are here for you. Can you trust Our love?

I can't do this. It's too hard.

We know this is hard and We are here. We grieve for you and what you have been and are going through. Remember the joy set before you. There is a way through.

I can't handle all of this. It is too much. It's overwhelming. I don't know what to do with all of this.

Stay steady in Our love.

I can't see You. Where are You?

Even in the darkness, We are with you. Put out your hand and take Ours.

I'm afraid.

It's okay to be afraid. You can face this with Us and with Jo.

Okay. You won't abandon me?

No, we won't and neither will Jo.

Are you sure?

Yes.

I'm such a baby! This is so stupid. I don't need anyone. I don't want to feel all of this.

Ask if any parts want to testify. It will help you.

Okay, does anyone have anything you want to say?

The True FAMILY won't abandon us.

They care and They give good gifts like Jo.

We can get through with Them.

True FAMILY is here.

Okay, thank you for your testimonies. True FAMILY, I feel pulled in two. It's hard. You are my only hope. Please help me.

We always answer this prayer. We are close to the brokenhearted. We hear your cry. We care tenderly for you. We have a way through.

Section XVI

Forgiving Self

One of the hardest parts of this journey is being able to forgive yourself. When memories of the things that we were forced or programmed to do surface, they are overwhelming. For me, these memories started in the womb when I didn't obey an order, so they killed my twin brother. The guilt and grief were incredible and became the catalyst for the feelings of "I don't want to hurt anyone" that you see throughout my journaling. Time and again, there was "no choice." We were forced to hurt others and take lives. Sometimes we thought we were doing a "good" thing as they told us the one we were to kill was evil and hurting others. They may have told us that we were "helping" God. Other times we were tricked or forced. It is soul crushing when these memories emerge. Even if God could forgive me, sometimes I can't forgive myself. Each time self-forgiveness has been a struggle, but one that is worth it. I understand the depths of God's love and forgiveness in a way that the average person cannot comprehend.

Don't Want to Hurt Anyone

Okay, but what if it happens again?

We can't fully know who is "safe" and who isn't. We get to trust True FAMILY step by step. We will likely make mistakes again. It is not about being perfect.

(I see the part with her hands over ears. She does not want to hear this).

It is okay. We are loved no matter what. This is truth. It is good news. Does this have to do with not wanting to hurt anyone?

Yes. We have to try harder.

True FAMILY is exposing this root in us. It will take time to work through this and to see from a different perspective, but we don't have to try harder anymore or to worry about hurting others. Of course, we don't want to hurt others, but the drive behind this is from our pain that True FAMILY is healing. We can't live and not hurt someone sometime. I know there's deep pain. I am not even aware of the lives we took and evil things we did, but the True FAMILY is in the business of restoration, healing and transformation. We are learning to let Their love in, to forgive ourselves and to experience new life. True Jesus, can You reveal Your deep, deep love to this part and any others who are ready to receive?

Yes, gladly. Our love never fails. Your sin is forgiven.

But you don't know how much the sin is.

True Jesus does know because He paid for it all on the cross. I am not fully aware, but I am willing to see in days to come as the True FAMILY walks us through this. We are forgiven for it all, already. It is already dealt with; we just get to receive it.

I can't. I need to pay for it. I need to be punished for all the bad things I did.

That is an overwhelming amount of pain and guilt that you do not need to carry. True Jesus has already provided everything.

Why?

Because He is love. He represents the fullness of the True FATHER'S love. Our fathers tried to love, but it was conditional on doing bad things we were told lies about. We were tricked and thought we had no other choice. But now we see that we do have another choice. I would like to invite you to receive all of the mercy, grace and love the True FAMILY has for us. This is really good news.

I still don't understand it. How could that be?

I know that it is incomprehensible, but it is true. We get to receive it.

No tricks?

No tricks, just incredible love. Please come try it.

Okay.

Thank you so much, True Jesus, for all that You are doing. I give all of this to You.

We so delight in this process. Keep it up step by step with Us. Receive more and more of Our love for you. Let your heart settle in Our love and trust Us to work it all out for good. We have a good, good plan. Our love never fails. Receive deeply today.

Thank you so much!

Target Practice

Memories had surfaced of theta skills training with archery. I would be raped by a man and then blindfolded and told to channel the anger and rage I felt towards him and shoot him with an arrow. It was justified since they told me he was a "bad" man. I was good at this and hit the target to kill, even though blindfolded. One time, without my knowing they switched the man out for a baby. I was so very devastated when I realized what they had tricked me into doing. This journaling was from shortly after this.

Jesus, do You forgive me? Is there any place in Your heart for me? I need to know because otherwise Your own words indicate to me that I should die. "But if anyone abuses one of these little ones who believe in Me, it would be better for him to have a heavy boulder tied around his neck and be hurled into the deepest sea than to face the punishment he deserves!" (Matthew 18:6, TPT)

It is okay, precious Adena. I know who you are. I know your precious heart. I know that you were forced to do these things. The guilt for these is not on you. Do not listen to the programming. Don't run. This isn't a time to run. Only We can help you. Do not be afraid. Trust and rest in Our love for you that never fails. We see and We know all. We know what was done to you to do that. We know the guilt you are starting to feel. Do not listen to the suggestions of the enemy. We are going to walk you through this.

I've told people I've killed people.... But babies, what will they think?

What We think is the most important. We have forgiven you. Can you forgive yourself?

I cannot right now.

Healing comes when you do. Love is here for you. Beating yourself up is no good. It will only harm.

But shouldn't I be punished for a while? I deserve it.

Jesus took all on the cross for you so that you could live and that you could be redeemed and restored. Do you want to meet those babies?

Yes, I do.

(Seeing happy children playing and laughing)

(children) We forgive you. We do not hold this to your account. Jesus paid for it all. Isn't that what you say? It is finished. There is no shame. No guilt.

You were a child yourself. This sin is laid to those who purposefully forced you into this.

I'm so very sorry. How can You forgive me?

(children) We knew this day would come and we've looked for it with great expectations of joy! We do not hold this against you. Do not hold it against yourself. We love you, precious Daughter of Zion. We forgive you. Now let the forgiveness flow over you and in you to heal every part of you. This is the day the Lord has made, rejoice and be glad in it.

True FAMILY, do You really forgive me? I did bad things.

We know. We have forgiven fully and completely. It is up to you to receive it deeply.

I don't want to. I want to pretend or bury it or die.

None of those options are healing or healthy. There is great activity to get you to stop this journey. We see and We know. These ones are cheering you on. Take courage, precious Adena, and do not be afraid. There will be more revelations to come, but this is your first fruits of joy.

How can that be? I did bad things.

Yes, and you are forgiven because of what Jesus did. We do not hold this sin against you. You did not know. Receive release today.

Jesus, I give You this great sin, this unforgivable sin. Will You help me?

Yes, gladly! I already have. Will you receive this gift?

I don't deserve it. The Scriptures say I deserve a millstone around my neck and to be drowned in the sea. Isn't this true?

You have asked for forgiveness. Because of what I did on the cross, you are forgiven and restored. This is restoration. This is what I want you to share tomorrow (in the service) -- the power of forgiveness.

I choose as an act of my will to receive Your forgiveness and their forgiveness. But I don't know if I can forgive myself…even though I teach this.

Forgiving yourself is also an act of the will. You can do this. It is just a choice for now until your feelings will follow. You do not need to wallow. We are here to love you, to hold you in your grief and sadness and pain.

I'm so very sorry. Please forgive me.

You don't have to keep asking because We've already done it. But you get to forgive yourself.

I don't want to, but I am willing to choose to forgive myself and to receive Your love and forgiveness. I choose forgiveness. I choose the path of love. Please protect me, precious True FAMILY. I need help like never before. I don't know what to do. I really need help.

We are delighted to do so.

Okay. I hide myself in You today. Thank you, precious ones, for your graciousness in forgiving me when I do not deserve it. I stand in awe of God's goodness. I'm so very sorry for what I did.

(children)We love you, Adena. We do not hold this against you. You are clean. Let it go and live.

Thank you. I choose life today. I choose joy in the Lord. I will see you again one day.

(children) We look forward to the reunion that will never end. We are doing what True Father has assigned us on this side to help in what is coming. It is so glorious! More than you can think or imagine! Be of good cheer. He has overcome the world.

A Few Months Later...

Started to read the gospels again recently. Today's reading is Matthew 18. True Jesus, this triggered suicide programming months ago. I don't know if I can face that today. But I want to be in Your Word. Will You help me to read this?

Yes, I am here, and you know the truth. Although you harmed many little ones, this was not your heart, and you would not have done this on your own. You've repented and been forgiven.

But have I really been forgiven? There's probably a lot more I don't know yet that I did.

This is an opportunity for you to trust that We have forgiven you. All of us including those ones whose lives you took or destroyed. You get to reaffirm forgiving yourself.

I can't. It's overwhelming. I don't want to hurt anyone.

We know this. This is what We are dealing with today. Your fear of hurting others will keep you in the cage of your own making. You can take responsibility for what was done and receive Our love and forgiveness and forgive yourself. This is the path of healing.

I can't.

That is a lie. You can choose to forgive yourself. It is possible. It is a choice. You might not feel like it, but you can choose to and rest in Our love. We don't condemn you.

I want to choose Your way. I want to choose to forgive myself. I want to live fully in Your love. Is that enough?

It is a start.

Can I read something else today?

You always have the option to choose. We are not forcing you. We are encouraging you to face this. If you don't face it today, you will need to face it sometime. Why not today?

Okay, I let go of deciding what I can handle today, and I choose to trust You. I do like verse 3 about becoming like a child to enter the kingdom of heaven. I choose Your way. Here I am. Just as I am.

Thank you! Take Our hand and enter in.

So, I have done all those bad things the verses talk about, and You say what my punishment should be. So do it… kill me! Get it over with! Better that I had never been born! Why did You make me?

Is it your true heart to harm another?

NO!

I know your true heart. You did not do those things with malice and intent. You were forced. Can you face this and forgive yourself?

Why is this so hard?

Keep reading…you are the lost lamb We are seeking. See how tenderly We care for you. This is how We feel. This is the truth.

Please come rescue all parts of me!

(I read through the rest of the chapter…)

So, the parable... if I don't forgive myself and my parts, You won't forgive me?

You have already been forgiven, but you hold yourself hostage and torture yourself. This is not My heart for you.

Okay. I choose to forgive all of me and my parts for all that we've done or not done. I don't want the torture.

See you got through the chapter and grew!

Why didn't I read the whole chapter before?

Because you got stuck in the suicide programming. It was important for you to complete it today, to see the whole context and Our heart.

Thank you! I'm glad.

So Much Pain

Images of me killing babies…Compassion to do it quickly. They are going to die anyway. At least the mercy of it will be that it will be by someone who cares. Waves of pain and grief. I can't stand it. Their faces. Oh God help me. I'm so very sorry. How can You forgive me? Jesus, how do You redeem such horror? How can anyone forgive me? Horrible. Horror. Terror. Pain. Run and hide. NOOOOOOOOOOOOOOOOOOOOOOOOOOOOOOOO OOOOOOOOOOOOOOOOOOOOOOOOOOOOOOOOO OOOOOOOOOOOOOOOOOOOOOOOOOOOOOOOOO OOOOOOOOOOOOO! Please Jesus, let it not be so.

Do you want the truth?

Yes, True Jesus, I do, I just wish it wasn't this truth. Please forgive me. I can't believe it is so bad. I'm so very sorry. Please help me. Please no. I'm so very sorry. Why didn't You stop me?

Are you willing to trust Me? We do work all things for good. There is redemption even in this.

How can there be? No one can forgive this. It's not forgivable. I am not forgivable.

We know you feel that way, but there is nothing that can't be forgiven. Jesus' blood paid for it all.

This is too bad.

Nothing is too bad for Us, Adena. We love you even in this. We know your true heart.

Please forgive me and let me die. I can't live with this.

Yes, you can. Your life is a testimony of Our goodness and Our love.

I can't bear it.

Yes, you can't bear it on your own, but We are carrying you through this. We have provided all that you need to walk this out in victory. We know the deep grief. We will help you through this. The enemy will not win. We are and have triumphed over him. The victory is already won. Do you believe this?

Somewhere I do, but right now in my pain and grief I can't. It is just too hard. I wish I could talk to Svali about this.

We know and one day you will. Be patient and trust Us for the timing.

Okay.

In the meantime, you can talk to Jo about this. She has walked others through this, and she knows. She will not reject you.

Okay. I give all of this pain to You and grief and loss. I'm so very sorry. Thank you for taking this for me.

It is okay, We've got this. In time, you will see the triumph of Our love and you will understand.

Hold me through this please.

We are tenderly caring for you. Do not be afraid.

Brotherhood Property

While traveling on a plane for a recent trip, True FAMILY revealed that the property we were going to be staying on (where our Airbnb was) was owned by the Brotherhood and that I had been there before. God waited until I was on the plane to disclose this to me, otherwise I probably would have backed out. But He had a purpose for me going. When we arrived, I found Albert Pike's book "Morals and Dogma" on the bookshelf over the bed. I also discovered numerous paintings throughout the house depicting the Queen of heaven as well as pedophilic art. This definitely confirmed some things for me.

Here I am True FAMILY. I am so grateful that You keep me through the night and sustain me in the day. I yield all that I am to You and ask for You to walk with me through this day. Show me any areas I need to process through with You. If there is any restoration to be done here, let me know. Is there a basement here? It feels like there is for use when rituals happen here. I submit this to You.

There is, precious Adena. You have authority here, as a survivor and having been here before yourself, to release Our glory here. My blood is more than enough. There are things that you can do that will confound the enemy.

I am willing, please show me. I would love to be able to stop things from continuing, through the power of Your blood.

We will show you. Do not be afraid.

Okay. I am willing. This feels crazy.

Do you believe?

I believe. Help my unbelief.

Gladly. Trust and rest today. Walk the grounds with Us today. Release forgiveness.

Do I need to remember or know anything before I do that or is it better if I don't know?

We will reveal more when you are ready. Let Us show you the way and timing.

Okay. Thank you. Keep me safe. I want to do Your will, True Jesus.

Remember to have the right heart in this. I am not commanding you to do this. I'm inviting you. I do not want you to do this because of "do what the man says" programming. I am inviting you to release My glory and forgiveness as My friend, in relationship, not like a master commanding a slave.

I'm still struggling with that programming.

This is where you get to practice. I am safe and gentle, and I only want you to do this if you want to. If you feel any shred of obligation, then don't.

I don't at the moment. I love to do restoration with You, but yet I feel that for some of my littles, tears are welling up. I don't feel resistance, just pain.

It is good to process this.

They are scared and want to hide. They don't like it here and don't want to go on the grounds alone.

Bad things happen here. We can't go on the grounds without a guard, or we get in trouble. We are afraid. We can't do this. Stay inside and hide. Scared. Very afraid. We hate it here. Slaughter. Babies dashed on rocks. Evil laughter. Pain. Pain. Pain. At the top of the hill. Dedications. Marduk. Evil. Blackness. Can't stand it. Fear. Dread. Pain. More pain. Basement. Darkness. Cool. Hide. When will they get us? Why do I survive, and they don't? Wish I could just die. Always the same. Over and over. Take the knife. Do bad things. Don't want to. Help. Will someone please help me? Where were You, Jesus? Fear. Panic. Dread. I hate this place and those people. We can't forgive.

Okay. I'm glad you let me know. I hope we can work through this this weekend. I am so very sorry for all that happened to you. I didn't know until we were on our way here that this happened here.

True FAMILY is with us and will help us through. You have questions that need answers. True Jesus, where were You?

I was right there with you the whole time and every time. I have never left you or abandoned you. I knew this day would come when We could triumph over them with Our love and set the captives free. This is the joy set before you. You've endured much. We agreed to the triumph of Our love from the beginning, to turn every trauma into triumph. We win, not them.

Why did it have to be so very hard?

I understand. It was hard for Me when I took it all on the cross. The horror of darkness I experienced. I would not ask you to go through anything I had not also experienced. Remember the joy set before helps us endure. We can turn every trauma into the triumph of Our love. That is the bigger picture. But in the present moment these ones need help in facing the pain and emotions. Can you face this with them?

I don't want to, but I know it is the path to healing and restoration. I know it will be worth it. Little ones who experienced this…

We are not so little…

Okay. Those of you who experienced things here, True Jesus is here to help us walk this out. He understands what we went through, and He's experienced it too. He understands. We can trust Him. He is able to turn it all for good. This is His promise. What do you need?

It is really bad. We participated. No one can forgive us. We can't forgive ourselves. Or them. They made us do this. Bad threats. Kill our children. No! Please no! Don't. Can't. Screams. Pain. No!

Okay. True Jesus understands and knows, and He doesn't hate us. He has already forgiven us. I'm so very sorry for what you went through.

Despair. Loathing. We hate ourselves. How could we do such things? We couldn't stop it. Easier to just go along. Numb. Fueling the defilement of the land.

You didn't feel you had a choice back then, but True Jesus is offering us the opportunity to bring restoration to the land through forgiveness and His blood. This is where we get to see the triumph of Their love and the possibilities of restoration. This helps us process these terrible things and have hope. You don't need to stay in despair.

It is better if we just bury this. We wish we hadn't come on this trip. Horror of darkness.

True Jesus can take that horror of darkness away with His glorious light. This is what He desires to do but He won't violate our free will. He invites us gently. This can be a really powerful time. But you get to choose.

I'm not ready. I'm too bad. Can't forgive.

I understand how you feel. Jesus respects your choices. Do you really want to stay stuck here? Do you want to keep carrying this incredible pain? You don't have to. True Jesus already paid for it all on the cross so you could be free. He says, "Let the little ones come." His arms are open wide.

It is a trap. A trick. No one could love us if they knew what we've done.

You shared some with me and I still love you. I am not ashamed of you. I know you only did it because you were forced with the threats. That is not who you are.

Really? How can I believe that?

There is this incredible love that True Jesus has especially for the very broken which is who we are. He cares so deeply for us and for what we've gone through. He has the solutions for it all and invites us to experience His True love that is greater than we can even comprehend.

Bitterness. Hatred. Pain. Despair.

He can take it all. We do not need to carry that anymore. It is all toxic to our spirit, soul and body. True Jesus offers to take it all so we can be free. This is really good news. This horrible place can be transformed into glory, and we can, in a measure, limit or stop what they do here. Wouldn't that be powerful? True Jesus is more powerful than any other being and He has a plan to bring restoration and healing and life to every place the enemy has brought destruction. This is better than revenge. We don't want to act in the same spirit they did, but in something so much better. You are the spokesman for the rest of them. Would you help me help all of them? True Jesus is excited to walk us through this if we are willing. But He won't force us.

Is He truly that good?

Yes, He is.

Okay, I am not sure everyone will want to cooperate, but I will see.

Thank you so much. I'm very grateful for that.

What about what they said would happen if we didn't "bury this forever?"

True Jesus is more powerful than they are and can protect us if we ask Him to.

Yes, please.

Okay. True Jesus is smiling. He cares and is happy to do this.

Okay. Where do we put all of this bad stuff? There's a lot of it.

True Jesus, would You take all of this pain, despair, hopelessness, pain, bitterness, sin, evil, hatred, rage?

Yes, gladly! I died and rose again so I could do this! Thank you all for cooperating! My yoke is easy, and My burden is light. Come and learn of Me. I am gentle and I care. I

understand your pain. I am the resurrection and the life. All the lives you took are safe with Me. They forgive you and I forgive you. Can you forgive yourselves? It is a heavy burden you were not meant to carry.

We want to get rid of it, but we don't know how.

This is why I say "learn of Me." I forgive you freely and completely. Feel My love for you. I do not blame you. I do not condemn you.

But You should! We did bad things.

I know what you did. But it was not your true heart. You did not want to do those things.

But if we'd resisted…

They would have just done it themselves and more. I do not blame you. Can you receive My love?

How can You love us? Maybe tolerate us and put us to work as slaves…

No. There are no slaves like that in My kingdom. Only those who willingly participate with Me in glory.

We aren't good enough.

You don't need to be. It is My righteousness I freely give you.

We do want to be free, but how can this be?

It is possible and it is the true life I have always intended for you. I have longed for this day with great joy. It is My delight to bring you into My glory and love. But I will not force you. This is fully your choice. I won't rescind this offer. It is always good. I am not tricking you or pressuring you.

Can we think about it?

Yes. There is no time limit. If you choose not to participate with Me today or this weekend in restoration, I will not look down on you or despise you. I only want to partner with you in this from your choice for freedom.

Why would You do this?

Because I created you and I deeply love you and I redeemed you from the hand of the enemy. I have already done this. I am patiently waiting for you because I deeply care for you. You are My treasure and My joy.

We don't understand this.

Yes, it really is good, good news. You don't need to understand it or figure it out. You can just receive it. You can try it out and if you decide you want to go back to the old way, you can.

Really?

Yes.

Okay. If you want all this garbage, we will give it to You.

I take it gladly, willingly and with great joy. Doesn't that feel better.

Yes, it does. The torment is gone. How did You do that?

It is what I love to do! This is the triumph of Our love! Isn't it wonderful?

Yes, it is!

This is only a fraction of what I can do. There are more layers. I can take care of it all.

We'll just take it step by step.

Perfect! Now that you feel this, can you forgive yourselves?

It is asking a lot.

It is about your freedom. You will feel even better if you are willing to forgive yourselves as We do.

(Just then, I see an image of dashing a baby on the rocks.)

It is too much.

They forgive you. They are safe with me. Would you like to see them?

Yes, but they must hate us.

No. They don't. They have been praying for you along with all of heaven. We are here for your freedom, not condemnation. We know the truth. We know your true heart. You do not need to carry this heavy burden.

(Babies) We *love you! We forgive you! Be free!*

Really?

(Babies) Yes! We do not want you to hold this against yourselves. We know the truth and we love you.

Okay. Thank you. We will try to forgive ourselves.

It will become easier. Thank you, True Jesus, for this! I am so very grateful. I choose to forgive myself. Is there more processing?

Yes, but not for today. Well done, darling daughter! We are so proud of you!

Thank you for loving me and forgiving me. I still don't understand it, but I choose to receive.

Section XVII

Dreams As Memories

For a survivor, dreams can be memories, or they can be actual or metaphorical representations of things that True FAMILY or parts want to communicate. Writing down our dreams and processing them with True FAMILY and with our parts is key to stewarding the revelations God gives us. Here are a few samples of "Dreams as Memories" from my own life.

On a Mission

I dreamt I was on mission with two other agents, and one was driving us in a big school bus. We accessed the target, a woman. When she got on the bus, the main guy had her drive and then got off the bus. Since I thought we'd done our mission, I wasn't paying attention. Another man was in the passenger's seat. I felt a nudge (from the Lord) to look up and I saw that the woman had fallen asleep at the wheel. I think she was drugged. I was tempted not to pay attention but felt the nudge again and looked ahead. We were coming to a place where there was a curve in the road with a river on the other side. We were headed right for the river. I jumped up and shook her awake and she stopped the bus.

I give this dream scenario to you, True Jesus. Was this a memory?

Are you ready to know?

I don't know, but I am willing. It felt like it.

Yes.

What do I do with this?

Do you want to look at each scene with Us? (There were more scenes, I'm just sharing this one)

Inside, parts are saying no. They are scared.

We are not forcing anything. You can rest.

Yet there is some curiosity from some parts who do want to know. Did You save me in the school bus? Was it You that prompted me? Were they trying to kill me and the others?

Ask inside.

Does anyone inside want to talk about this memory? Did True Jesus nudge us to pay attention?

We were drugged too.

Who was the young blond woman?

She was expendable. It was a set up. They wanted to see how you would react even with the drugs. Testing your skills. They were surprised you were alert early on. They wanted you to use other skills when it was "too late".

Did I hurt anyone?

Yes. You were supposed to.

I'm so sorry.

We're used to it. It happens. We have to. Don't like it, but no other way.

What if there is? I'm learning that there is another way.

Too dangerous, especially for you.

Why do you say that?

You don't know who you are.

I do want to know.

Not supposed to. Keep the secrets. Bury it. You shouldn't be remembering this. It will only get a lot of people in trouble. Stay comatose.

That doesn't sound like life.

It's the only way.

Remember how True Jesus nudged us in the school bus? He saved us that day.

But you could have done it with your powers.

But He was more powerful. They couldn't stop Him from alerting me to danger despite the drugs.

That's true. They were surprised. It caused quite a stir. They were upset, furious.

Can this give you hope that there is a way out into a different life?

I don't know. Not sure. Maybe. Keep talking.

Many other parts are discovering how powerful True Jesus is and have hope. He is also kind and loving and doesn't ask us to do bad things to other people.

Depends on your definition of bad…

True. He does help people get out of the cult. They (people still in the cult) certainly think that is bad, but I've heard many stories of getting out. Those who are out are much happier and peaceful. They are living new lives that they love as they find hope in True Jesus. It would be good if you'd at least consider thinking about this.

Tired. Done.

(The next day, we picked up the same conversation…)

We are here and want you to know that you are Our beloved daughter in whom We are well pleased. Rest in Our love today.

I want to. How do I remember? I felt despair last night until I did some prayers. Keep me steady in Your love.

We will help you remember step by step. You can rest. Your work is to rest in Our love and to pay attention to what We show you and what is surfacing. We will give you what you need when you need it. This is resting and trusting. When you listen and read stuff, you tend to want to hurry up and get there. It is not bad to read and listen as We direct you, but how you receive it is important – from a place of rest. It is all

preparation. Your inside realm is listening and absorbing and processing as you read/listen to faith-filled things. Know that more is happening than you know, and you can rest in Our love. We are the Author and Finisher of your faith, healing, and life. We can do more as you rest and trust in Us and the flow We have for you.

Okay, but when not much is happening, I feel like I should be doing something.

That isn't resting and trusting. Yesterday was significant because of the dream and you did some processing last night. You can ask Us questions if you want to go further.

I wasn't sure. How about working on forgiveness or restoration stuff in light of that dream?

Those are always great things that We love to do with you. Intentionally choosing forgiveness is a beautiful part of the process.

I just don't want to spiritually bypass if I need to feel or remember more.

This is about not trying to figure it out or putting things in an order. If you feel prompted to forgive or want to ask about restoration, you can.

Okay. I want to forgive all those who were part of the school bus set up and release blessings and restoration to all involved. I feel like I need to forgive myself as well for being a part of acquiring the young woman. Is she still alive?

No. She is safe with Me. She is at rest.

I'm sorry for any part I played in that.

Because the set-up didn't work out as they planned, they took it out on her in a ritual.

Was it at my hand?

Yes.

I'm so very sorry. Please forgive me.

You have already been forgiven. Let Us wash the guilt away.

I deserve a lot of punishment for all that I did.

I took that punishment for you already. There is no need. There is just the invitation to rest in Our love as she is.

How can You forgive me?

We knew all about this and how We work all things for good. You did not do this willingly. You were more merciful than others would have been. We were with you and with her each moment. We held you both in love and sorrow and hope.

How can You love me when I did so many bad things?

This is who We are, drawing you all with loving kindness. This is why True Jesus died to redeem and restore. This is love.

I choose to receive it even though I don't understand it.

That's Our girl! We love you so tenderly through this. Don't be discouraged.

Would she have been spared if You hadn't alerted me?

No. She would have died anyway.

Okay. I give this to You. I am so sorry.

We know. We see your heart.

I don't want those skills. Can you erase them?

We can work with you to dismantle the demonic as well as the structures used so that door can be closed. It is a process.

I want the bad stuff and the incentive/rewards "good" stuff to go as well. I repent and renounce using them. Please wash me and cleanse me of every defilement. I don't want this anymore, in any way, shape, or form. Please hold all of this safely until we can deal with it.

Yes, darling daughter. We are delighted to do this for you and to walk you through this as you are able.

I'm really sad about the girl. I have tears but I am not in a private place, so I can't fully release it. I give this to you to hold. I'm so sorry.

We've got this, too.

Decoy Suitcase and Drugging

I dream that we are in a very large house with other people. We'd stayed overnight. I woke up early but can't find my suitcase. It's a large silver suitcase. I slept in a large common room used by others. There are other suitcases there, even other small silver ones, but not mine. I will sometimes see a suitcase that looks like it but when I get close to it, it is not. I'm embarrassed as I see others and I'm obviously wearing yesterday's clothes. I mentioned to a few people that I can't find my suitcase, and some tried to help me find it, but we are not successful. Some of us gather at the table and I think we are going to have breakfast, but then I realize it is 3am and I wonder why we are up so early. There is food available. I go over and cut some of the food up on the plate. Then I realize no one else seems interested in eating and it's not appropriate for me to do this. I walked away.

One woman sees me do this and she thinks I'm doing something good with the food. I'm still trying to find my suitcase and I'm starting to get desperate. One woman realizes I'm one of the speakers and is honoring me, but I'm embarrassed because I have not showered, and I am still dressed in yesterday's clothes. She shows me the program with my name and picture on it, along with others. It is me, but I don't recognize the picture. There are kids around too and one man in particular is working with them. He also seems to be the leader here. I don't understand how my suitcase could just disappear. It is a very frustrating dream. True Jesus, I give this to You. I'm so very sorry I don't have my suitcase. Can You tell me about this dream?

Can you trust Us?

Okay, I give this dream to You. You are my Provider, and You can supply whatever I lack. I don't like that creepy place.

What do you feel like?

It feels like part of the system. It felt like magick was involved too. Also, I was awake in the night before the dream (3am) and I felt good, but then after waking up from the dream, I felt sluggish and almost drugged. I'm having a hard time getting up and moving. I don't like this feeling. What is going on?

There's more to this dream than you know.

Why do I feel so out of it?

You were drugged.

How? Why? When?

You will have the details and remember when it is time. For now, give this to Us and trust and rest.

Why do I feel so yucky inside?

The suitcase is the decoy to not know what is really going on.

Oh. So, what does that mean?

Ask inside.

We don't like that place! Bad things happen there. Bad things. Get away. (There is a brief pain in the back of my head).

True Jesus, please help me.

We are here and We will help you recover.

I want to die. The frustration of the suitcase is easier than the truth.

You desire truth in the inward parts.

Yes, I do. I am grateful and it is hard. Please help me.

We are here. Invite these ones to the Lion of Judah. He is here.

Hey everyone, there is a safe place with the Lion of Judah. He is safe and comforting. He can help us feel better after that dream.

We hate that place. They hurt us there.

But you were a leader too?

We had to. No choice. They know our gifts. Can't resist. We are special.

What if there's another way? Try the Lion of Judah and see if you can get relief from the bad stuff.

Okay.

Thank you for helping me, True FAMILY. I choose You today. Show me the way.

We are so very proud of you.

But I couldn't find the dumb suitcase.

It isn't about the suitcase. Focus on what it is about. Keep your eyes fixed on Us. There are many opportunities to drift. Stay focused on Us. There is a way through.

Okay. Thank you. I still feel very drugged. I want to go back to sleep.

Move around and drink some water. It will help.

Can't I just go back to sleep?

No. Focus on moving around. Drink some water.

I don't want to. Why am I resisting?

You feel the pull to sleep. It is more than natural sleep. Get up and move around and drink some water. You will feel better.

Okay. Who inside keeps saying, "I don't want to live?"

(Several say, *"Me!")*

I am here to listen. What's going on? I want to help.

You can't. It is too late.

Why is it too late?

Nothing can be done. We are hopeless. Too bad. No choice but to die. Too painful to live. Mean. Bad. Stuff. Just escape. So much easier.

I feel the pull, especially with the drugged felling. It is better since I got up and walked around and drank water, but still feel the pull to death. Why?

It is what they want. Circling. Circling. Waiting to devour.

(I see tigers circling.)

If these are entities, True Jesus can handle them.

No, they keep us in line. We would be really bad if they didn't.

I think there is a better way.

Scared. Frightened. Cowering. They are too strong for us. Have to do what they say even if we don't like it.

I know that True Jesus is stronger. He can help us. True Jesus, can You clear my head? Are these parts or entities or both?

Both.

True Jesus, please separate my humanity from these entities. Can You also speak the truth to my parts. Let them know that You care and there is a better way. I just want to go to sleep.

Stay awake with Me. I've got this. More is going on than you know.

Please help me. I want to stay present.

Remember who you are.

I want to give up and just slip away. It would be so much easier. The tigers are mesmerizing. Just give up.

Keep focused on Us, Adena. We are here. This is a place to overcome. Do not look at the tigers but at Us. We are holding you gently, tenderly, and We care. Life is worth living. Wake up.

I'm trying but it is so hard. Where are You? Can't You do something? I want You to. Please help me. Why is this so hard?

There are multiple layers inside and out.

See, this is why I shouldn't be in ministry. I can't. I'm too messed up. I just want to die and slip away forever into nothingness.

Stay present, Adena. We are here. There is so much worth living for. You know the call on your life. You know why We created you.

But I can't make it. This is too hard. I'm drowning. Sinking. I'm afraid. I can't do this anymore.

Help is here. Your journey is unique. We've called you for such at time as this. You've agreed to this journey.

Why did I? It was dumb. I want to die.

Stay steady in Our love. We know the battle is fierce, but you are fighting. Ask all of your parts to testify. It will help you in this.

Is there anyone who wants to testify to the goodness of God?

Yes, it is worth the fight. We are glad.

We can get through with True FAMILY. They are kind to us. They don't hurt us.

We see the struggle but believe that True Jesus can get us through.

We can do this with True FAMILY.

Thank you for encouraging me. I choose Your way, True Family. It feels a little better. The heaviness is lifting a little. Thank you.

We are so proud of you! You are an overcomer. We have called you to bless so many. Do not be afraid.

I choose to resist the cult system and all it represents. I choose the joy of the Lord. I choose You, True FAMILY. I trust You to help me through. I still want to sleep.

This is not a normal thing. It is important that you resist this as well.

Why is it so hard?

They do want to re-access, but you can resist it.

Why won't You do it for me?

It is important for you to develop strength of will to resist when they try this, especially with the drugs/magick. You can rule over this as We give you strength.

I've not felt a pull like this before.

Nor will it be the last, but each time you resist, you are building strength as an overcomer. This is strength training.

I don't like it. I just want to sleep. But I am waking up a little bit more. Thank you. Wow! This is hard. Please help me, True Jesus.

We are here and proud of you. Keep resisting until this is completely over. There is more going on than you know.

I give all of this to You. Thank you for helping me through.

Section XVIII

Dissociation

As mentioned earlier, dissociation is a way to cope with overwhelming trauma. It is the way we survived. There is no condemnation in this. BUT now we get to learn a new way of operating with True FAMILY towards wholeness. It is not easy, but it is well worth it.

The Dissociation Room

What about these parts that want to run away? How do I help them?

Listen and love. Ask them why.

Dearest ones, why do you want to run away?

The pain is too great. We don't want to remember. It was really bad. They are really bad. They did horrible things to us. We had no choice. We didn't like it. It hurt really bad. They stuck things in us. Needles and penises. Yuck! No more! We are very angry. We don't want anyone to touch us.

I'm so very sorry for what happened to you. There is hope and healing with the True FAMILY who won't hurt us. They won't stick anything into us. They pour out Their love and They give us options and choices. They do not force us.

We feel safest if we are isolated from all others. We've sectioned off this space to be safe. We don't like boys. They are bad. They stink. They hurt us. Boys are bad. They killed the girls. Bad man. Bad man. Bad man. He got us. He won't let us go. We are tied up around our necks. We can't breathe. We have to do what they say no matter what. We can't get away. We hate them. Bad boys. They do bad things. They cut us. We bleed. We bleed some more. They do bad things. We hurt bad. We can't move. They will find us. We hate them. We are paralyzed by fear. We don't like needles and drugs. It makes us crazy and do bad things. We don't want the spinning wheel. Of fortune. They tease us. They lie to us. We don't like this. We want to run away.

You are not on the wheel anymore. We are safe with the True FAMILY. They will help us to recover from what was done to us and even more. This is really good news.

But is Jesus a boy?

Yes, He came as male. However, He is loving and gentle and never forces us. He doesn't do sexual things to us. He doesn't do sex magick. Neither does True Father or True Holy Spirit.

We don't trust anyone anymore. We can't. It is too hard.

I understand. The ones who should have been your protectors weren't there. But now we get to experience all the protection available through True FAMILY, which is more than enough. Nothing is impossible. And we get to take back what the enemy has taken from us. How does that feel?

We are afraid to hope. Things have been too bad. They did bad things.

I'm so sorry that I suppressed you and your memories. I am good with hearing what you have to say and for True FAMILY to help us through this. Together we can do this. We don't need to be stuck anymore or to desire to run away. We can stay right where we are because True FAMILY is keeping us safe. Is that okay?

We can try it, but not sure. Can we just stay in the room?

What is in the room?

Just a TV screen.

This is probably the disassociation room. I know it feels better than facing things, but it won't bring any healing. You always have a choice.

It's better than the programming room.

Yes, but you are still close to it and there is not full protection from what is in the programming room. When you come into where True FAMILY is, you have more protection and safety and love and its lots of fun. I know dissociation and programming feel good in the moment or better than the pain, but it won't heal you. Do you want to be healed?

Yes, we do. But it is really hard. Can we crack the door open?

Yes, you can. You can let True Jesus into the Dissociation room too. Or do you feel more comfortable with Holy Spirit?

Holy Spirit. Can we suck our thumb? They won't let us do that.

Yes, you may. Holy Spirit is here. She is willing to hold you if you are willing.

Will She hold us while we are watching the screen?

Yes, She can do that.

Okay. We'd like that for now. No more. This is enough.

Yes, beautiful. Just know there is much more to explore. True FAMILY, help all of me to receive Your love.

We are here for every part of you, including in the programming room. These are not off limits. They simply are open doors to more harm than good.

How do we close them?

It will take time and process. Be patient. Remember these places and parts were developed for survival over time. It will take time to deconstruct all these things. You are safe and whole in Us always, and there are places to explore in Us.

I say yes, True FAMILY, to all that You are doing. Thank you so much!

It is Our joy! All things are possible, dearest Adena. Receive Our love today without measure. Come to the ocean of Our love.

True and Counterfeit Shalom

Teach me about Shalom.

It is more than you know and is a being whom you can engage with. But be aware, there are counterfeits as well. Those shalom beings who have fallen corrupt are counterfeit shalom, giving false peace and false rest. Be aware of their presence and why it is different from true shalom. Feel the frequency difference.

Okay, thank you. Anyone inside connected to false shalom?

Yes. They keep us safe and dead.

That doesn't sound good. True Jesus is here to give us life and true peace, true shalom.

It is easier to be dead and didn't Jesus say to die daily? We are just following this shalom.

It is a twisting of that Scripture. He is not saying for us to connect with death like that. He is the way, the truth, and the life. I would like to get rid of all false shaloms. We don't need them anymore.

That's what you think. We need them. They keep us docile and passive until we are needed to fight.

That doesn't sound good. There is a different way to do things.

Not interested. We just want to bliss out with this shalom.

Even if it isn't true?

Fantasy is good. We don't want to face reality. You don't either.

Yes, I know that it is not easy to face the truth about what happened and what is happening, but I am learning and growing with the True FAMILY. We are learning to do things differently.

Yes, we've noticed, but not ready.

Okay. Just know that I am ready to face this when you are.

We just want to sleep longer. Bliss out.

I hear you. I honor this coping mechanism that has worked for you. Just know that there are other ways to do things, too, that can be more beneficial.

We don't want to try anything new. Too hard.

True Jesus can make it easier for you.

Oblivion is better.

Oblivion is not your friend. You are missing out on things because of it.

To each his own.

True FAMILY, can You help these ones? Help them to see that Your way is better…

Yes, We are doing this over time, gently in love. Be patient with yourself. You have some new information.

I am trusting You today with this. I can't do anything.

Yes, partner with Us in rest and it will come.

Okay.

Our Cages

…We like cages. We feel safer in them. We curl away in the corner and hope they don't notice us. We don't want to draw attention to ourselves. We like cages. We feel safe in them. It is better than outside where bad things happen. It is scary, but it is better than outside. We like to hide away. We don't want

to be seen. We don't want them to see us or to find us. If we are really quiet and don't breathe, maybe they won't see. It is better this way. We can fade away. It is okay to die. Just die. Nobody cares, anyway. Last breath. We don't exist. Gone forever. Forgotten for good. Please put me in the cage so I can go away forever. Buried. Gone. No more. At last. Thank you. Death feels good.

True Jesus, I don't know what to do with this. Can You help me?

Yes, We are here, and We care. She is not forgotten. Many "deaths" in many cages. It is time for rescue.

But she likes it there.

That doesn't mean she needs to stay there.

But it is very scary. She is very scared. Life is too hard. Death is easier. She wants death. Oblivion.

Can you face her secret wish?

Not right now… maybe with Jo.

Okay.

Forgetting

Listening to some of Svali's previous interviews on a podcast. I don't remember most of it. This is similar to how I "forget" movies, some more than others. I don't like this. Why does this happen?

It is about parts programmed to not remember things. You have a lot of it going on in many different arenas, but hidden enough so it is less noticeable, especially to others. This is increasing as they are running "blank" programs.

I don't mean this but…I almost would like a complete blank for everything.

It wouldn't change what was and is and it would erase the destiny We have for you.

I know, but it would be a whole lot easier.

Not really. I know it seems that way, but We have the true path of safety and overcoming for you. It is worth it.

I know that in my head, but everything inside is screaming, "Run! Blank out!" …. but I know You know my true heart and I want to stay here with You, no matter how hard this is. Please help me.

We are here and will help you to remember who you really are.

Facing Lockdown

You are on lockdown to survive.

I've tried not to be.

It's not full lockdown and there is no condemnation. You could not fully survive this without it.

But if I fully trusted You, I could.

It is like asking a 2-year-old to drive. I did not expect that of you, although you expect it of yourself.

I tried really hard.

We know. But it is about relationship, not trying hard.

I can't get it right.

Yes, you aren't meant to get it perfect. It is okay to make mistakes and to not have it all figured out. You can rest in Our love and Our right-eousness. Remember this. We cover you on this journey.

I couldn't fix it.

Yes. You weren't meant to. Only We can work it all for good as you trust Us.

I want to die. I failed.

I died so you could live. There is only ONE perfect sacrifice. It is not you. Can you rest in Our love?

I want to.

It is good to acknowledge how you and your parts feel. Bring everything into the light for healing.

I wanted a way of escape, but I didn't know it would be this hard. Yet, I know You've made it easy in some ways as You've walked me step by step. But then it is also confusing. Did I make all this up? Maybe my memories are fake. False. Maybe I'm just really deceived.

Would Jo lie to you?

I don't think so. She has been honest with me.

She experienced righteous suffering when reading your journal. You felt it was to help you know this is real.

Yes.

Can you believe that?

Yes, but…

Remember all the other confirmations. You are not making this up. There is much more that has gone on than you know. We have brought you on this journey of love to show you who you really are and to bring you out of darkness into Our marvelous light. We do this gradually. You are making such beautiful progress.

But I make mistakes. I'm so sorry.

We can help you through each one and use them as a springboard to success in Our love. We work it all for good when you trust Us. You are learning keys and tools that you are sharing with others. Remember who you are.

Will you forgive me?

We have, even before you ask. It is a done deal. There is no condemnation in True Jesus.

But I deserve to be punished. I don't even know it all, but You know the depths of it. You know every life I took. I'm brokenhearted. Shattered. Fragmented. Too many pieces.

It is not impossible. We love the work of restoration. We are not ashamed of you. Paul called himself the chief of sinners and yet walked boldly in his calling. This is what we've called you to. Don't be ashamed of your journey, known and knowing.

You are too wonderful for me.

It is Our joy and delight to demonstrate Our great love through you. You can go on all night about your sin and unworthiness, and We will keep on sharing Our love for you and plans for restoration. Bring everything into the light.

I can't.

We can help you.

They will pursue me.

Can you trust Us for a way through? Remember Our plans we showed you in the session with Jo.

Will You really keep me safe?

"Now until Him who is able to keep you from falling and to present you faultless before the presence of His glory with exceeding joy…" (Jude 24) Do you believe it? We are able.

I want to. I want to bring You exceeding joy. I give You my doubts and confusion. My fears. My uncertainties. I take ahold of You. Hold me. Help me. Keep me safe in Your arms of love. Please show me what to do.

Gladly with great joy.

The Great Wall

Inner realm, how is everyone doing?

We miss you, Adena. Many of us are doing well, but others are not. There are things stirring. Strange dreams.

I am so very sorry. I want to be more attentive and to help with connecting you to True FAMILY. But it is hard right now. Please forgive me.

We do. We are here.

I acknowledge that and I honor you. Do not be afraid. I know True FAMILY is good and They will help all of us come to wholeness. Is there anyone who has something specific you want to share this morning?

Lots of bad things we haven't shared yet.

What keeps you from sharing?

Big wall. Big wall. Big wall.

True FAMILY, do You see the big wall?

Yes, We do. It is there from the enemy so you would not remember.

How do I bring this wall down and should it come down?

When it comes down, there will be much happening, and the time is not yet. If it comes down too fast, there can be some damage to littles and to you. We see and know this. It is crumbling a little in places. It will come down. We have the right timing, and the enemy cannot stand against Us. The book you are reading does have some keys, but it shows the people being very scared and afraid. You do not need to be afraid.

Is anyone else afraid?

Yes, we are terrified. We know some of what is there, and it is really bad.

Thank you for sharing. We are going to give this wall to the True FAMILY to manage. They know how to bring it down gently so that we are not harmed. We are safe and secure in Their love, and we can trust Them. We do not need to be afraid. Is that okay?

Yes, we are grateful, but we are hurting because of it. Some of us are under the wall.

I am so very sorry. True FAMILY, what do we do with some who are under the wall?

We are ministering love to them as We speak. We are tending to their needs even while they are in this position. It is okay. This is why it cannot come down quickly because of where they are. It must be done gently so they are not harmed. The crushing weight of this is a burden to them, but We are here for them.

Can they be extracted?

They can but it is not an instant thing. You are now aware of them. This is progress. Do you trust Us?

I trust You.

We will accomplish this. The wall will come down, but gently so that none are harmed.

I entrust them to Your care. I see parts in the wall who are facing up and also down. Parts in the wall, I honor you and I am here to let you know True FAMILY have plans for a rescue. Be patient and trust Them and Their love for you. It is coming.

We will die if you bring the wall down.

That is why I am leaving it with True FAMILY. I know that They have a way of extracting you that will lead to life.

They say if we come out of the wall, we will all die. We don't want you to die. We will take our punishment.

Punishment is not with the True FAMILY. There are consequences to our choices, but They do not punish us.

But the system does. And we punish ourselves. We know this. We've heard about it.

You can receive love and freedom even where you are. True Family honors you. You are not being punished.

We are here to help you out, Adena. We must remain otherwise there would be a complete breakdown and everyone would die.

I know this is what you've been told. However, it is not true. True FAMILY can provide freedom and love.

Oblivion

The water was not blue.

Yes, because it is not in the same dimension. You slipped between and into this one.

What do I do with this? Can I work through this now or with Jo this week?

Do you trust Us?

I am choosing to trust You.

Then look around you.

She (a part) has her eyes closed. She is falling (sinking) slowly. I don't see anything else.

Wait and watch.

Are You with me?

Yes, We are here. You are safe with Us.

Is there a bottom to this place?

Not like you think.

I don't understand.

You don't need to. Rest and trust in Us.

Is this Oblivion?

A form of it. There is trading here. She doesn't have to feel or know things here. She can trade it for Oblivion. Release. They feed off of it.

I see them now. Hideous, swirling around her. She thinks she is alone, but she isn't.

Yes. That is the deception. This is where the unburdening happens. Then she can enter in.

She is let in and is given something in a bowl to drink. It is red. I don't want to think about that.

It is okay. Stay steady in Our love.

She is given things here. She can rule here. It is cold and heartless. There is no love here.

She doesn't know that. You can see the truth because you've asked for it.

Why can't she see how hideous they are?

She sees it very differently. This is a refuge for her. She sees adoring fans, bowing and worshipping, not the revealed trickery you see.

She is so deceived. (I suddenly experience a pain in my head, in the upper left corner…)

Yes, We can help her. But she will have to wake up.

She will be distressed to see them as they are and what they are doing to her.

Yes. We are here.

Is this the time for her to see?

You get to choose. It will not be easy.

I desire Truth in the inward parts.

Underwater earthquake. Terror and pain. No more Oblivion. Darkness swirling. Vicious. Pain. Jesus, come rescue!

I will always answer this prayer.

She seems lifeless and the bites are bad. Infected. Pain. Terror. What can You do?

There is healing, but not in this realm. I can take her to a safe place.

Yes, I repent on behalf of myself, my parts, and my family bloodline and all associated bloodlines for accepting this place as a way of coping with the pain and trauma and receiving worship while being devoured. I am asking for Your blood, True Jesus, to thoroughly destroy all agreements, covenants, contracts, oaths and vows, rituals, dedications and baptisms related to under the sea and every demon and fallen being, principality and power connected to it. I renounce and relinquish all titles, offices, crowns, scepters, authority, privilege or anything else, including gifts given here. I am asking for the power of Your restoration, True Jesus, to come into this place and into this part of me. I want to be free of this and to face what I need to.

She's still stuck. What do I do, True Jesus? Please clear this trading floor. Please set me free.

He who the Son sets free is free indeed. I have called you out of darkness into My marvelous light. See it?

Yes, I can. Thank you. She is not in good shape. Can You help her?

Gladly.

That was quite awful. Thank you for bringing truth and setting me free. I don't want to trade in those waters. Is there anything remaining?

This is a process. Go with Us step by step. We are here.

She doesn't want to face Truth. She wants to sleep.

Yes, and that would not be safe at this point. She can rest, but the temptation is to the other Oblivion in the sky.

Do I have to go there today?

No, you aren't ready.

Will you keep me and all this safe until I am?

Yes, gladly.

Why is it so much?

You were trafficked in all places – above, on, and below. You know this.

Yes, but I don't like to look at it. Can't it be simpler? Can't it just be "taken care of?"

There is simplicity in just taking Our hand and walking it out step by step. You don't need to understand it. There were many dimensions that you could operate in. The enemy exploited this but see how We have plans for restoration. Remember that wherever you have been, We have given you authority over. This means that as you walk out healing, there are many ways for exponential restoration and many to be set free. This is the joy We've set before you. Do not be discouraged by what you saw today but trust Us as We take you step by step.

I believe You. Yet it seems so crazy and maybe I just made all this up.

Take Our hand. Don't try to figure it out. Trust and rest.

Okay. I am grateful. Thank you. How does she rest not sleep?

We have sent many true guardians to watch over her and to keep her from sliding into the other Oblivion. She is safe for now.

Thank you.

Too Much Attention

There are so many reaching out to you in love. You are uncomfortable to receive it.

I don't like the focus on me and would prefer to hide. I don't like this much attention.

Go a little deeper.

Attention is bad. I don't want attention. It hurts and leads to bad things. Don't see me. Don't know me. I'm invisible. I want to be, at least. Keep the focus somewhere else. Oblivion.

This time around, we aren't going to go to Oblivion.

Good choice. You can stay steady in Our love and stay present instead of going there to hide. That was your coping skill, especially in the really hard times with high elite. It was the only way you were able to get through. It was also how you dealt with attention. Learning to stay present and to receive being seen, heard, and known in a healthy way is important in this season. People delight to be with you and to give.

Why?

Because of who We are in you. This is Our grace to you.

Just want to hide. Oblivion. I don't like the attention.

Do you want to overcome this and step into the fullness of your destiny?

Yes, but I can't face it right now. Too many things.

Do you trust Us with what you can handle each day?

Okay. I want to stop running and face truth.

That's the start.

I had attention. Was "special." Resulted in lots of pain and darkness. Attention is bad.

Then you don't want attunement? (To be seen, known, heard and understood) That is part of attention.

I know it is necessary and the way we are created. Yes, I want to be attuned to, but…being seen is dangerous. Hiding is better.

Hiding leads to death. Being seen and known in love brings life.

I want to choose life, but…death is so appealing.

Where is that coming from?

Despair. I can't handle this. It is overwhelming.

Can you trust Us?

Can You stop saying that? It is too dangerous. Hiding is best, safest. Go away, everyone! No one is safe. Hide. Die. Slip away. Can't face life. Despair. Pain. Loss. Trouble. Forget it all in Oblivion.

Stay present, precious Adena. We are here.

I can't.

See where that is coming from.

I don't want to. I want to be blind to it all. Can't see. Can't feel. Oblivion. No one can get me here.

Remember the picture? That is an illusion. When you go into Oblivion, they devour you.

Not true. Don't remember. Forget.

Help me, True Jesus!

You've seen what Oblivion really is. When you can face things in the light of Our Love, there is freedom and love like you've never known.

Too risky.

You want to continue to be devoured?

Well, no. but…

You can always choose Oblivion, but it leads to death and destruction.

I want to embrace death.

Where is that coming from?

See how bad I am? I can't do anything right.

We are here. You can choose to be seen and known by Us or not.

I do want it, but death is easier.

Facing life in love is more powerful than death and is the true desire of your heart. What is coming up is some deep pain and fear. You can face this and overcome.

I don't want to.

Are you a guardian?

Yes.

What's your role?

To keep Adena in Oblivion. She isn't cooperating but we want her back. She needs Oblivion.

Did you see that the other day? Oblivion is not a safe place, but a place of trades and devouring. We don't want that.

Bad things happen if we don't obey.

I know it seems that way, but we are learning to trust in True Jesus for help and protection that is clean and doesn't involve horrific torture.

But we can get lost in the torture. We can go to Oblivion for safety.

I know that it seems safe because you are deceived into thinking that, but really it is a horrible place of pain.

Pain is good. We need it to protect us.

This doesn't make much sense since you go to Oblivion to "escape" pain and get more torture. Why would torture be good?

Because we can get a way to Oblivion.

Is Oblivion also an entity?

Yes.

I come out of agreement with these things. I repent on behalf of myself and my bloodline and all associated bloodlines for believing the lie that Oblivion is a place of safety. Please cleanse me and wash me in Your blood, True Jesus. I want to be free of death and oblivion. I renounce them and its hold on my life. I choose life and love in True Jesus. I choose to stay present and steady in Your love and to remember who I am. Thank you, True FAMILY.

There is more, but you can go back to sleep and rest in Our love, not Oblivion. Stand up against the draw to that place.

Thank you that I got a little more sleep… I am trusting You today for strength and rest. I really need help.

We are here and will help you.

I want to be completely free.

Yes, they want you to have the illusion of being "free" while still having some level of control. Remember, there is a line they cannot cross. Take courage with this and choose boldness.

Yes, You said I would have to walk this out publicly and I don't like that. I see now more and more why – this attention means death. How do I handle this? How do I overcome?

Step by step with Us. This won't be cured overnight. We know the vulnerability you feel, but it is an opportunity to press into Our heart and love for you. We are able to protect you. We are able to provide for you. Can you receive it?

We always come back to this, right? Help me to answer all the responses (i.e. emails people have sent me lately). They are all kind and caring and I am grateful for their love, but it is scary and frightening inside.

I don't like it. I want to run away. Everyone, please leave me alone!

Let Us comfort those terrified parts.

I can't stand this! I want to die. Oblivion, here I come.

No! Let's stay present with True FAMILY. Let's not go there. Remember what happens there. It is trickery.

But it is so nice to blank out. To pretend. We like it. It helps us cope.

We are choosing to trust True FAMILY instead of Oblivion. They can help us through this without getting consumed by the entities in Oblivion. You saw it. It is not a pretty picture.

But it feels good at least for a time.

I understand. I know this is hard. We can make it with True FAMILY and Jo will help us.

She probably hates us because we can't "get it together."

No, I don't think so. Bu you can ask her tomorrow if you want.

It's dumb.

She will understand.

We don't want anybody. Nobody is safe. Everyone leaves and betrays. We hate them all.

I hear you and, from what we've experienced, I understand. And we get to work towards freedom with True FAMILY. They have solutions to all the things we are facing.

It's not possible.

True FAMILY, I don't want to keep cycling.

Is that impatience?

It just seems a waste of time.

What your parts need is attunement and patience and love. There are ways to diminish cycling, but you also don't want to spiritually bypass. Your impatience will actually slow things down. You are going through a lot and your inner realm is feeling a lot. You are suppressing a lot of it and that is why parts want to escape to Oblivion. As you can face this in love, more pressure will come off and you will experience more freedom. We are very patient with you and so is Jo. You can rest and be and write what comes without editing.

I'm not editing!

Where is that coming from?

I'm trying my best!

Is it about your efforts?

No, but I have to do something.

The main tasks for you are to receive Our love and to trust Us. This is why We say this so often.

Okay. I give all of this to You. I choose Your way. I choose to receive Your love and rest and trust in You.

Thank you, precious Adena. Be gentle with yourself. We love and care. So does Jo.

I don't want her to. I'm bad. I want to hide, run away. Scream and vanish. Die. I don't want anyone to care for me. I don't want anyone to love me. I don't deserve it. Ever. I can't make up for it, so it is hopeless. Can I ask You to kill me like Moses did? Or curse the day I was born like Job?

My children have suffered and feel deeply. We recorded their accounts in Scripture so that you would know you are not alone in these struggles.

I need to be alone. Isolated. Away from everyone so I don't hurt anyone. I can't do life anymore. I don't want to live. I hate this.

Your feelings are real and understandable. We do not condemn them. Neither does Jo. She knows and understands and cares. You can't change that. You can't prevent people from caring for you.

But if I disappear or die, then that will take care of it. I could run away.

Yes, you can do that, but it would not change people caring for you and it would cause them great grief because you are deeply loved by many.

I can't handle it.

That's right, but We can help you through. Remember who you are, and the joy set before you. We understand this deep despair and We can carry you through it.

I'm fragile right now.

We know. It is okay to be fragile. It is okay to need.

NO! We can't.

True FAMILY, You know I have a lot to do this morning, and I have to move on. I want to stay in the light of Your love. I am asking for You to minister to all these ones and all this brokenness. I can't do this day without You. Please help me.

Gladly! We wrap you in Our arms and We carry you through this day. Know that We are with you and can supply all that you need as you can receive it.

Okay, thank you.

Done with Life

Remember why you spent most of the time in your room as a child. You felt safest alone.

Do we have to go there?

No. You can when you are ready.

I hate life.

We understand. There is a way through.

Yeah, yeah remember the joy set before. Don't You get sick of this?

No, We don't tire of speaking truth to you.

Because I need it. I don't want to need anything.

There's lots of anger here.

Yes, this is too complicated and takes too long and we can't do it. You expect too much of us. Just leave us alone. We hate you. No place safe. Die.

It is not a game. Recognize Reckless.

I want to do intentional harm.

What will that accomplish?

Get some rage out.

Yes, there is a lot of it. There are healthy ways to do that.

I can't.

You have a choice.

I want to hurt others so they will go away.

Do you really?

No, but I feel it. Everyone, go away. I can't stand it. Leave me. Leave me alone. I hate you. I don't need you. I'm fine by myself. I should go away. Disappear. No more pain. Oblivion.

You can step back from the edge. You can make another choice. We love you.

I don't want You to love me. Love hurts. It is too painful. Everyone leaves. No one cares.

You know the truth.

But this is what it feels like.

Yes, it does feel this way. It is okay to acknowledge it. Just be aware of where it can take you.

You bet I want to self-harm. It's the only way. Suffering. Loss. Pain. This is my life.

There is another way.

I can't find it. It's too hard. I want to give up.

You can. Yet, how many people would that devastate?

Why can't I just be isolated and alone and not affect anyone else?

That is not how We created you. You are created for relationships.

I know, but it doesn't work. I want to die. I should die. I don't want Your love. Let me go into Oblivion. I don't want to talk to anyone.

There's a lot of pain here.

You bet.

You don't have to carry all of that. There is a better way. True FAMILY cares and has a way through. I know it is repetitive but that doesn't mean it isn't true. I am sorry for all the pain. I am willing to hear about it when you are ready.

Go away.

Okay. True FAMILY, can You help this precious one? I am so sorry for all the pain she carries. I know she is a key in this season.

Yes, We will attend to her as much as she is able to receive. We will carry you through. Stay steady in Our love.

This was the most vocal she has been in a while.

It is good to bring it into the light. Don't be discouraged by this. Stay steady in Our love.

Okay. Thank you.

We are here and We are a fire of love all around you. Our glory is in your midst – that means in you and your parts! This is the hour for great deliverance if you choose. Do not be afraid of this. You can face this. We will help you.

Later….

There is a beautiful place of attentiveness and trust, not hypervigilance and oblivion.

I can't find that. I only know hypervigilance and oblivion.

We are happy to help you. It is okay.

It's too hard. It feels overwhelming. Hypervigilance and oblivion are easier.

But remember what is really going on. True ease is when you trust and rest with awareness. This is relational. Hypervigilance and oblivion are not relational. Relational is easier.

Relational is scary and hurts.

We can help you heal the deep hurts. Rest and trust.

Ocean of Pain

I don't know how to process stuff or what self-care looks like. Reading the book "Women, Food and God." Although it is not a Christian book, I appreciate the insights. What am I running from? How do I stay present? How do I face pain? But the question is what pain? In one sense, I have a great life… even with all that is going on. I love what I do. I am well-loved in our community. Life is good and fulfilling. And yet these things that surface… That's what makes it hard to believe. The amnesia denial programming is so thick and deep and wide. If I just focus on the now, the "present," then I'm enjoying time with dear friends and life is good. Some things are hard, but mostly I'm happy. If I don't listen inside, it's really pretty good. I'm good at blocking things out. It's easy. No pain. But I know it is not really true, and it is not healthy. So how do I look at this? True FAMILY, I need You. I do desire TRUTH in the inward parts. I don't want to live amnesic to those that cause pain and whatever else is there. Please help me, True Jesus. Is it real?

Being fully alive is worth the fight to remember.

I feel fully alive.

Remember the illusions We've shown you recently. They want you to feel alive, so you don't remember.

Does this mean all my relationships are an illusion?

No. They are genuine and you are doing wonderful things partnering with Us. *And* there is another reality that is equally real that they (the cult) don't want you to know about. With both sides open and healing, We get to do amazing things together. It is "the joy set before you."

The pull is strong. Things are good. Why focus on this other?

You would miss the best We have for you. Sometimes this is the hardest temptation. You can avoid the pain and focus on

the good. Others have chosen that. This helps you to have compassion for them.

Ah, so if I do the same, they still have me in their control?

Yes. It takes courage when things are good to face the pain when you can avoid it.

Okay, but that barrier is so damn thick. I don't know how or what to do.

You don't need to. Remember this is Our work. Your part is to just put your hand in Ours….

Right, right… Alice in Wonderland. Pain and darkness. Forget. Forget to remember. I can't. Pain. Torture. Death. Will I ever have actual memories or just these feelings and thoughts?

They will come. Be patient with yourself. Trust Us for this journey.

I hate Alice. She's so dumb. I hate the movie. I hate her. I hate the whole thing. Just fix it! If You are so powerful, just fix it.

I can fully restore you. I could do it instantly. You would skip all of the keys for helping others and miss the relational aspects. And the reward. As well as the destiny We have for you.

I DON'T CARE!

Deep down, We know you do. We know your true heart. We know the desires of your heart. This is pain talking, desperate to avoid facing what seems impossible. You can always choose that path. We will still love you. But We know what We created you for and how you will be most fulfilled.

There's just rage and pain, like an inferno. I can't control it. So, I give it away.

You thought that was the only way, but they use that rage inferno for their purposes. They offered you amnesia in exchange. There is no condemnation. It is how you survived.

But now it is keeping you from all that We have for you. You get to choose.

Do I start by repenting, or do I need to ask parts?

Ask inside.

I am so very sorry for the pain and rage you experienced. I know you thought the only way was to give it away, but they tricked us and used it for their purposes to hurt others and do bad things. We can do things differently now.

You are trying to hurt us. We are happy to be oblivious. Isolation is a blessing. Bliss.

It isn't real.

Who says?

There is a better way that brings life.

Just leave us alone.

Alone is the right word. Even though you have love all around you, you can't fully experience it, because you can blank it out at any time. This isn't the way True FAMILY has for us. They have something much deeper than we know. It is available, but it means facing this and stopping the system control.

We aren't controlled. We choose this. It is better. Better than pain.

I understand that it seems easier, but we are actually missing out. It is stealing from us. Remember the images True FAMILY has been showing us? We didn't know. We thought we were alone, but more was going on. Yes, this is painful to face, but the rewards are worth it. You could just try it and see.

Too painful.

We have good support with Jo and others. True FAMILY will help us through.

Pain. I can see it but not really feel it…waves of fire like the ocean. Never ending. We can't go there.

I can understand. Let's see what True Jesus can do.

He can't.

Let's see. True Jesus, would You show us what You can do about this pain ocean?

(Talking to parts…)

Do you see He is walking into it, and He is okay? He is making a pathway through it. Would you walk with me on that path? See He is holding back the pain. He can help us manage it, so it is not overwhelming. You can take my hand if you want. We can go to Him.

Maybe. Just a few steps. But what if He lets the pain flood us and burn us forever? Hell. Damnation.

No. He won't do that. He loves us deeply. He has a way through if we will trust Him. Look into His eyes. They are kind. See the tenderness He has for us? We can do this.

I'm afraid.

Me too but look at Jesus. See His smile. We can do this with Him.

He's not burning up.

No, and He won't let us burn up either. Just take a step.

Okay.

Jesus, meet us here.

I am here. We can face this together.

Thank you.

The walls of amnesia seem impossible to you, and they are. But when you take hold of Our faith, it is done. You are trying to do it in your limited strength. Work with Strong Girl to let go. It will come. Have patience.

Okay, thank you so very much. I'm grateful. Please keep me focused on Your faith and Your love!

Being A Living Sacrifice

Here I am, True FAMILY. What's coming up this morning is a "living sacrifice" distortion. Why have I had to sacrifice and blame myself for everything that happens? Can You help me?

Yes, darling Daughter of Zion. We've grieved this in you. This is not a condemnation. However, this distortion has so many ramifications and prevents you from fully living a "true living sacrifice" life that is meant to be a joy and a blessing! The counterfeit can seem close. It looks pure and holy and yet it is twisted and comes from the system. It is Our delight to walk you through this.

But I'd rather be the one to be sacrificed. I can take it.

That isn't the job We've given you. That is the job the cult gave you.

We have to do it otherwise everything collapses. See Adena stopped doing it and her marriage is gone. She's lost everything.

She has what counts most. What if there is another way? We are here to help.

We don't know any other way. Tight, rigid confines keep us and others safe. They will hurt them (our loved ones) if we don't. We agreed to this, and we keep our promises. Die daily. Living sacrifice. This is what the Bible says. We must do. We must obey. No other way. Pressure. Squeeze. Pain. We can take it. Sacrifice for others. This is how we become holy. We can take it, they can't.

True FAMILY, I come out of agreement of being a living sacrifice in the cult system. I am asking for every agreement, covenant, contract, oath, vow, ritual, dedication, and baptism to be completely disintegrated under Your Blood, True Jesus. Please untwist this distortion in me. I repent on behalf of myself, my family bloodline and all associated bloodlines for this. Please help me.

We gladly do this, and We work tenderly with the parts of you who are programmed to be this. It takes process, not just a declaration of repentance.

(I feel a wave of nausea. I see the rituals associated with being a "living sacrifice" and the torture involved. It is overwhelming).

We showed this to you so you can understand and not spiritually bypass. This is a deep work to overcome with your parts. Can you trust Us? We do the work. Your part is to say yes and be tender with your parts in the process.

I just want to be done. I know that is not what I teach, but I'm so tired of this.

What's under that?

I want to get it right and be perfect.... I hate this "layer upon layer" work.

Seeing the layers is the first step and then it is working gently with the parts for as long as it takes. You know this and it is hard to walk it out with patience. Remember that impatience cost Moses at several points. You can learn from him. Repentance is a good thing and often is the starting point, but you get to also embrace the work of patience and love. You can easily extend it to others, but you struggle to do so with yourself.

I just want it to be over with. (The tears start to flow…).

We know and We hold you gently through this. Your part is to trust and rest

But I want to do something. This is excruciating. How can I help anyone when I'm so messed up?

It is not you, but Us in you. Take the pressure off of you. We can speak through a donkey. It is Our delight to flow through you to others. This is Our gift. You do not need to be perfect, have it all together, or be the living sacrifice. Look

through the Bible. All of the ones We called were not "qualified" because of being perfect. They just said yes to Us. You've said yes to Us. That is all that is needed on your part, moment by moment, as We show you how to walk this out.

I know this in my head, but…

The training is deep and from conception. You can't unravel this. You can't hurry up the process. You get to accept *you* right where you are, because We do. You get to let Us love you. You get to let others love you.

There's resistance.

Yes, and for good reason. Have compassion. Let the barriers down.

I'm trying really hard.

Let. Not try.

I can't.

Why?

Must stay loyal otherwise. My baby. No. No. Please no.

I'm just copying Svali. This isn't true.

Would you let Us be the judge of that?

I can't face it.

Do you desire truth in the inward parts?

Yes, I do.

We can give you the courage to face this.

But what if I am wrong?

Why would you feel this much emotion if it wasn't?

Okay, but I don't want to know.

Why?

It's too hard.

See, True FAMILY, it is too big of a mess. I can't do this.

Did you just pray to relinquish what you could handle today?

Yes.

Feel the storm within. What are you avoiding? Can We get you through the storm?

Theoretically, yes.

Practically, can We?

Well, yes. You have been so very faithful to me. Why do I doubt? I just repented for it in the prayer, but see, I am back again. It is hopeless.

Cycling. Slow it down. Stay present. There are solutions with Us. It is a process, and We are not afraid of it or of you. We have a way through. You have a lot going on. Let yourself off the hook and just be.

But I have so much to do.

Yes, there are things that are pressing, and you have a choice. We can help you to take it step by step and you will get done what is needed and you will also receive rest. But if you try to do this in your own strength and use work as a way to avoid facing things, it will delay your journey and the things We have for you. We have been proving Our faithfulness to you and you are seeing this. There is so much more that you aren't seeing. The invitation is to rest in Us and take it step by step.

Okay. I give this to you. I let go of control. I choose Your way. Please settle me in Your love. Am I safe here? I'm scared.

There's a lot going on and you are always safe with Us as you trust and rest. When you try to do it on your own, you are vulnerable. This is a new skill, and it is okay to make mistakes.

Mistakes are costly.

We can work all things for good. When a child is learning to walk, there are many falls, and it is okay. There is no condemnation. Just take Our hand and take the next step.

I don't like being a baby.

You missed many steps growing up. This is not your fault. But it requires care in rebuilding the foundation. We can do this in you while you are doing what We've called you to. It is harder, but it is possible. We have uniquely created you with the grace to do this. This reveals the triumph of Our love. Receive Our grace. Strong Girl and Good Girl are vital and can learn how to flow with Us in deeply rewarding ways.

What do I do with the parts who are saying we can't, we won't, we are afraid of failing, and all of that? I don't want to keep cycling, but I want to be honest about what is coming up.

Breaking the programming is about believing the truth.

How do I believe? The lies are so deeply engrained.

Take some time to worship and finish prayers. It will help. Reading and engaging with Scripture. The pattern We showed you for Sabbaths will help. The journaling is good, but you also need the other components to help stabilize you. See how these elements stabilize you.

Okay, thank you. I choose Your way. (I took some time to do the above and then resumed the conversation with the True FAMILY…)

That did help. Thank you so much. I see how these things need to be in balance and in Your order and way so that we can stabilize. Thank you for showing this to me and please teach me how to walk this out and how to help others.

With joy! Relationship is the key. Done on their own, these things will burn out and dry up, but in the flow of relationship they are the keys to life. The relational piece comes first. Otherwise, the rest will be done in striving. There will be that tendency anyway, but the relational part can draw you back. You can feel the difference.

Yes, thank you!

We allow you to experience things and make "mistakes" so that you can feel and know the difference. We don't see these as mistakes because we are working them all for good for you and others.

I am grateful! Your love is amazing, and Your ways are past my understanding. At the same time, all this makes sense as You show me. Let me stay steady in Your love. I give this time to You and ask You to help me stay in the rhythm of Your grace. I know I could just work and closet away. Help me to do what is on Your heart that is needed for my healing and restoration.

Take it step by step, hour by hour. Don't get stuck in what you have to do but enjoy. Take time for you.

I don't know how to do that. I know it is needed.

We are happy to teach you.

Okay.

Section XIX

A Few Memories

I've included a few memories that have surfaced over the last couple of years. They may be triggering to some, so please make sure the Lord is releasing you to read them. I hope for those of you who have experienced this, you can know that you are not alone and that there is hope!

Memories from England

One of the countries I was trafficked in was England. Memories of this part of the world include images of castles, dungeons, cages, ceremonies with royalty, and more.

Parts are in panic mode. What's going on?

We don't want to say.

I feel you and I am here.

We can't talk about it, but something is up. Bad things are coming. Run and hide. Cages. Blank. Blank. Blank.

(I feel parts starting to disassociate…)

We aren't there anymore, in the trauma, and we don't have to blank out. We can ask Jo what happens when someone passes. She may know. *

No one can help us.

Can you let Jesus help you so we can settle down for the night?

No! No! No! It's too late.

It's important for me to get some rest tonight.

You just care about yourself. You don't care about us.

I'm sorry. I do care. It's just that we need to work together so we can heal.

It's not possible.

I believe it is. Jesus can help us. He is True Jesus, not the bad ones.

We don't believe in any of that anyway.

I remember the cages in England a little. Do you want to tell me more?

We're all going to die.

I know it feels like that right now, but there is hope.

Hope for what? Who wants to keep living in a cage?

I'm sorry you are still stuck there. There are other options.

You don't know the half of it.

I know. I am willing to hear if you would be willing to tell me.

Maybe, but not tonight. You won't be able to sleep at all if we tell you.

Jesus, I need You. Am I making this up? This feels crazy. I'm not trying to disbelieve but I don't like how this feels.

I am here. It is real, but these are also things you don't want to face. We won't make you. There are some things coming up to be prepared for. We will help you step by step and you don't need to be afraid.

I don't know how to walk this out. I don't want more to go on because it feels so crazy right now. I don't want to be paranoid, but I want to trust You. Can You help me?

Yes. Note the concern from tonight. We will help you as you are able to handle it.

I want to be able to. Can I just get it over with?

You've also wanted to be functional and that is why it is slower. You are doing great work. Can you trust Us with the timing?

Okay. I give this all to You. I need to sleep well tonight; can You help me?

Yes, the inner realm is riled up and it will take a little bit to settle. You're not believing them doesn't help.

How do I help them to settle?

Sing a song.

Will that work?

Try it.

Okay. Good night.

* Here I am referring to what to do when a handler passes away.

Auction

I am here. I am with you, Daughter of Zion. Do not be afraid.

I'm struggling. I don't know what to do. I feel this swirl of confusion. Please ground me in Your Word.

You haven't been taking time to read Scripture like We asked. This will help. Let Us lead and guide you gently.

The word "auction" came up while I was drifting during prayer…

Yes, there were auctions.

What do I do with this?

You can talk with Jo about it.

But I don't have any real memories of it.

You don't need to.

What if I don't want to know?

You don't have to go there. There are other things you can address.

I feel hopeless.

It is okay. We are here. Trust Us to lead and guide you. You did shut down. This is not how We do it. We lift the burden. There is a difference.

Okay, thank you. I want to do it Your way.

We are so glad! We have a way through for you.

Why am I having distortions* again?

These are some of the results of the access. Don't be disturbed by this but trust Us. You can work through this.

I don't like that.

We know. But will you trust Us?

How can I trust You when You continue to allow these things to happen?

There is purpose in all things. Remember it is much bigger than just you. You are here for such a time as this. Be encouraged.

What if I am wrong?

You are doing what you know to do with the best of your ability. Deep inside you know the truth. The programming interferes and is where you back down. This is an important step if you don't want to fulfill the plans of the cult system.

I'm afraid of the consequences. Or it may be just nothing.

Yes, you know the pattern. It is a crossroads.

What if I'm not ready?

We are with you and have been preparing you. Take courage. We work all things for good.

(A little bit later, we continue the conversation….)

Thank you so much for clearing my day. It feels much better! You are so good at that.

We love to flow with you and to help you manage all that is going on. We see and We know your heart. Trust and rest.

Do I need to pursue the auction subject anymore? Any parts want to share about auctions?

We hate them. Buying and selling flesh. Yuck! Bad things. Pain and torture… made to do things. Expensive. High class. We hate it. The way they look at us. What we have to do. Chained. Pain. Backwards. Painful. No love. Some better than others. We hate the cruel ones. Make us do bad things. Bloody mess. Bad. No choice. We hate them.

Thank you for sharing with me. I am so very sorry.

Not your fault, you don't remember. We go somewhere else to endure. Jesus takes us sometimes and keeps us safe until done. He is good. We hurt for the others. Many of us. So many. Some don't make it. Many don't make it. We lucky but I don't know… maybe not. Maybe better to go away forever to Jesus. Bad things so hard. We hate their body parts. We want to kill them for what they do to us. Merciless. Access programming. Can't help it. Must obey. Do bad things. Can't help it.

Yes, I'm sorry. Only Jesus can help heal this bad stuff. When I drifted in prayer, were you trying to get my attention?

Yes, it's the only way.

I'm sorry I've kind of shut down the last few days. I was overwhelmed.

We know. It is okay. It is a lot to handle. We interrupt less if you give us a chance to speak.

Okay. I want to do that more. Thank you for letting me know.

We go now. Too hard to talk about.

Okay, do you want Jesus to come and comfort you?

Yes.

Okay, thank you, Jesus, for hearing and knowing.

I am with you always. I am proud of you for facing this. Trust Us to help you walk through this.

Can we shut down the auction houses?

There are things that you can do, but not alone. Wait to address this with your group. It will trigger some.

Okay. I put my trust in You. Please help me to hear correctly. (A little later) I'm so distressed, True Jesus. Please help me. When I open up to feel, it hurts so bad. Can You hold me?

Yes, We are holding you. Even when you don't feel it, We are here. We never leave you nor forsake you. Trust and rest.

What do I do with this ocean of pain? All these little ones from the auction are crying out…

Let Us meet them. Each one. We are able to handle this. It is more than you can handle right now.

*Distortions for me are when an image shifts from something good and positive to something evil or scary, sometimes in connection to God. This can be a part doing this as "protection" against intimacy with God or demonic or programming.

Memories From NASA

A number of survivors were programmed through NASA and participated in experiments there. I was a part of a failed experiment where lives were lost. These memories haunted me until I was able to find peace in True Jesus.

Jesus, are You real? Are You the true Jesus?

Look to Me and you will see. See My eyes of love for you. I am so very proud of you. You have come so very far. Do not be discouraged! You are making good progress, and We are here with you step by step, every step of the way. You are seen and known. We are so very proud of you.

Thank you! Can You help me today? There are so many things going on and I want to do what is on Your heart.

You get to flow today in any way you want with Us. There's no legalism here. If you want to do something fun and creative, you can. Laugh and have fun.

Thank you so much! How do I receive Your love for today?

Let Us have your pain. We will help with all the parts. None of them are too much for Us.

What do I do with these things? Are they true? Did they really happen? Was I involved?

Yes, you were. We will help you process and give you confirmations so that you can receive healing.

I am struggling to believe it. It seems so far-fetched. I don't blame my family for not believing. Especially if I have trouble believing it. I would be happy to retract all of it. I don't want any of it to be real.

You can do that, but would you find healing?

No. I do want healing. So, I am willing to face this stuff. But it is really hard.

You all were abused together. Remember the opportunities for restoration.

I really need help with this. I don't want to speak them out.

Yes, We know. Do you want the truth, or do you want to live a lie? Do you want to participate in restoration or bury this?

I want to bury it, but I've come too far for that. I have seen Your goodness and Your grace, and Your restoration and it is so beautiful.

So, I will choose that route. I just don't know what to do with it right now. Do I do some research?

You can, but it will stir things up. You can choose to wait until closer to your next session if you want.

I want to throw up.

We know. It is okay. You knew you had ties to NASA....

Yes, but I didn't want to believe it. I don't want to believe any of it.

It is okay, precious Adena. You can take this slow. We are with you. Do not be afraid. Nothing is impossible with Us. Our vision is for beautiful restoration of all involved. There are ones who are trapped from this horrific event. You can partner with Us for restoration.

I am willing. I give this day to You. I submit all that I am to You. I am believing in You, the one true and living God, for all that I need. Will You show Yourself powerful on my behalf?

Of course! It is Our great joy to do so. Just remember to let go of expectation and embrace expectancy of Our goodness to you.

Alice In Wonderland

Although there was some previous Alice in Wonderland processing, I'm including some more here. For context, this was triggered when I didn't attend a meeting because I was afraid of being overwhelmed and wasn't sure who was going to be there. I found out later that the people who were at the meeting were ones I would have felt comfortable with, and I could have joined in, but was afraid of being late. This triggered the Alice in Wonderland programming.

It was good to reach out and be honest—this is a win-- and it is good to see how strong this programming is to never ever ever ever ever be late. I didn't know you were there. Thank you for letting me know. What happens when you are late?

Bad things. Ruins it all. Punishment. Severe. Must be on time. Cannot come late. Scared. Terrified. Bad. Eternal punishment. Zap. Electrocute. Bad, bad, bad. Don't be late. Once it has started, cannot come. Banished. No hope. Bad. Very bad. Tricked. Bad. Timing. Precise. Must stay in time. Fatal. Timing. Must keep time. Accurate. Internal clock. Taskmasters. Keep time. Don't deviate. Seconds count. Must be on time.

Thank you for letting me know. I didn't realize this was such an issue.

You wouldn't because you've always been good with time. Keep on time. Big punishment if off. Keep the time. Can't be late. No matter what. Seconds can make the difference between a successful mission and failure. Life or death. Split second. Keep the time.

That sounds very stressful.

Yes. Bad.

There is another way.

Can't deviate. Never.

True Jesus, I don't know what to do with this. I give it all to You. I want to be in Your timing and not the timing of the cult system. What do I do with the internal clocks and timekeepers? I see the white rabbit. I don't want to follow him. I'm afraid. Time bomb.

Look to me. Can you see Me?

I'm trying.

Okay, listen for the sound of My voice and let it steady you.

Okay.

Notice the ringing in your ears decreased.

Yes. Thank you.

Keep steady. Don't run. Stay present. I'm here.

But I want to run.

That is what they want. Take a deep breath. You are okay.

Okay.

You will need to deal with time clocks as part of dismantling this program and breaking through the amnesia.

I can't.

On your own, yes, but We are here to help, and Jo can help. She knows what to do.

Can you keep this in a safe place until Monday?

Yes, I am able.

You won't let anything bad happen to me?

No, We will keep you safe. Alice can climb into Our lap.

Will she be safe there? She doesn't know what to do. She sees the Cheshire cat. He says it doesn't matter where she goes. There's no place that is safe.

Listen for My voice and let her come to Me. It is dark, but she can follow My voice, not the moon. Listen carefully and walk to the sound of My voice.

Okay. Must be good. Must be good. Must be good.

It's okay. We've got you safe.

But they will know I didn't do it right.

I can protect you. It is okay. You are safe with Me.

But I deviated. There will be punishment. Bad things. I can't do this.

Stay present and don't run. Listen for My voice. It is okay.

I'm scared.

I know.

I can't go any further. Can I sit here in the dark? Can You come to me?

Yes, I never leave you nor forsake you.

Why can't I see You? Are You the One with kind eyes?

Yes, I am True Jesus. I am here for you. Take My hand.

It feels big and warm.

Yes, I am able to keep you safe. Rest and trust.

Okay, I give this to You, True Jesus. Help me!

I am here.

Okay. They say I have to be a good girl otherwise they kill the others. I try really hard. I'm trying really hard. Really hard. But it is never enough.

That is a heavy weight. I've not asked that of you. I just ask you to be My friend. To have relationship. To be real. I don't want you to be stressed. You can rest and trust.

But we must be perfect. Otherwise, bad things happen.

It doesn't have to be that way anymore. You can be you.

What about the punishments? Death. And more death. Must keep going. Can't stop. Must be good.

What if you didn't?

Fatal. Fatal. Fatal. We all die.

What if there's another way that didn't involve those deaths? I died and rose again so that you don't have to perform or be good, just receive what I've done.

Impossible.

It might feel that way, but it is true, and it is possible. Do you feel safe with Me right now?

Sort of.

Take a deep breath. I'm here. Stay present with Me. I will help you.

I want to run away.

What would that do?

I can't trust anyone. Everyone betrays. Everyone is bad. No one is safe.

I know this is what it has felt like. But there is a way through. Take a deep breath.

Are You going to force me?

No. You are free to go at any time.

Okay. Do You do bad things to little girls?

No. I don't. I won't ever. I mean that. You've been tricked before, and I understand why you struggle with trust. It is okay. I'm not mad at you. I don't hate you. I'm not trying to get something from you. I'm here for you. You can receive when you are ready.

Okay. Where's Jo? I want Jo now.

It is okay. She will be here on Monday. It's okay. You are safe here.

Okay. But what if she doesn't come?

She has been faithful and consistent. Rest and trust. Remember she is a gift.

I can't receive. I'm too bad. Nobody gives me a gift that doesn't come without a price. Always a price tag. Have to be really good. Perfect.

You are looping back. It is okay. I'm happy to reassure you as much as you need it. I'm speaking the truth. Stay present. You don't need to follow the white rabbit or see the Cheshire cat. You can see Me and if you can't see Me, you can remember Jo and her patience with you. See her smile and know that it is okay. This is Our gift. It's going to be okay. Let things settle. We will keep this safe until Monday.

I feel so fragmented. I have a lot to do today. This is important, but I need to move on. I need to give this to You.

You can. We will help you settle and move forward. I know this was unsettling, but you did well. We are here for you. You are safe and secure in Us. It's going to be okay.

Section XX

Attachment Pain

One of the hardest areas for survivors to face is attachment pain. God designed us to be connected relationally. With mom first and then dad, we are meant to bond deeply to establish security, trust and love. When this doesn't happen, we develop coping mechanisms. We avoid intimacy at all cost and push relationships away or we are very anxious and needy/clingy. Often, we are a combination of the two. Those of us with complex trauma will have both working within us, causing us to have conflicting "push/pull, I love you/I hate you; I need you/I don't need you" experiences and feelings regarding others we are in relationship with. This is where the deepest pain lies.

The good news is that with True FAMILY, we can be reparented! It takes time, but the deficits can be replaced with secure attachments. We also need a healthy community to help us stabilize and demonstrate what unconditional love is. It takes great patience and understanding to be in a relationship with a survivor, whether the person is a friend, a spouse, or a family member. One minute, a survivor loves you and the next, they are running away or attacking or clingy. This is also where we learn the relational skills we missed growing up. For more on relational skills, check out *Transforming Fellowship: 19 Brain Skills that Build Joyful Community* by Chris Coursey. Healing happens in relationships. We can't do this on our own.

Letting Love In

Just putting things on the paper will help to relieve the pain and let Us hold all your parts. She is not the only one. Invite all the others who were involved so that they can have a clean fluffy blanket too. Everyone is welcome. No one is excluded. There is love here.

We don't deserve it. We can't … They said we can't …ever have anything to do with Jesus… They say He is bad.

That is all a lie. He is the best! We can overcome all the evil through Him.

We are not strong enough to overcome anything. We must do what they say…

No, not anymore. We are free through Jesus and what He did for us.

Lots of Jesuses died for us but it never worked. Then they beat and raped us. We don't think it is a good idea.

Those were not the True Jesus. The reason they faked Him and did all those bad things was to keep you in bondage and under their control. The only true freedom comes from True Jesus. He is available to all of us. This is true life. He deals with our shame and pain and all the bad things we did. He forgives. He sets us free.

Too good to be true. It is a deception.

I'm sorry you believe that. It keeps you from so much more. You can try it. You can always go back to the old way of doing things if you choose.

Maybe.

Lots of fluffy blankets for anyone who is willing to try…

Why do I still feel nausea, True FAMILY? I need to go to sleep. Is anyone keeping us from going to sleep?

Trust and rest. There's more who want to say stuff if you will let them.

You know I don't want to go there.

Yes, but that is what is needed.

Okay, I'm willing. (To my parts) I know you all are thinking that Jo doesn't want to come see us in person because we are bad. That isn't true. She knows True Jesus and how to love even those who have done bad things. She doesn't hate us.

Yes, she does!

No, she knows other people who were abused like us. She has helped them to experience freedom. She is not turned off by us or what we've done.

But everyone hates us.

Not Jesus.

Yes, but He must love us. He's God. But she doesn't have to.

But she has a heart like Jesus and so she cares.

We know it will happen again (rejection). We can't be that vulnerable. Danger! Run. Hide. She's got to hate us soon. It will happen again. We don't want that. Keep her away.

Is this because you don't want to be vulnerable and needy?

Yes. Love hurts too bad and fails in the end. Nobody could love us if they really knew us and knew all that we did. Garbage. Trash.

That isn't how God sees us and Jo doesn't see us that way either. She's worked with lots of other people like us.

Then she is crazy.

No, she has God's love in her. He gives her the strength to help us escape.

But it hurts too much. You can't get attached.

True Jesus, is it okay to have healthy attachments?

Yes, darling daughter. You have asked for this. It is My joy to bring to you healthy relationships that are full of love and not rejection. Do not be afraid.

Okay, thank you! Can we go to bed now? Will you all cooperate so we can sleep?

Maybe, eventually.

Jesus, can You help us?

Gladly. Rest and trust.

She Hates Us

I know everyone's struggling with not having an appointment next week (with Jo), but it is going to be okay. True FAMILY is with us. We will be okay.

We don't want to ever see her again. We can't. She hates us. She doesn't want to see us.

I know it feels that way, but the truth is she has other things that she needs to do, and she needs to rest. This is life. No one can be there for us all the time. I am very grateful we went this long without missing sessions. It will be okay. She doesn't hate us.

How do you know?

Because she is caring and compassionate. She carries True Jesus' love. She is not mad at us. Only the True FAMILY will always be there for us.

But we are very scared. Lots of things are happening.

Yes, and True FAMILY is here no matter what. We can trust Them. This is an opportunity for us to learn trust.

We can't. Nowhere safe. Cages. Hide. Goodbye.

We can stay present even when we are disappointed, sad, or scared. True Holy Spirit, can You take these little ones, hold them, and comfort them?

Yes, I'd be very glad too.

But we can't see Holy Spirit. We want Jo.

We can see Holy Spirit in our heart. She is always available and wants to hold you close. It is okay. Listen to the sound of Her voice. She is singing to you. Can you hear it?

Yes, it is nice.

Okay, let Her hold you and rock you. It is okay. True Jesus, please help me through today. I need you.

I am here and I am delighted to help you through today. I have you safe and I have Jo. It will be okay.

I'm struggling to trust You.

I know. It is okay. We are going to walk through this. Remember that it is through the storm that your trust grows as you experience Our care and protection.

"On/Off Switch"

How did you feel in the dream?

Jo was distant and professional.

Is that what you want?

It is safer and easier. I am just a client.

Would you like Us to set the boundaries of your relationships?

I guess so but this is easier. For now.

What are you afraid of?

It is easier and safer to be "distant and professional."

That wasn't the question.

I can't.

Why?

Because. I thought we were going easier today.

You always get to choose. Do you want to face this?

No.

Why not?

It hurts.

Do you want to bring it to Us?

Okay. Here you go. I don't want any of it. Leave me alone. I can't do it anymore. I will go far away. I don't need anyone. I can do this on my own.

Well done. What do you want to do about that?

What I want to do and what I choose to do are two different things. I want to bury it and forget it. I am choosing to bring it into the light of Your love and trust You with it.

Good. So, you can be honest with how you feel?

As honest as I can be.

Let the light of Our love shine. You can let love in. You can receive love and care from others, including Jo.

So, I wasn't as anxious about Jo being gone because I'd removed her to "distant and professional?"

Yes. Is that what you want?

No. I choose Your way. I put my trust in You. Thank you for revealing this. How do I walk this out?

We will show you step by step. You are used to using the on/off switch with relationships. It is how you survived. Would you give that on/off switch to Us? You've asked for healthy relationships. This will mean submitting them to Us. This is your safety.

I repent for my on/off switch in relationships. I recognize that is not how You do relationships. You want to show me a new way. I have used this to protect myself. I repent for that, and I ask You to be my Protector especially in relationships. I choose Your way. I give You this switch and I choose to keep my relational circuits on and appropriate as You show me how.

Yay! We are so proud of you. Thank you for releasing the on/off switch to Us. This won't be easy to let go and walk this out with Us, but the rewards are great.

I don't trust you. This won't work. You are leaving us too exposed and vulnerable. We hate you.

Is this towards me or True Jesus or both?

Both. You both are crazy. On/off switch is best. Safer. Easier. Clean. Tidy. You've stolen from us.

I am sorry, I didn't know how you feel and how you depend on that. I am choosing a new way with True FAMILY. I know this won't be easy, but I do believe it is the best way. They have proven faithful to us over and over again. I would like it if we can cooperate with Them.

Can't we have it back for a while? You need it now. You won't be able to handle the emotions with Jo being gone. What are you going to do?

I have other friends and True FAMILY is here. I am okay. I'm actually doing quite well.

"Needy"

While worshipping at the keyboard, some parts were wanting to hurry up and send some journalling to Jo. Other parts, not so much.

Shut up you babies! We don't need to send anything to Jo! We can do this on our own. Stop whining.

Babies crying.

Get over it!

Quiet.

Hey, let's work this out. We don't have to shout at each other. Why don't you want to send anything to Jo?

(I sense parts backing down…)

We are afraid.

What are you afraid of?

It's too much. We can't share anymore.

Jo has heard all kinds of things. I don't think anything we say can shock her. She is God's gift to us for this journey.

But it will end. It always does.

With the True FAMILY, it doesn't have to end.

We can't hope. It hurts too bad.

I understand. This isn't easy. True FAMILY will help us through.

But they're being babies. Being needy feels vulnerable. We can do this on our own. Tough it out.

It is okay to be needy in this season. We missed a lot in our lives, and it is okay to have needs and express them.

NO!

Why?

Not safe.

Why don't you feel safe? Jo has been faithful and caring to us.

We just can't. Too risky.

If we just stay locked up, we won't fully live our lives and fulfil our destiny. We will be lonely and afraid forever. I don't want to do that. I want to learn to trust and live free. I understand your fear and believe that together, with True FAMILY, we can open up to live a beautiful life.

You already have a beautiful life.

Yes, but much of it is controlled in different ways. True FAMILY is helping us come into true freedom. Let's walk this out together. Are you dragging this out so that the journaling will be too long, and Jo won't read it?

Well, if it works…

I think working together makes more sense. Together we are stronger. We don't need to fear because True FAMILY is with us, and They have given us support in many different ways. Jo is one of them. I want to fully hear you and understand. I don't want to drag things out forever, so will you cooperate?

Okay. Sure.

Thank you!

Section XXI

Good News!

I want to close this book with an experience that might feel like it is not good news but ultimately it is. It is connected to what I believe is coming with the mass exodus from the cult system and the restoration of what God is doing. I hope you will be encouraged with the ultimate restoration that is possible.

I woke up from a dream where I am slowly building info against the cult and being careful and cautious, noting who is a threat.

We seem to be on something like a train. When I return to my office (possibly on the train), there's a woman, whom I know is connected to the cult, standing suspiciously in front of my filing cabinet that has all the info I've collected in it. I ask her something and then I see another woman. She approaches, and then a third one from behind. I know that I have two "strikes" against me and that I can have four strikes before disaster happens (i.e. I am taken in or eliminated by the cult). I ask the first woman how long I have, and she says, "24 to 48 hours."

True FAMILY, I need You desperately in this. Is this dream about parts communicating threats or impending events?

Yes, darling Daughter of Zion. We do have a way through. Stay steady in Our love. Keep moving this morning.

I'm really tired. I was really hoping to rest over the holiday but spent the whole time working and putting out fire after fire. And there is so much more to do. Next week is packed. Show me how to rest in You.

Remember that all of this is an opportunity for greater trust and learning to lean on Us instead of your own understanding.

Oh, yes, I see. I'm sorry. I was not fully giving all of this to You and trying to manage it all myself. I don't know how to fully rest, and it comes at such a pace, all this "stuff" … I feel I'm shutting down with all the attacks and stress. I don't want to do that. I want my heart to be open to You and what is needed. I'd like to rest and experience Shabbat, but it seems that is when the attacks are the most intense from them.

Just take it step by step with Us. Relax through Shabbat and enjoy time with Us. We will give you grace. You are here for a reason. Remember the canopy of Our love. See the angels We are sending. You are not alone. Can you find Us in the storm? Can you join Us resting in the boat while the waves crash around you? Can you find the rhythm of Our grace in the rocking boat? We are here.

It's hard, but I'm willing if You will help me.

It is Our joy to do so. Find joy even here. Remember that one day all of it will be exposed and nothing hidden. Those coming against you will see. Can you trust Us until then?

Okay. I am willing. I give all of this to You. Thank you.

(Next day) Thank you for seeing me through the night. I feel good overall and at peace. Is there anything I need to know? I don't want to think everything is fine if something has happened.

Your preaching to them last night was powerful.

Was it real or just my imagination?

It was real. It was a simple proclamation of your allegiance to Me and We loved it! They will try other tactics. Be aware.

I feel like You are inviting me deeper into Sabbath rest and I want to understand that and enter in. I am seeing an "envelope of time" that I can step into and enjoy safety, rest and peace in a special way. They seem to attack hardest on Shabbat, so I do want to appropriate what You have provided for me.

Yes, this is Our special time with you. It is "rest training."

So not magical thinking, but intentionally practicing rest in the storm? Okay, I'm seeing it more clearly. This is why the cult wants to destroy Shabbat. So we miss what You've provided for us.

This is an important part of healing. It is not so much the outer expression as the inner one. Not that the outer isn't important, but simply that is where legalism can come in and the point of Shabbat can be missed.

Okay. I want to practice today. Can my inner realm practice too?

They need it the most.

Okay. Inner realm, we are going to practice rest today with True FAMILY. It is like an envelope of time we get to step into and practice rest and trust, dance and hugs. How does that sound?

Yay! We like that.

Not all of us. Bad things happen on Shabbat. We hate Shabbat. Rape, torture, pain. Sadness. Loneliness. Isolation. Slaughter. Distortion.

I am so very sorry for that. I wondered at the resistance. I can understand that it would be really painful. I understand your desire to avoid Shabbat and how you dread it.

Yes, that is how it is. We can't enter in.

I know it feels that way. I want to do whatever it takes to help you heal and find freedom from this and explore the restoration True FAMILY has of Shabbat. You see, they think they can destroy the good gifts God has given us, but we get to triumph in Their love. We can have a degree of "revenge" when we, with True FAMILY, can celebrate it in the way They intended. Can you see that?

Yes, I guess so. But we are sad.

Yes, and True FAMILY knows that. It is not that we can't mourn the loss. We don't have to "just pretend." True FAMILY knows the depth of our pain and are glad to help us walk this out in triumph. That is better than being a victim. True FAMILY is inviting those most wounded on Shabbat to come to a special place with Them. You don't have to dance or hug or celebrate. They are focusing on your healing and deep rest from the pain and torture of Shabbat. How does that sound?

Too good to be reality.

That is what They love to do! Love makes a way.

Okay, is this our envelope in time?

Yes, True FAMILY always wants to heal and give freedom and minister to us, but especially on Shabbat. Remember True Jesus healed a lot on the Sabbath. It got Him into trouble, but He wanted to demonstrate His tender care to relieve suffering, even on Shabbat.

We are used to just the rituals and pain and torture. It is hard to imagine anything else.

They understand and will work with you gently in this. If you need to share anything with me, I am here.

Black betrayal.

What does that mean?

Not saying.

I understand you may not be able to share yet but know that I am here, and I care.

You can't do this!

What?

Enjoy Shabbat. It is not meant for that. We have to do what we are told.

Did you know True FAMILY created Shabbat for enjoyment and rest and peace?

You don't know what you are doing.

What if we could see Shabbat differently than what we were trained in by the system?

You don't know the consequences! Must keep Shabbat their way.

Did you enjoy that?

No. But that is not the point.

For True FAMILY, it is. They give us choice and the freedom to choose. They gently invite us to see things differently and to enter into Their rest and joy and peace. They can also protect us from the consequences the cult is threatening you with.

Disaster. You already have three strikes. This is your last opportunity.

We are choosing to trust True FAMILY no matter what. They are able to protect those we love.

Do you see what I see?

Yes, I see the knife to the throat of those little ones. True FAMILY, I am asking for Your help. Only You can help us through this. These lives of the little ones are in Your hands. I appeal for mercy and for the blood of True Jesus to protect these ones. Unless these precious ones are martyrs for You and then I trust You even in this.

If they allow that they are no better than the cult.

I understand how you see that. True FAMILY knows the end from the beginning. They have a plan through it all for the triumph of Their love. You will one day see the fullness of this and be amazed. Their perfect love and justice will triumph over all. True FAMILY, please intervene for Your glory.

It is not time yet for the fulness of that to be manifested. Can you trust Me even in this?

Yes, but I don't like what I am seeing.

Can you stand with Us no matter what the consequences are, trusting Us to work it all for good?

I am willing. Please help me. This hurts really bad.

Yes, and We are here with you in the pain.

What about the envelope of time?

They are entering in. Can you?

Only by Your grace and Your help. Did I really see that or was that wrong?

You saw.

That was hard.

Yes. They are entering Our rest here with Us. Do you see them celebrating with joy unspeakable?

Why won't you let me go too?

It is not yet your time. Remember the plan from the beginning.

This feels crazy.

Do you see their plan for destruction and Our plan that, either way, leads to life? This is the triumph of Our love. Even in death, life is found in Us. There is an ultimate triumph over death when it is thrown into the Lake of Fire. Until then, We have a way through even this. Every life is in Our hands. Can you believe this?

I want to. It is hard. We've seen too much death. We've participated. I'm so very sorry.

Can you leave it in Our hands?

Okay. How can I enter into the envelope of time after seeing that?

You can. Remember the joy. Remember where they are now.

Why do You save some and not others?

Remember We are the Author and Finisher, so We have a really good plan that ends well. Can you believe that?

Yes, but it still hurts my heart.

Where are they now?

Joyfully with You, but then let me come too.

It is not cruel for you to stay. There is much more We have for you there. These agreed to a short time on earth. You know this.

Cognitively yes, but it is hard in practice.

Remember you are surrounded by this great Cloud of Witnesses. There can be great joy, even in the pain. Can you find Us here?

I want to. I choose Your way. I choose life in You. I choose rest and peace and joy in You. I give to You the things I don't understand. I put my trust in You.

This has more meaning than you know! Well done!

Is this my 4th strike?

Yes, but it is good news when you see it from Our perspective. It is closing a door to access, although it will be difficult to walk it out.

So their plan is to take me in or eliminate me? What is Your plan?

Life and life more abundantly. Can you embrace that?

I want to.

Well done.

I haven't done anything.

You are pressing through honestly and We love this.

Okay. True FAMILY, I am still hoping I am wrong in this, but if it is true, then I boldly declare that I forgive them for what they just did. I release Your restoration to them. I declare that the blood of the martyrs is the seed of the church. In this case, I declare it is the seed of the mass exodus from the cult system that You, True FAMILY, have ordained. I declare that many will be set free as they see the true reality of who You are as the Resurrection and the Life and that nothing is lost with You.

I declare that I forgive you and True FAMILY forgives you and there is a way through for freedom, even from this. While tears run down my eyes, I will stand and declare the faithfulness of True FAMILY and Their goodness, even in this. I testify to principalities and powers and thrones and dominions, True FAMILY triumphs over it all. You will not win against Them. Their love triumphs. I call those in the system out. You do not need to continue to do what you are doing. It doesn't make sense. We were lied to and deceived, but now the door is open for restoration, healing, deliverance, and freedom. You can have new life in True FAMILY. No matter how bad, or how long, or anything else, nothing can separate us from True FAMILY's love. Look at me. They have and are delivering me from the pit of hell that I lived in. You can experience freedom too.

(Cult members and entities are throwing things at me, but True FAMILY is protecting me).

Can you see that you cannot harm me? True FAMILY ultimately protects and has a way through. You cannot harm me anymore. I have chosen True FAMILY. Come while you can. True Jesus, can You allow them to hear the sound of the singing from the ones they thought they destroyed?

Explosion of joy!

(I am seeing and hearing the babies/children singing and dancing before God's throne with incredible delight and the cult is able to hear it as well)

See these little ones are not destroyed, as you thought, to use as leverage against me. They are free and rejoicing in the presence of the Lord. You did not win. You cannot win. I see you trembling. You too can experience this joy with True FAMILY. You can come out of the cult system and receive true life. It is not too late. You can experience it too. This is the triumph of Their love and the power of the blood of True Jesus. It is available for you, too. That's all I've got, True FAMILY. I am trusting You to do the rest.

Yes, We are delighted! Thank you! We love to partner with you in this and more. This shifts things for you and for them. Can you see it?

Yes. Dimly, but I am grateful. This does bring joy to Shabbat. Thank you so much!

Epilogue

I don't fully understand God's ways. For example, I struggle with parts of the last chapter in this book. Why is suffering and death allowed?

But I know that He is good and has a way through. This is where I have to stand on the promise that God works ALL things for good as we love and trust Him. Death does not have the final word and suffering can be transformed.

I also know this -- No matter what *your* situation is, restoration is possible.

I have to believe that there is meaning that can come from our pain and that trauma can be turned to triumph through the power of the blood of True Jesus and the incredible love that True FAMILY has for us. This love encompasses even our perpetrators. While we must process the pain and emotions, seeing the joy of restoration gives us the courage to continue the journey. I believe this is what Jesus experienced as the "joy set before Him." This joy enabled Him to endure the cross and overcome. It was the joy of restoration that His death, burial and resurrection would bring.

As I have mentioned, I believe that the best "revenge" is seeing those in the cult system and our abusers restored and joyfully embracing relationship with True FAMILY. As survivors forgive, bless, and release restoration to those still in the system, God moves mightily to bring transformation.

I invite you to participate in the mass exodus from the cult system through your prayers, and if you are a survivor, through your forgiveness and partnering with the Lord for restoration. Our healing has ripple effects into eternity. I know that I am coming out today because of others who went before me. They set the example and prayed for my freedom. I am truly grateful to them for breaking through very difficult circumstances and standing true to God. Their bravery made a way for me.

You too can make a difference for others!

This is bigger than just our own personal healing. Yes, we definitely get to see a massive internal "revival" within ourselves as we heal and as our parts come to True Jesus. At the same time, we also get to be a part of the mass exodus from the cult system and witness the incredible glory of God!

If this rings true with you, I invite you to explore the resources available within Transformations Community. Whether you are a survivor yourself, know someone who is, or simply have a passion for this mission, there is a place for you in Transformations Community.

Feel free to explore what we are all about at www.Transformations.Community. You can also reach out to me at adena@transformations.community.

I look forward to hearing from you!

Stay Connected!

Thank you for reading *Windows Into My Soul.*

If you enjoyed this book, you can find additional content at www.transformations.community. Join the free mailing list there to get details about new books, events, courses, and other exciting updates!

You can find regular content on YouTube at Testimony Mountain: From Trauma to Triumph

Please consider leaving a high quality review on Amazon.com so others can find this book more easily.

Other titles by Adena Hodges include:

3 Easy Steps Towards Revival
The Inheritance

About the Author

Adena Hodges is the founder of Transformations Community, a non-profit ministry for survivors and the people who love them. She is also the creator of the Transformations 2.0 Curriculum and Group Support model, which is an on-line learning and Zoom-based group experience that focuses on trauma education and healing through relationship with both the Trinity (i.e. the True Family—Father, Son, Holy Spirit) and others in community.

In addition, Adena is the host of Testimony Mountain, a weekly YouTube and Rumble video podcast focused on releasing stories of the power of God's love to transform lives through teachings and guest interviews.

Prior to her current leadership roles, Adena focused on prayer ministry in churches, developing a strategic prayer model for pastors and leaders that impacted many churches and prayer teams while also building community. She holds a Masters in Christian Leadership from William Jessup University.

Adena is passionate to see people restored and walking out their true identity in Jesus. She loves to teach, write, and facilitate group encounters with God. As a complex trauma survivor herself, she understands the complexity that faces those who have experienced similar things. She has discovered keys that has helped herself overcome that she is honored to share with others. With a compassionate heart, wisdom, and practicality, she inspires those she mentors in groups as well as those she ministers to in one-on-one counseling sessions walk out their transformed life.

Windows Into My Soul is Adena's third book. Her first two books were written before memories surfaced of her trauma. *Three Easy Steps Towards Revival* was written while she was an intercessory missionary in her local house of prayer and embodies three of the powerful prayer tools that impacted her life. *The Inheritance* is loosely fictional as well as partly autobiographical. It is a light-hearted tale that also has an impactful message of redemption and God's love. Her fourth book is in the works and focuses on the theme of biblical paradoxes. It is scheduled to be released in late 2025. All of her works can be found on Amazon.

As a Christian leader for most of her life, as well as a survivor of mind control and SRA, Adena straddles two unlikely communities. Most churches do not know how to help survivors and are not equipped to do so. Adena has a passion to see this change through education and compassionate care. If you are a church or ministry leader who would like more information about survivor issues and how you can help those in your congregation who may be struggling with complex trauma, please reach out to Adena directly at adena@transformations.community.

If you are an individual who would like more information about how Transformations Community can help you or someone you love heal from trauma, please visit www.Transformations.community to see what we are all about. You can also reach out at support@transformations.community.

Made in the USA
Columbia, SC
16 March 2025

55231698R00228